A FUNNY THING HAPPENED
ON THE WAY
TO THE DARKROOM!

A FUNNY THING HAPPENED
ON THE WAY
TO THE DARKROOM!

Photographers' True Stories & Anecdotes

MARGARET LANSDALE

Toronto, Ontario,
1997

ISBN 0-9681931-0-2

Canadian Cataloguing in Publication Data

Lansdale, Margaret, 1928 –

   A funny thing happened on the way to the darkroom! : photographers' true stories & anecdotes

Includes index.

ISBN 0-9681931-0-2

   1. Photography--Humor. 2. Photographers--Canada--Anecdotes. I. Title.

TR139.L35 1997   770'.02'07   C97-900567-1

Printed and bound in Canada by
Seldon Printing Limited,
Hamilton, Ontario

For additional copies contact:
Margaret Lansdale,
18 Ashfield Drive,
Etobicoke, Ontario,
M9C 4T6
Phone/Fax: (416) 621-8788

Dedicated to my sister
Sheila Adie Carter

❦

"Sisters are Special"

Sponsor's Honour Roll......

We give special acknowledgement to the following corporate and private sponsors who have given financial support for the production of this book. It is heartwarming to know, that despite the stringent economic times we face, these sponsors believe deeply in the purpose of this book –

- AMPLIS FOTO INC.
- AGFA FILM
- ARRI CANADA LIMITED
- DEXTER COLOUR CANADA
- HARWOOD PHOTOGRAPHIC LTD.
- KODAK CANADA INC.
- LISLE – KELCO LIMITED
- M&A PHOTOVIDEO INC.
- NIKON CANADA INC.
- POLAROID CANADA INC.
- TECHNIGRAPHIC EQUIPMENT LTD.
- THE PHOTOGRAPHIC HISTORICAL
  SOCIETY OF CANADA

- RICHARD D. BELL
- RAY & SHEILA CARTER
- EVA DZILUMS
- DAVID JAMES & JACKIE ENTWISTLE
- LESLIE & PHYLLIS EVANS
- AL & GAIL GILBERT
- JOHN, LEE ANNE & CAMERON LANSDALE
- ROBERT C. LANSDALE
- MURRAY & BESSIE LAWS
- JOHN NARVALI
- DOUGLAS & BARBARA PAISLEY
- EVERETT ROSEBOROUGH
- CHRIS & DIANNE SHELDON
- STANLEY J. WINDRIM

Table of Contents

Foreword....

ORDER
OF
CANADA

EWALD RICHTER

It is indeed a pleasure to help introduce this Canadian book to the world, which has been so long in the making. For the past ten years, I've enjoyed the humour and unique details from the lives of professional photographers as presented by Margaret in her column. She has the capacity to seek out the stories that become timeless legends. Now the collection will be enjoyed by a much greater audience.

Malak oc of Ottawa

Our family studio dates back seventy five years during which time the stories in this book have taken place. Digital computing is fast changing photography and ere long our whole system of creating photographs will become a distant memory. Margaret Lansdale has tirelessly collected those tales which make the lives of professional photographers – interesting, challenging and above all humorous.

Al Gilbert CM *of Toronto*

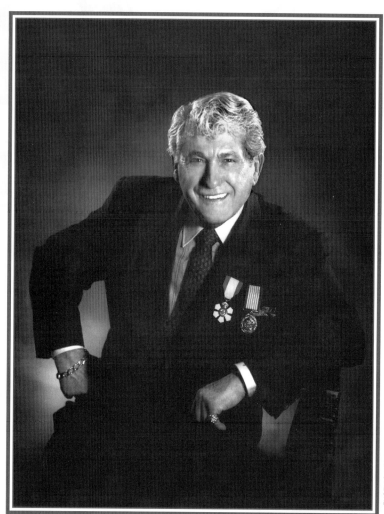

EUGENIO MEDEIROS – GILBERT STUDIOS

Introduction....

Principally, this book is the culmination of ten years of columns which ran in *Exposure Ontario,* the journal of the Professional Photographers of Ontario Inc., and articles produced for the *PPOC Professional Photographer of Canada* magazine. In addition, I've culled through my taped interviews to bring forth material never committed to paper. I am fully aware that the book is too long – almost overkill in some areas, but it seemed destructive not to acknowledge as many photographers as possible and preserve their stories for history. I think the best of the collection has been presented here. I apologize to those who have been left out or who feel I severely edited their best story; hopefully I haven't made any permanent enemies in the process.

But my story telling didn't start just a decade ago; even as a child (Margaret McGibbon Adie) returning from school or dancing classes, I just had to perform before my parents to re-create all the wonderful things that happened during the day. When I first entered the world of photography as a teenager in Glasgow, Scotland, I was enthralled by the variety of adventures I was thrown into. Every assignment brought me into contact with new people, new insights, new challenges. I would burst forth with my experiences that evening.

I am a product of my parents, My mother taught me the love of the arts while my father, –a product of a boys boarding school, taught me to appreciate books. A book was a gift, – a reward to be cherished. When it came time to emigrate from Scotland my suitcases were heavy; many possessions had to be left behind but I took all my books.

Bridge-of-Allan, Scotland

I chose photography as my profession, initially as a challenge to my father who expressed the opinion that careers for women were very limited. In my naivety, I chose to be a press photographer and go the limit in covering dangerous assignments –conquering the world. Scanning the telephone book I stabbed at a business listing: *The Scottish Press.* I applied for a job and found myself working, not in the newspaper field but rather, for a wedding photography agency. It brought its own excitement and pleasures as we photographed all levels of society and travelled to the far corners of Scotland for the weddings of farmers or the aristocracy. After World War Two, our family briefly moved to South Africa, then returned to Scotland, before a final move to Toronto, Canada. Each location brought a new job that gave experience in a different field of photography, –portraiture, –industrial, –advertising. It wasn't until I came to Canada that I finally arrived at my original goal, –the hurley-burley of press photography. On the staff of Federal Newsphotos of Canada, a small press agency, we served the Toronto Star and a roster of papers across Canada.

It was at Federal that I met my future husband, Bob, and on one of our first dates he took me to a meeting of the Commercial and Press Photographers Association of Canada. A great way to start a courtship! Little did I know that I would become involved in photographers' associations for many more years to come. Now if you ever get two photographers together, they will immediately start to tell stories about their escapades and problem assignments. It was during these years of meetings, seminars and conventions that I got to hear some of the best tales that photographers can relate. It wasn't until 1985 that we heard of an escapade by Robert Streeter (see page 157) that sent us tittering all the way home. It was then and there I decided I must preserve all the stories and assemble them into a book. I thoroughly believed I would have it all wrapped up in three months. To promote the idea the stories first became a small column in the PP of Ontario magazine and gradually expanded into a full page. The months dragged on a year, then the year became five and unbelievably, a decade. It is heartening to think how the members stood by me during all that time, withstanding my pestering for new stories and always looking forward to my next column. It was gratifying that those I interviewed were so willing to reveal their inner souls, their mishaps and their mistakes.... all in the name of humour.

Well, Bob and I finally arrived at the point in our lives where we said "the book" had to be done now. We surely had enough material with the topics varied to satisfy every reader.

Here is the collection: –preserved for history... –offered for pleasure.

The Federal Newsphoto team ready to tackle the Royal Tour of Canada.

Acknowledgements....

Producing this book has been a family affair as the people who have come to my assistance I regard as personal friends and part of my family. Through my involvement with the professional associations I've come to meet many people who have gone the extra mile providing assistance and directions smoothing the path to bring the book to fruition.

Eva Dzilums must be the first person to be thanked for her belief and confidence that I could produce a column of interest for the readers of Exposure Ontario. Her extended tenure as editor provided the smooth continuum of the column. My thanks to those who phoned in the middle of the night to provide that 'last anecdote' to complete articles on time. If my spirits were low and it became an uphill struggle to gather enough material, often a few words of encouragement or a surprise letter with a humorous tale always seemed to arrive to spur my efforts onwards.

I am indebted to Everett Roseborough in so many ways, for his variety of support, including the tedious proof reading of the book.

To secure extra illustrations I've pushed friendships to the limit by requesting special portrait sessions be completed on short notice. In addition, my gratitude to all those who scoured their old files for missing pictures or removed prized portraits from their walls and couriered them to me.

Almost near the completion of the book, we unexpectedly realized that without promotion and publicity the book would never get sold. That is when the 'friends' came forth offering opportunities to spread the word, – distributing flyers, producing magazine articles and providing Trade show exposure. Their groundwork opened the gates to success. In particular I wish to thank Suzanne Despatie (PPOC), Eileen Gilbert (PPO), Jim Watson, Roger Sands, Andy Petersons, Ted Smerchansky, Douglas Boult, Mark Robinson, Murray White, Gerard McNaughton, Bill Silver, Frank Cava, Daphne Carlisle, Patti Livingston, Richard Bell, and Aldo Vetesse. For special directions in promotion my gratitude to Jack Arno and to Al McLellan. My apologies to anyone we may have overlooked.

Appreciation and gratitude is extended to Al Gilbert of Toronto, Malak of Ottawa and Michael McLuhan of Owen Sound for their extra special input.

Although we have a special page for our honoured corporate and private sponsors, I wish to give thanks to those who added their substantial support by purchasing books prior to publication. This combined support has eased, somewhat, the financial costs to produce the finished book.

Last of all I thank my husband, Bob, for grooming my rambling words into the published columns and reworking them to form the contents of this book. Bob and his computer have magically transformed the text and photographs into this presentation. Through it all it has been a team effort.

FRANK W. GRANT

If ever there was a Canadian version of the movie hero "Indiana Jones", then it must be Frank Grant MPA, formerly of Toronto whose stories and escapades are legends. If you ever hear this Australian describe his adventures, then you will understand why we adopted him as a great Canadian character. Here he relates a few of his favourite stories.

"I was flying in a helicopter," says Frank, "up through a mountain pass in north-eastern British Columbia. We were scouting a location when the weather turned really rotten with buffeting winds. I wanted to shoot out the open door as the plastic bubble gave distortion. The pilot suggested that I prop the door ajar with my foot and poke the lens through the opening. Well, we were at 1100 feet between two rather large mountains when a freak wind caught the door and ripped it completely off the helicopter. It flew into the rotor blades causing us to lose the main power. You can't imagine the terror when you suddenly realize you're going to crash. The rear stabilizer prop was still working and started to make us go round in a dizzying counter rotation while the big overhead blades gave us just enough lift to glide down at a very steep angle. We landed bloody hard, breaking both of the skids and cracking the bubble of the aircraft. I came out of it OK but the pilot had neck whiplash. The turbine from the engine started a fire in the trees behind us, so we were busy as hell scampering about putting that out with the extinguishers, lest it spread and consume the whole aircraft. When everything settled down we realized that our radio had been knocked out, so we were on our own and were forced to hike some 13 miles through incredible bush. I swear, I must have been bitten by every darn bug in British Columbia. I'll never forget that hike; It took us five and a half hours before we stumbled onto a road and flagged down a ride. It was a terrible experience but we were damned lucky to escape. As for the 'copter, –it was a complete write-off."

"In 1959," recalls Frank, "I was sent over to Hong Kong with Jack DeLissa of the Toronto Telegram. The hope was to get into Red China which was starting its program of 'The Great Leap Forward'. We had been promised visas, but when we got there they didn't even want to know our names. As far as they were concerned the border was closed to the western world. Using Hong Kong as a base we started chasing down other stories. We went over to Portuguese Macao with the intention of photographing a family as it went back through the no-man's land to the big customs gate with the Red Star on top. Jack and I went up to the area in a bicycle rickshaw and were sitting like lords in the back seat. It was a beautiful view encompassing the Portuguese gate, a stretch of 100 yards and then the Communist gate. I put a long telephoto lens on my camera to squeeze the scene together. To top it off, there was a family of seven heading back to China. It was really quite a shot and I figure that this was a picture made in heaven. So, I'm shooting away like crazy

and am ecstatic how its all falling into place. I felt something nudging me in the ribs but thought it was Jack who was sitting on the other side of me. I looked up to find a Portuguese border guard with a sub-machine gun poking in my side. They took away my cameras and threw us in the slammer. We were in deep trouble as they spoke no English. Finally, we were able to phone the Canadian Consul in Hong Kong who, thankfully, cleared up the whole mess. It turned out that another photographer had been killed just three months before, doing exactly the same thing. We didn't know, so it was nice to live to tell the tale."

Frank was commissioned by the Canadian Tourist Bureau to photograph in the Nahani Wilderness National Park deep in the interior of the North West Territories. He arranged to take models with him and fly in with a pontooned Cessna aircraft. The location is wilderness, being some 250 miles from the nearest civilization. The scenic background was to be the mighty Virginia Falls which are twice the height of the worthy Niagara Falls. Arriving over the area the pilot chose to set down on the river above the falls where the water was smooth. His intent was to put the passengers on shore where they could make their way to the base of the falls by foot. The plane landed about 800 yards above the falls and was taxiing towards the shore when the engine conked out. Try as he would, the pilot just could not get that machine to fire up again and every moment the plane was drifting closer to the brink of disaster. Try and try again... the sweat was running down everyone's faces with their white knuckles clenched at their safety belts. The plane swept ever closer to the precipice, then started turning in wild circles as they slipped into a whirlpool a scant 125 feet from the very edge of the roaring falls. It looked like they would be the first Cessna to go over the Virginia Falls. Well... with a thrill to all... the motor did catch and the pilot roared that plane right up onto the nearest river bank, much to the relief of everyone.

Of course, they still had the prospect of taking off later from their precarious location, but the pilot assured Frank that he would tend to the engine while the party made off for the photographs. With white faces and wobbly knees Frank and the models clambered some three miles down to the base of the falls, completed the assignment and then toiled back up the hill again. By this time the pilot had completed his inspection and had worked out a scheme whereby they would be safe if the engine conked out again on the start-up.

Before shoving off they ran a long rope from one of the floats to a tree at the river's edge, around the tree and then back to the plane where it was secured to the other float. They pushed the plane into the river and everyone clambered aboard except Frank. He was given the task of sitting on the pontoon to release the safety rope at a given signal. While the pilot fired up the engine, revving it to test the power, poor Frank was hanging on, a precarious foot and a half from the whirling propeller blades which threatened to cut his head to pieces. Water spray and blasting winds whipped at him. When the motor was running smoothly it was up to Frank to cut the rope loose; but he had only been provided with a very blunt knife and sawing through the rope was a hell of a problem. The pilot was screaming to 'Hurry Up!' but under the duress of the propeller blades and thrashing winds, Frank could only see his life flashing before his eyes. Finally, the knife broke through and the plane leapt away to freedom. Frank inched back to the safety of the cabin, mindful that if he fell into the river, there would be no chance of rescue. But they made it successfully back to Vancouver.

"I was in Rajastan in North-West India to take stock photographs of camels in desert settings. We travelled by car part way, then transferred to camels to reach the the most primitive scenes. The temperature reached 118 degrees Fahrenheit and I was cautioned not to over exert myself. But I was so inspired by the scenery, I was running up and down the dunes and nearly keeled over from the exertion.

My guide came prepared with a local lemonade, called 'Limca', to offset my dehydration. In the morning he had loaded up with the Limca and filled a cooler with ice, bought at a strange looking mud hut. I saw where the ice was buried in the ground and it was dirty and rancid; but that didn't deter me when the mouth watering mixture of ice and lemonade was offered. With the incessant heat and the rocking of the camel, all I could constantly think was: 'When am I going to get my next drink of Limca?' It was an incredible experience and it's a wonder I didn't come down with Belly-Belly on that trip."

Frank was assigned to Newfoundland during the epic photo-shoot for the book 'A Day in the Life of Canada'. His first stop in St. John's was to confer with the Chief of Police of the Royal Newfoundland Constabulary. As Frank describes the scene, "There I was in my tacky khaki's, standing before this spit-and-polish officer who must have been wondering what this elderly hippy from Upper Canada was up to. I produced a letter of intro-duction from Governor-General Sauvé and as soon as he started to read it, I could see him stiffen to attention and there was a radical change of attitude. 'I think we can accommodate whatever you want to do, sir!' he said. So I requested that I have two policemen and a cruiser available at 4 AM, down by the waterfront where the trawlers come in. I wanted to show the patrolmen in the middle of the night, with all the ships lit up in the background. Sure enough, on the dot of the hour, a super-polished cruiser arrived with police-men dressed in immaculate uniforms and shiny boots. They co-operated beautifully, as I had chosen a tough shot to do which required an eight second exposure. I took straight time exposures for the harbour scene, then thought I would try something more creative by adding lighting to the interior of the cruiser with a mini-strobe flash. I had to run a long sync cord underneath the car, through the far door and down to the strobe at their feet. I had just got it all attached when, over the police radio, came an alert of a break-in just a few hundred yards down the road. Well, in a flash-of-duty, they took off without a warning. I was lucky my camera didn't get dragged away as it was attached to the sync cord. Luckily, it slipped off the camera and was dragged, snapping like a whip-in-the-wind, as they disappeared over the hill."

"Thankfully, it was a false alarm, so they were back in a cou-ple of minutes. My cable was still streaming along behind so I picked it up, plugged it into the camera and it worked fine for the rest of the shoot. And that, my dear friends, was the picture cho-sen by the editors for a double page spread in the book."

ARTHUR LICHTMAN

Arthur Lichtman of New York City recalls his high school years when he was working as a freelance photographer for his home town newspaper. "I was assigned to cover the unveiling cer-emony of a painting, dedicated to a deceased lay religious leader. He was considered a local 'saint' for many charitable deeds to the community. The priest extolled eloquently the virtues of the deceased man who had supported the church so benevolently. The framed picture was already on the wall and, at the appropriate moment, was unveiled to great applause from the gathering. I grabbed some shots using a Busch Pressman and flash bulbs. Back in my darkroom I developed the film and discovered to my chagrin that the picture had been covered by glass and my flash had reflected directly back at the camera. The image of our benefactor was completely washed out but the frame and the rest of the scene was still OK. Undaunted, I rushed back to the church and took another shot of the picture, then processed the negative and, by double printing, put the new image into the empty frame of the original shot. It worked great! The man was now back in the frame and the picture looked perfect. I delivered it to the newspaper which ran it in the following edition. A few days later, phone calls began flooding the paper - all centered around my photograph. It looked like a bigger story was unfolding with overtones of a mir-acle. I had, in my rush, mistakenly printed the negative of the 'sainted' patron, backwards. The dignitaries of the first shot were standing normally but the man in the picture was now looking in the wrong direction towards the priest —sure proof that a miracle had occurred and that the man was indeed a saint! It all sorted itself out after a few days... but unfortunately, I lost my job with the paper."

MURRAY LAWS

In the early 1940's and 50's Murray Laws CPA SPA HLM of Hamilton did newspaper photography and, one evening, got a rush call from the Toronto Telegram. "There had been an explosion in our area, so I was asked to check it out and see if I could get pictures to them in a hurry. When I arrived at the scene, I found a small frame bungalow that had been built up on concrete blocks. The explosion had lifted the house into the air, neatly blew out a row of blocks all the way round, and dropped it back again. When I checked the insides it was like a midway Crazy House with the floors slanting in all which ways. Outside was a European character who couldn't speak English and was walking in a daze, back and forth in front of

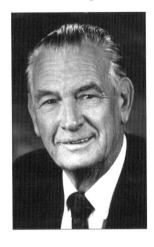

the house. It appears he had attempted to take a bath, so the land lady had put on the water heater - a Ruud heater, the kind that heated continuously until you turned it off. She had lit the fire but he had forgotten to turn it off. The steam pressure continued to build until it finally exploded. The tank, about five feet long of heavy metal, took off like a rocket through the house and then out through the roof, disappearing into the dark night. We couldn't find the tank but shortly after I arrived there was a commotion of yelling and screaming across the street. I hustled over to investigate and found a young lady in hysterics. It being a hot summer's night, she and her boy friend were out on a blanket in the back yard when this 'thing' came whizzing down, thudding into the ground about three feet from them. It buried itself at least two feet deep which shows how fast it must have been travelling. The girl was absolutely paralyzed with fear and I guessed she never would neck in the backyard again. The Telegram used a three-picture spread of the event showing the man walking outside the house, the damaged house and the couple in the back yard with the tank!"

ERNEST W. LEE

Ernie Lee MPA SPA HLM formerly of the London Free Press recalls an assignment where he stood his ground to capture an exclusive scoop while other photographers ducked for cover. The

picture got world wide usage in newspapers and magazines with many front pages and covers.

The occasion was the inaugural run of the Canadian National Turbotrain between Montreal and Toronto; a crowd of reporters and photographers were aboard to record and publicize the activities. A number of press people were in the observation dome admiring the scenery and photographing the facilities.

Ernie saw a truck in the distance, approaching a railway crossing. He thought little as it disappeared from view, thinking that it had taken an underpass beneath the rail line. But suddenly, a cloud of smoke and debris came sailing up over the nose of the train, heading straight back towards the exposed position in the dome. The truck and train had obviously crashed, bringing death and destruction suddenly on the scene. Other photographers dropped to the floor as panels from the broken truck came slicing through the air, but Ernie's instincts forced him to stand his ground. In a burst of three shots on his Nikon the moment was gone forever; it paid off handsomely. The first negative was the only one useable showing the debris flying over the top of the train; the other pictures were unprintable due to the dirt that coated the exterior of the dome. Much to the chagrin of the railway publicists, the picture and story got tremendous play in the Canadian media as well as in the U.S., Europe, India and New Zealand.

JAMES TAMPIN

James Tampin FBIPP of London, England has come through many an episode in his life as a press photographer. He visited Canada as President of the British Institute of Professional Photography to meet with his North American counterparts.

Mr. Tampin's career in photography began abruptly when he phoned a local newspaper for a position and had to leave school when, to his surprise, they accepted him. The Chief Photographer threw a 4x5 Speed Graphic in his lap and told him: "If you want to be a press photographer find out how that works!" It didn't matter as he ended up with a much older camera that used glass plates. It had a focal plane shutter and was so heavy that he had to balance it on his shoulder. Recalling his earliest assignments Jim explained, "On a typical Saturday, I would be given 12 jobs and 12 slides [one sheet of film per job] with which to shoot them. I would rush around to cover all the football matches, often arriving when the teams were resting at half-time. With no time to spare, I would drag them back on the field, throw the ball up and bang off one shot of them 'heading it away'. Then it was off to the next match. We had a dreadful darkroom to work in, up on the top floor. One night, I left the water running to wash some prints; the drain clogged, causing a flood that brought the ceiling down on the editor's office below. We got a shiny new darkroom down on the ground floor where a flood couldn't do as much damage!"

"Early electronic flash was powered with more dangerous voltages than are used today. On a night assignment with my first strobe-flash, the police had captured an escaped killer and were going to sneak him out the back of the house. There was a pub next door with a high wall separating the two gardens, so, I dragged several tables out of the pub and stacked them against the wall, one above the other, and then put a chair on top from which I had a clear vantage point. While waiting the hours away, the heavens opened up and it poured like it had never rained before. I got thoroughly soaked. As the police brought out their man, I fired off my wet strobe-pack which exploded with a WHAM and a cloud of smoke. The whole charge grounded through me and I felt like I had been struck by a lightning bolt. It's a wonder I wasn't killed but the picture turned out and it made all the papers."

"I've been through all the equipment phases: flash bulbs to mini-strobes, glass plates to 4x5 sheet film, roll film cameras to 35mm Nikons. Everything has become miniaturized and automated, but with extra bodies and a selection of lenses I still struggle out with 40 to 60 pounds of equipment. I never learn!"

"I got the urge to travel so I did a stint as an Army photographer, then moved to Kenya for about five years covering Rhodesia and Bahrain, as well. Those were changeable and exciting years as the various British protectorates gained their independence. I was really on the hop shooting both stills and TV newsreels as lots of things were happening. I photographed Ursula Andress and Peter Sellers at the Victoria Falls. When Peter was asked to do something different for the press, he stood on his head. That photo got world play in all the newspapers and magazines. The Queen Mother, during her visits, was a lovely lady to work with. When the press was barred from a reception during which she made a portrait presentation, she came out to us and asked what photos we would like staged. Another Royal favourite was Prince Charles with his bald spot. It seemed every photographer was trying to get a similar shot. By the time the Prince cottoned on and asked if we were after his bald spot, we blandly said 'No!'... By then we were after pictures of him with any lady that might be his girlfriend. Charles took it all in good fun. The free-roaming wild animals, like crocodiles and elephants, always amused the visiting golfers from Europe as they made their way around the hazards of the course. I was chased by an irate elephant with his ears back and his trunk down; so I knew he wasn't bluffing that time. My wife said that half a second later and she would have driven off without me!"

"In Kenya, they were training local Africans for television to replace the white cine crews. One of the new crews was sent to record President Kenyatta as he opened the Royal Show at Nairobi. The President spoke for hours with the result the film spool finally ran out. The crew hadn't learned to carrying a spare, so a little man crawled onto the stage, tugged at the speakers trouser and explained the problem. The President therein intoned to the crowd: 'We must stop while they fix the magic.' There was a pause for some 15 minutes while they reloaded the magazine with new film in a black bag, returned it to the camera, did a test and then gave the OK. Mr. Kenyatta picked up exactly where he had left off, as if he had never lost a beat. Where else in the world would a President do that for the media."

"The urgency to send wirephotos, immediately, pushed me to the limits to find darkroom space where I could do the processing. I've gone from the poshest air-conditioned darkroom down to a broom closet underneath a stairwell where I had to crouch on my knees. The photos were flush-washed in a communal toilet before transmitting them on the wirephoto in my bedroom. There was many a time that I put the wet film back on the processing reel then ran for the last plane home. Each time, I had to convince the airport authorities to let me, personally, carry the tank on board so that the water would not leak all over the place."

"We often recorded violence during our African stay. I travelled to Sharpeville to cover the protest meetings that were planned. It was a long hot day and everyone was milling around, but nothing in particular was happening. I chose to bide away some time in one of the cooler pubs and by the time I returned, all the press had left for home. That was when everything erupted into a riot and the shooting ended in a high death toll. All of the photographs printed throughout the world were my exclusive photographs."

"I have the dubious distinction of leaving my mark at the NATO Headquarters in Germany where they have a photographic section in the basement. This was during my Army stint. We received a shipment of Glacial Acetic acid and I was busy transporting it to our area when I slipped and smashed the bottle on the floor. There are seven and a half miles of corridors in those self contained buildings which are four stories high. The fumes of the acid spread to every section on every floor, burning eyes and noses for days and days."

"Now that I'm back in England, the news game has changed drastically with everything cut throat. With the threats of violence to diplomats and the Royal family, the authorities have been forced to pen the photographers into restricted areas... no more free roaming these days. You either get a fixed point-pass where you get only one chance, or you get one of the few "rotor" passes where you travel with the VIP's. The rotor pass [pool] requires that you supply prints, at cost, to all the other media. I concentrate, now, on feature stories for the weeklies, but we still seem to put in eight days a week. My wife is always suggesting that I take a day off. Well.... maybe next week!"

ANTHONY ATTANYI

Tony Attanyi MPA HLM, retired now in Calgary, Alberta was a sports photographer in Hungary during the Second World War. From the roof of his apartment in Buda (Budapest) he witnessed the American Airforce bombing the industrial sections of the city.

As the war continued, the bombs fell ever closer to the downtown district. Tony worked for a sports magazine and on a cold November Sunday in 1943 he was rushing back from the Hungarian Fencing Championships to process his pictures to meet the deadline. "I was just on my way up the stairs to the lab," recalls Mr. Attanyi, "when a bomb hit the building next door. I was sent sailing through the air and smashed against the wall by the blast. Dust as thick as fog engulfed me while debris tumbled all around. When I got my wits back I found I was unhurt but my ears were ringing like crazy".

"I picked my way up to the lab and had a real shock. The windows were smashed in and a fine powdery dust, an inch thick, lay all about. That powder got into everything, into closed boxes of paper, inside the enlarger... absolutely everything. It looked like we were out of business. But the electricity was still working so that meant the magazine would still be going to press. Our photos had to be ready by 11 PM and we had to find some way to process the pictures. It was a daunting challenge but we started by nailing two blankets over the windows to keep out some of the cold, then began clearing up the mess. There was no such thing as a vacuum cleaner so the dirt had to be scooped up by hand."

"All the chemical bottles were in a second room and luckily were undamaged by the concussion. We developed the films and sought out the best location to dry the negatives. An inner office with little damage had the least dust so we hung our precious films to dry there. Then we set to work to resurrect the print darkroom. The enlarger was a white ghost, inside and out. We did get the job done and on time... but what an experience. It took months before we were back to normal with the feeling of dirt and grit –gone!"

BRIAN BOYLE

Brian Boyle of Scarborough, Ont., remembers the visit by HRH Queen Elizabeth to the Royal Ontario Museum to open a brand new gallery. "After clearing security, I was instructed where I would be allowed to locate, what I could do and what I could not do. Above all there was to be NO FLASH and that created a real problem for me. ROM galleries are dimly lit, at the best of times, so that meant renting a fast lens and testing the area with colour slide film. Early, on the day of the visit, I did a quick tour of the gallery and found the lights had all been adjusted to shine higher on the walls thus ruining all my preparations. 'Effect' was the lighting designers explanation. In a panic I ran around readjusting the lights down to people height. It took quite a while but I made it just in time as the Royal party arrived. It is panic moments like that which you remember for years after the event."

PETER BREGG

Peter Bregg is now settled in Toronto as Photo Editor of Maclean's newsmagazine; but for some 20 years he experienced the thrill of chasing the hottest stories throughout the world as a photojournalist. "I still go out on photo assignments," says Peter, "but the game is now changed to meet the needs of the magazine. Everything is done by committee with the photos selected by space and style requirements. Its different from the hectic days when I worked to capture the most dramatic pictures, edited the film to select the one best shot and then transmitted it on the wirephoto. If you were on the front page the next day, then you knew you had made the right choice."

It all started in 1966 when Peter, right out of high school, joined Canadian Press in Ottawa as a copy boy. In the intervening years he's lived through a flurry of interesting events in fifty different countries. "When I joined CP," recalls Peter, "I had never taken a photograph and it was only when Lynn Ball taught me to print pictures in the darkroom, that I started to take an interest. Eventually, I was allowed to carry back exposed film from assignments and develop them for him. My first camera was a 35mm Topcon and then a 2 1/4 Rolleiflex with a Braun Hobby flash. The photographers at Canadian Press and the Ottawa Citizen took pity on me for all the mistakes I made. They offered advice and I learned slowly. I'll always remember my first break when I actually got a scoop. It was March 17th 1967, as I was walking up Parliament Hill to deliver copy to the Press Gallery. As always, I had my little camera slung over my shoulder. My attention was attracted to some soldiers taking photographs of other soldiers, dressed in a different coloured uniform. The news copy that I was delivering, was hot on the unification of Canada's three armed forces with the announcement that there would be only one uniform. I realized that these guys must be wearing the new green outfit. I stepped up to take a photo with my little camera, but a military policeman jumped in front of me just as I was clicking it off and said I couldn't take any pictures. I processed the film but it

turned out underexposed and quite thin; with so little experience my print was so bad, I threw it in the waste basket. Back in the office I mentioned what had happened on the Hill to the news editor. Everything did a quick turn-around when he saw my cull print and it was shown to the photo editor. A good print was rushed through by one of the photographers and, in no time, it was sent out over the wire services along with the story of my encounter. Next day it was on the front page of the Globe & Mail, in the Star, used by Time magazine and by papers all across the country. The biggest thrill was the caption that credited the photo to Peter Bregg - Canadian Press PHOTOGRAPHER.... not just the copy boy. That was when I decided I had to be a press photographer."

"In 1974 I began working for American Press (AP) out of Boston and, in a stroke of luck, joined the team covering President Gerald Ford's visit to Salsberg, Austria. I was to concentrate on Mrs. Ford, shooting a full length of her costume on every occasion for a fashion layout. Our photographers were allocated to the photo stands or sprinkled about the airport at strategic locations. As junior photographer of the seven man team, I wasn't assigned a spot. So rather than duplicate the others I chose to stand in with the public, hoping the President might shake hands with some of the crowd. It was raining slightly as Mr. and Mrs. Ford descended from the plane and umbrellas were popping up to provide protection for him. I thought it would make a cute full length of Mrs. Ford so used the 300mm telephoto to grab a shot. The motor drive ran off a burst of film and, by luck as the first shot clicked, the President lost his balance. With the mirror working so fast you can't really see what is happening. It was only a minor stumble and Mr. Ford was back on his feet, quickly. I sent the film in for processing with every one else's and was surprised, when we got back to the office, to see a full sequence of 8x10 prints spread out on the editors desk. I couldn't believe it when the credit was given to me for the dramatic coverage. All other photographers had their views blocked while I had a clear vantage point, looking straight up the ramp. If the camera hadn't been up to my eye to photograph Mrs. Ford, I never would have got it. I have to say that 90% of my best pictures are made by luck alone."

"Being in the thick of the action, sometimes causes photographers to be arrested; I first ran afoul of the law while covering a women's protest in Montreal. Mayor Jean Drapeau passed a by-law to prohibit demonstrations during the Grey Cup festivities. On my way to cover the Miss Grey Cup pageant, I was diverted to a group of women protesting that very by-law. They were chained together and wearing FLQ bandannas. The police decided to evacuate all the media so that no pictures could be taken while they arrested the women. I left the area, doubled back through the alleys and, in the darkness, was able to slip inside the circle of women where I crouched down and hid. As the police commenced to round up the women I stood up and started taking pictures. Well, they grabbed me right away and tossed me into the nearest paddy wagon. I didn't mind that because I could then get pictures of the gals being thrown in with me. Unfortunately, my flash-head came off, landing just outside the door, and I needed it desperately for more pictures. When the door opened again I grabbed for the flash but one of my cameras flew up and hit a policeman on the forehead. He started to scream so I was yanked out of the wagon, taken to the station and charged with criminal obstruction, assaulting a police officer plus two other charges based on the by-law. Next morning when I appeared in court, fifty of the arrested women stood to cheer me as the only male to join them. It took some four years before all the charges were dropped when the Supreme Court of Canada finally threw out the by-law as unconstitutional."

"My next arrest was in '73 while in Vietnam covering Canadian troops involved with the ICCS peace team. On my first day, I was heading for the base church at Transanuut Air Base when a Major of the South Vietnamese Police swooped down, questioned me on what I was doing and hustled me off to the brig. They had a couple of South Vietnamese soldiers in there, as well, and it seemed the Major was very angry with them. His tirades

evolved around their attempt to grow mustaches while their hair seemed too long as well. The Major suddenly pulled out scissors and cut off half their mustaches. It looked very painful and I thought I was in for trouble, too, as I had a mustache and my hair was a little on the long side. Finally, the Canadians were called and they sent over their military police who had strong words with the Major which hastened my release. I was told not to walk around the base unescorted - that being my only crime. I was travelling with reporter Ray Dick, who wrote a column about this escapade and the next day Claude Wagner, the Defense critic in the House of Commons, raised the question about security for the Canadian journalists. Prime Minister Trudeau replied: 'Yes, the Canadian government is doing everything possible to help and protect Canadian journalists in Vietnam, especially MY FRIEND, PETER BREGG.' I was sent a copy of Hansard with the item underlined in red ink. I don't know if my stature went up any higher at Canadian Press but being recognized as 'a friend of Trudeau' might have helped when martial law was declared in Poland, some years later. I was able to secure a visa into Poland and talked Canadian Press into sending me there. I had a very good five-week trip shooting everything: soldiers in the streets, farms etc. But getting the pictures home was a different matter. The finished pictures had to be cleared by a censor who stamped them on the back and put them in an envelope with a fixed seal like those used on your electric meter box. I then had to take the package to the airport to go through the military office before it was allowed on the plane. If the seal was broken the package was rejected. I brought along a sharp razor blade to slit the leading edge of the envelope then insert extra prints and reseal the opening with a glue stick. I always held back from the censor those pictures which I thought were too sensitive such as: line ups for food, empty shelves in the stores, or run-down property."

"Iran was a different situation; very dicey at the time as they had just kicked out the Americans and most Westerners, but Canadian Press managed to get visas so we headed off to Iran. Little did we know when we registered at the Canadian embassy and were being briefed by Ken Taylor, that we were sitting on top of a major scoop. At that very moment six Americans were hidden down in the basement, and four days later Ken Taylor spirited them out of Iran. When we heard of the escape, my reporter thought we better get out as the Iranians would surely suspect we were part of the plot. But we were never harmed and stayed in Tehran for three months until replaced by another team from Canadian Press. At that moment in time, the Russians were invading Afghanistan and all the Westerners were being kicked out. I went to the Afghan embassy, claiming to be a tourist in Iran and wanting to stop at Kabul on my way through to Pakistan. The young people at the embassy obligingly cleared me with a visa, so I gave over most of my equipment to my reporter. He headed back to Toronto while I hopped aboard a plane for Kabul with a back pack and one camera, like a regular tourist. In a situation like that, which happens all too often, the photojournalist is completely on his own to ferret out the story, photograph it and then get it back safely to the home office. There was no problem getting into Kabul, but within an hour of checking into my hotel, a plain clothes policeman was watching me from a room across the hall. Every time I left my room he would come out and follow me downstairs. When I ordered up a taxi, he would phone somebody and shortly a cab would arrive which I am sure was one of theirs. I couldn't take pictures since they were watching me so closely. To play a game, I would open and quickly close my hotel door; my policeman would come out looking up and down the hall for me. Then I would open up my door and do the same."

"While in Kabul I was asked to locate a French photographer who had arrived before me and had gone missing for several weeks. I learned from the French embassy that he was safe and would return in several days. I finally found him, received his film and headed off for Pakistan by bus. That was foolhardy as rebels repeatedly stopped the buses and shot anyone they thought were government agents. Luckily, that day we joined a convoy of Russian trucks heading in the same direction. We passed through the Khyber Pass at sunset and I visited an Afghani refugee camp at Peshwar. Nearby is a town called Dara which is like a Wild West show, complete with wooden sidewalks. Dara is a manufacturing trade center for guns with the rebels and tribesmen testing the rifles and pistols out on the sidewalk. Its quite unnerving to have one of these guys suddenly start blasting away beside you... but it did make good pictures."

"When I tried to fly out, all the flights to London were booked so I opted for Karachi. Arriving at one in the morning, I didn't want to spend all night looking for a place to stay so left it up to the cab driver to choose the closest hotel. It cost 75 cents a night and came equipped with filth, grime and bugs. By 5 AM I was out of there and headed for an intercontinental hotel to clean up with a shower. That evening I caught a flight to London and spent the summer in Ottawa."

"By September, Iraq and Iran were at war. Western correspondents were devoting their coverage to the overpowering Iraqi forces. To show the other side of the story, the Iranian embassy in Ottawa phoned Canadian Press asking if they wanted visas. In short order, I and a reporter were off to Iran and set up an office-home with a staff of eight Iranian photographers, translators and teletype operators. Three weeks into the tour four men with machine guns burst in, searched us and hustled us into the basement where we sat blindfolded on the floor with our hands over our heads. An hour later we were carted off in two mini-vans to a hollow sounding warehouse. About four in the morning I, my reporter and a French photographer were taken away to a house and given a bedroom to sleep in; we were relieved to take off the blindfolds. Packed into one bed with the Frenchman's feet at our noses, we passed away the remainder of the night. Morning brought a group of teenage students who fed us tea, bread and honey, then began questioning us about places back home. The students had all received their education in Canada, America or Europe so it was a friendly conversation. But once in a while a question would creep into the conversation: 'Do you know many Iranians? Do you go to Iranian homes? How to you get your money?' They were pumping us to see if we were part of a counter revolutionary plot and if we were exchanging money on the black market. Finally we were returned to our office to find it thoroughly ransacked and all the wirephoto and camera equipment confiscated. Next day at the Foreign Ministry, we were told we had to leave but, if we wanted to come back, we would have to apply for a visa! Since nothing was flying out of Tehran airport, the only escape was a five hour bus ride to the Turkish border where we caught a flight to Istanbul. After a few days there, we again applied for visas, thinking that stranger things have happened in the past. Lo and behold we got our visas, so we were back on the road to Iran like Hope and Crosby. On crossing the Turkish border, we found it was a Holy day so couldn't get a bus to Tehran. The only thing available was a sheep truck –no sheep but all the smell was still there. That took us some twenty miles to another village where we hired a driver and a car. He was to take us to the nearest city where we might find a hotel and proper transportation. An hour out of town, the car spun out of control and flew over an embankment, rolling over and over, four times for sure. Luckily, we got out with just scratches but the car was a total wreck, sitting on its roof. Some villagers took us to their home and put us on the bus the next morning to Tehran. So we were back on the story as if nothing had happened! The Danish embassy, who were handling Canadian affairs, retrieved my cameras but not the darkroom or wirephoto equipment. Now, I had to take my photos to a censor for clearance who then used MY wirephoto equipment to transmit the images, charging a dollar a minute for the service. They used an egg timer to calculate the charge. I was spending about $600 a week to use my transmitter. It eventually appeared they were going to release the hostages, but that was when they told me I had overstayed my welcome and I would have to leave."

"So by New Years, I was flying off to London. There, my bosses suggested I try again for a visa, but it did not work that time. So I went to Paris and was given the stall for ten days. We reasoned that if the hostages were to be freed then they most likely would go first to Algeria; so we applied for a visa and got clearance to go to there. I was, in fact, relieved to hear of the Iranians refusal. In Algeria, I waited a week covering the negotiations leading up to freeing of the 52 Americans. I was so overjoyed to think that this story, to which I had been attached for six months, was finally coming to an end. I followed them the last leg of the journey to their hospital in Germany; then it was back to Ottawa to a somewhat normal life."

JOHN McNEILL

John McNeill recalls for us when he was a photographer for the North Bay Nugget. "One evening I was sent rushing to a train station where something was amiss. It was one of those old fashioned wooden buildings notable for big decorative windows. I found all the windows blown out into the street and every car in the vicinity with their windshields shattered. Two policemen had an old wino in custody who was visibly shaken and was muttering something about 'striking a match'. Details of the devastation were pieced together to reveal that

the men's washroom had recently been refurbished with metal dividers forming the new cubicle. The wino was sitting on one of the toilets when he heard someone enter the adjoining stall. The new arrival apparently put a stick of dynamite in his mouth, lit the wick and blew his head off. The metal walls directed the blast towards the ceiling thus saving the life of the wino. The hapless victim was found wandering about, deaf as could be and shaking from the shock. All he could mutter was: 'I heard him strike the match... I heard him strike the match!' "

"Early in my career I bought a Speed Graphic and started shooting weddings. I was asked to photograph the marriage of a couple whose family had close ties to the church; quite a few nuns and priests were guests. I was hovering around taking pictures during the reception when the couple rose to cut the wedding cake. As the groom stood up he almost pulled the cover off the table along with all the dishes and the cake. The table cloth was trapped in his zipper and few missed the connotation in the gaff. Being so young at the time, I was embarrassed and never took the picture. The question remains: What had happened to get the cover caught in his zipper."

John eventually joined the Toronto Globe & Mail but a North Bay experience crossed his path several years later. "In the North I was sent on an assignment to cover the 10th Anniversary of a nudist colony. I took a number of photographs of an exceptionally pretty Belgian girl by the water's edge. She was an excellent model and unabashed, so we got along very well. With the shoot over, I headed back to the paper never expecting to see her again."

"Years later, I was located in Montreal working for the Globe and Mail. The elevator in our building broke down one day, forcing me to take a different exit route to the mezzanine. As I was passing a ski shop I heard a voice excitedly calling my name. It was a pretty blonde store clerk and she was beckoning to me. So I walked in and waited while she served some customers. She looked vaguely familiar but I was perplexed as to where I had met her. She turned and asked: 'You don't recognize me?' At that I remembered the pretty girl from the nudist colony and I blurted out: 'Oh! I didn't recognize you with your clothes on!' There was a gap of silence with the customers stiffening in surprise; the young lady blushed a brilliant red. Since I had only met her for that short assignment at the nudist camp so, in all truthfulness, I had never seen her with her clothes on!"

DAVID CHOO

David Choo MPA of West Vancouver, British Columbia recalls: "Before coming to Canada twenty years ago I worked for the Malaysian Information Services as a press officer in Sabah which was the former British colony of North Borneo. One day I was assigned to cover the victory celebration of a new government Minister; he was to make his maiden speech to 5,000 of his constituents in a village outpost. It was difficult for him to speak in English as a second language, but because of the British colonial influence it was deemed fashionable to speak in both his native tongue and in English. So he gave it his best shot. With loudspeakers booming he declared, 'For all your help and support during my last ERECTION, I thank you from the bottom of my heart and my WIFE'S BOTTOM!' "

"Shortly before Prince Norodom Sihanouk was overthrown as Head of State of Cambodia by a military coup, he paid an official visit to Malaysia with his wife. The day before his departure, he toured the zoo in Kuala Lumpur, capital of Malaysia, and I happened to be covering his visit. He was intrigued by gestures made by a group of orangutan who kept hitting their left fists with their right palms above their heads. Obviously, someone had impertinently taught the apes to make the foul gesture."

"The Prince asked the Malaysian Prime Minister what the big apes were doing. The Minister turned red and purple with embarrassment, but being a quick-witted politician, replied that it was the Malaysian gesture for 'goodbye'."

"The next day all the dignitaries and thousands of school children turned out at the airport to bid farewell to the Prince. Before entering the plane, Prince Sihanouk and his wife turned to the crowd, raised their arms and did the 'Malaysian goodbye' - which was much to the amazement of the spectators. The 'goodbye' was, in fact, a version of the middle finger gesture!"

LES JONES

Its a far cry from the beautiful mahogany and brass Lancaster view camera that initially perked his photographic interest back in England but now, Les Jones of Toronto wonders if he should add a fire extinguisher to the roster of modern equipment he carries while on sports assignments. Les runs a photo agency specializing in minority sports such as soccer, rugby and hot-air ballooning. It gives him the opportunity for trips and assignments to all parts of the world.

On two occasions, Les remembers that his camera bag caught fire causing a flurry of excitement beyond that of the surrounding sports event. Two batteries, floating loose in his case, accidentally aligned and connected with a metal flash bracket. That created a short-circuit causing the batteries to overheat and smolder ominously. On another occasion during a soccer match in Mexico, a 300mm lens, standing upright in his bag, focussed the rays of the hot midday sun on the inner lining. "I happened to look over at my bag," recalls Les, "and was stunned to see it actually in flames. The lens had acted as a magnifier to burn into the material. I haven't done that since!"

His biggest surprise was when he unwittingly started a 100 metre sprint at an international track-and-field meet. "I was in close to the starting position, hoping to capture the tension on the faces of the runners as they kicked off for the dash to the finish. To make sure I caught the initial sequence, I began firing my motor drive just as the Official Starter counted down and got to the word 'steady'. At the first CLACK of my shutter, the keenly tuned athletes thought it was the starter's gun and were off in a shot... only to be called back on a false start!"

TED GRANT

Ted Grant CPA of Victoria, British Columbia is one of Canada's leading photographers. In a career spanning over 45 years he has covered major news and sports events, political and advertising campaigns and worked on feature stories for magazines such as National Geographic. Ted has travelled in almost every country in the world, developing a style that captures a rich naturalness in a moment of time. He is the only photographer to be awarded both gold and silver medals for photographic excellence by the National Film Board of Canada, while in 1990 he was given an honourary medical degree by the USSR Academy of Medical Sciences. Yet it wasn't until his wife presented him with a camera in 1950 that he took any serious notion to photography. Since his first published picture in 1951 by the Ottawa Citizen he hasn't stopped supplying illustrations for all media. Grant moved to Victoria in 1981 to slow the pace of assignments but he has been busier than ever.

"In my early days as a photographer I covered many stock car events, often locating myself in the infield only a few yards from the edge of the track. One day a concerned safety manager made me move from my normal shooting position to a safer place. In the final race of the afternoon a major crash occurred at the west end of the track which forced me to squint into the sun to try to find a picture. I didn't see a huge wheel come flying through the air directly at me and it was only at the last second I tried to duck... but it was too late. As they loaded me into the ambulance the safety manager came rushing up to see who had been injured. That's when I gave him the sarcastic, 'Thanks for the place of safety!' "

"During the 1972 Winter Olympics in Sapporo, Japan there were many media representatives who discovered the wonder of the Orient for the first time. The crew I was working with had never been in Japan and the first thing they wanted to try was a visit to a bathhouse. Because of my previous assignments I was delegated to organize a visit to an appropriate place of bathing. I loaded my charges into a mini van and away we went with the usual off-colour remarks as to what they expected during their experience. However, it was a subdued shy group as each was directed to separate bathing rooms for a steam bath and near-boiling in the deep hot tubs. After this ordeal each was wrapped in a huge towel, given a glass of almond-scented white cream and sent to the massage room where the masseuse would work the cream into their bodies. The last photographer, as he came into the room, was followed by a group of giggling Japanese girls who worked in the bathing rooms. They were chattering and pointing at our friend who was carrying an empty glass. 'It didn't taste very good. What was in it?' he asked. Then, we understood why the girls were giggling!"

"Street children in Saigon thought up many ways to make money during the Vietnam war. Some were expert thieves who could slip a camera off your shoulder or pick your pocket without you even knowing it. One of the more imaginative schemes was the banding together of half a dozen urchins with shoe polish and brushes. One would make the first approach asking: 'Shine your shoes mister?... 500 piasters.' That was about five U.S. dollars and your reaction was to tell the kid to get lost. But as quickly as you refused, you were surrounded by a horde of little businessmen chanting the same:'Clean your shoes, mister?' It would have been easy to push them out of the way, but each had a fully charged brush in his hand. If you were foolish enough to refuse, there was a flurry of brush strokes leaving your clothes blackened from top to bottom. Needless to say the quick response was: 'OK kid, clean the shoes!' "

"I never realized that a long telephoto lens, mounted to a pistol grip, could look so much like a machine gun. I was in Bethlehem, just after the Six-Day War in 1967, looking for picture possibilities when I encountered three men, dressed in traditional Arab clothing, coming towards me in the distance. The setting, the lighting and the composition presented a perfect photo. I quickly raised my tele-lensed camera to my eye, holding it by the pistol grip. Just as quickly the three men flung their arms above their heads in submission. I was so surprised by their action I accepted their surrender without firing a single shot... not one picture at all."

"I was up in the Canadian Arctic, at Mould Bay in the Northwest Territories to be exact, when the inside of our helicopter filled with smoke. A red fire-light flashed on the instrument panel and the pilot worked feverishly to get us from 3000 feet down to the ice-pack without crashing and burning in the process. We dropped like a fast falling rock with the smoke getting thicker. Since the outside temperature was at 55 degrees below zero with a 30 mph wind, we didn't know if we were going to freeze or fry to death. Scared... you bet! The skipper yelled to grab a fire extinguisher and be ready to jump as soon as we hit the ground, then open the engine compartment and start pumping at the fire. A photographer wouldn't think of passing up a situation like that, so I grabbed a camera in one hand and the extinguisher in the other. I was kneeling on the floor, waiting for contact, when I realized, 'OK stupid, how are you going to open the door?' I reluctantly put

the camera down and leapt out running to the far side of the copter figuring I was going to be the hero-of-the-day. I grabbed the nearest handle, flung open what I thought was the engine hatch and there staring at me was... THE LUGGAGE COMPARTMENT! Luckily the pilot knew what to do."

"Here is some advice for travelling photographers. In some tourist cities, professional photographers are charged for the right to photograph historical sites and locations. I first encountered this practice in Rome at the Forum ruins. There is an admission fee to enter the arena but when I tried to go through with my equipment bag and a tripod I was asked if I was a professional photographer. 'Yes,' I replied, 'from Canada.' Immediately, I was told there would be a fee of l00 Lire for taking pictures. In Canadian dollars that was only one dollar and I could live with that. One dollar, I thought, was reasonable for the privilege of shooting amongst the ruins for a day. But then my interpreter found the fee was to be charged for each and every exposure which meant a 36 exposure roll would have cost 3600 Lire. That was more than I could live with. So we returned to the car, stowed our excess gear and slung a couple cameras around our necks. With film stuffed in our pockets we returned as tourists and paid the standard entrance fee. By day's end I had 30 exposed rolls of film and you can figure how much money I had saved. Sometimes it pays to be a tourist."

Ted Grant has been involved with his share of Royal Tours of which he recalls the following. "I received a panic call from the press liaison at Government House in Ottawa, during a visit of H.R.H. Prince Charles. 'We need you right away. A car is on it's way to pick you up for photographs of the Prince.' Arriving at Rideau Hall, I was told there were several groups of people to be photographed with both colour and B&W required and with the shooting done outdoors. Some of my magazines were still loaded from a previous assignment, necessitating a quick reload and a change of lenses to meet the situation. While kneeling on the grass, working over the equipment, I realized someone had stopped beside me and was watching the proceedings. Then a voice plied me with the usual questions on photography, lenses, cameras and film which greatly interrupted my concentration. Trying to be polite while preparing the cameras, I pondered:

'Why do amateurs always pester me with questions when I'm in a panic?' I was just about to tell the pest to get lost when I looked up and did a double take. The interested amateur was PRINCE CHARLES, himself!"

"Royal Tours, with their organized photo opportunities, force photographers to repeat the same pictures every day, thus making the whole tour boring. You must keep your ears tuned for the side stories such as this little item involving H.R.H. The Duke of Edinburgh. During a tour of the Arctic a luncheon was catered by the local women with assistance by young girls doing the serving. The main course finished and a shy young lady was clearing dishes from the head table. As she neared the Prince she became flustered. Finally she mustered her nerve, stepped beside the Duke and blurted out: 'KEEP YOUR FORK DUKE, THERE'S DESSERT COMING!' "

"The Queen, Prince Philip and their son Prince Andrew were visiting Upper Canada Village in Ontario with the usual walk-about to allow people to see the Royals up close. Prince Andrew was some distance ahead of Her Majesty when a Provincial Police officer approached him. Taking Andrew by the elbow the officer said, 'You'll have to move along son, the Queen's coming.' An alert liaison officer stepped in to save the day with: 'Pardon me Sergeant, have you met Prince Andrew?' "

"When Her Majesty visits Canada, the arrival point is usually the RCAF base in Ottawa where all the media gather for the first stories and photos. At the start of one of these visits, two RCMP officers, who I am sure were the biggest in the country, ushered the gaggle of photographers to a predetermined position. One officer drew an imaginary line along the tarmac with his boot and in a voice of total authority announced, 'Gentlemen, DON'T cross that line.' Then the officers posted themselves, like pillars, at each end. The photographers arrange themselves with the first row kneeling and the rest standing behind. All knew that to cross the line would mean the wrath of the guards. On one occasion, photographer Louie Jacques of WEEKEND magazine took off and crossed the line, a split second before the Queen was to appear from the plane. He headed for a more advantageous spot with a guard in hot pur-

suit. Everyone expected the photographer to be dragged away or sent to the rear of the scrum with little chance of pictures. The officer ordered Louie to 'move it real quick and get back in the pack'. But Louie's reply was so cool and so imaginative that it stunned the officer. 'Oh, I can't do that,' he said, 'I'm shooting COLOUR.' At that moment the Queen appeared, Louie got his shot and the Mountie finally ushered his photographer to the back. After that there was always a rope to cordon off the press."

RAY McFADDEN

Ray McFadden is proud to have worked for the old Toronto Telegram for over 26 years and always on the night shift by choice. "1945 to 1962 were the best years," recalls Ray, "when we worked out of the aged Bay and Melinda building that reeked of old style journalism. The newsroom wasn't the clinical computer room of today. The nightman on the City Desk wasn't a hard nosed editor but a knowledgeable capable guy who enjoyed every challenge. Usually, there were a couple reporters pecking out their stories on ancient typewriters in two-finger-style while the police radio constantly squawked in the background. Ears would perk to attention when a reporter sniffed some action on the radio even though the police dispatcher might try to disguise what was happening. We, Tely types, prided ourselves as the underdogs of the Toronto papers. With lack of manpower to blanket a major breaking story, we had to dig deeper and cover all possible angles. With some modesty, I think our coverage was superior to that of the Star or Globe because of that extra effort."

At times being a press photographer can require putting your life on the line. Ray relates a story from the late 1940's when a drug store was robbed one evening. "A citizen reported two men with guns running through a cemetery so I rushed to the scene for pictures. On arriving, a posse of police, strung out in a line, was systematically combing through the grave stones. It was an eerie scene, everything black except for the flashlight beams. The police with their guns drawn were slowly moving forward probing each darkened crevice. That's when I had a brilliant idea to position myself well out in front of the advancing line. I could already see the photo making the front page. I waited 'til a cluster of lights neared my position then took aim and fired my flash bulb. The gloom of the night instantly gave way to the brilliance of the bulb and therein I knew I had made an error. In that instance of light, I could see ten startled policemen swinging their guns in my direction. As the blackness returned I fully expected a hail of bullets to come whizzing towards me. I was quickly surrounded by a horde of policemen and berated by a tough sergeant for nearly getting had my head blown off. He was right, it exemplified a news-photographer ignoring his own safety in the heat of a story. The search quickly switched to another location with a report one of the robbers had fired at a policeman. The gunman had missed but it sure scared a smooching couple when the bullet struck the side of their parked car. I think myself lucky as I might have stumbled into that very robber while roving ahead of the police."

"To be a good news photographer doesn't mean you have to be blessed with an excess of brains but you had better be prepared to react fast and do battle with any unwilling subject or rival photographer." That's Ray's philosophy behind another story. "A local Torontonian, high in the ranks of the underworld, was flown back to Malton airport for questioning about a recent heist. Star photographer Gord Powley and myself for the Tely were waiting at the bottom of the stairway as passengers disembarked from the plane. Finally we spotted Inspector John Nimmo (nicknamed "Spiffy" because he was always well dressed and looked more like a male model than a policeman) as he made his descent with a dame cuffed to his wrist. She was a pro at dodging photographers and covered her face with her free hand. Nimmo took his prisoner into the Customs office, so Powley and I raced around to the exit door for a second chance. No sooner had I got into position when a mean looking guy planted himself squarely in front of my camera. I ducked to the side and he followed, letting fly with a steam of ugly words which implied that I wasn't about to get a picture (the woman later proved to be his sister). My reporter dashed in shouting, 'She's coming around the building on the outside.' So we charged off in pursuit and caught Nimmo just as he was coming round the corner with the suspect. I got my Speed Graphic up to my eye when a huge fist came crashing into the viewfinder knocking the lens and bellows clean off the front tracks. I'm swearing at this big hulk and frantically pushing the camera back together, determined to still get the G* D* picture. I ran to get ahead of the broad with the hulk again in hot pursuit. My temper flared and I wheeled to let the bully have it. But my assailant had pulled a gun from his pocket and was at the instant of taking a shot at me when two plain clothes detectives tackled him from behind. That was a very close call indeed! Now, if there is a funny side to this story, it must be that while I was being harassed, Gord Powley was having a field day taking great shots of the woman and even recording the gunman pulling the rod from his hip pocket. But it shows what a good guy Powley was, as he handed me a plate holder which showed the gunman chasing me. The Tely printed it the next day. One of the detectives later admonished me, 'McFadden, you're a damned fool. Don't you know **** beat a murder rap three years ago.' Even now I won't mention his name as he might still have a spare slug with my name on it."

ROBERT E. LANSDALE

As a press photographer during the 1950's Robert Lansdale MPA HLM of Etobicoke, Ont., was assigned to shoot the first Grey Cup game ever played in Vancouver, British Columbia. All the film was processed immediately in a makeshift darkroom under the stadium with pictures wire-photo'd to the Toronto Star for that day's editions. By the time the game was over, there was only an hour left before Bob was scheduled to catch a plane back to Toronto. Getting to the plane was no problem, but taking all the negatives WAS a problem.

"There before me," says Bob, "was a sink full of very wet 4x5 negatives and we had no possible way of drying them fast enough in that make-shift darkroom. Well, they had to go with me so we started scouting around for ideas and materials. I finally bundled them in thoroughly-wet blotters which was then wrapped in bread loaf wrappers and candy packages that I found up in the stands. The flight to Toronto was an all-night milk run that stopped at every city across the Western Prairies. This stretched-out schedule could mean a mass of stuck negatives by the time I got to Toronto, so at every stop I ran for the men's washroom and filled several wash basins to separate and rewet each film. This created quite an attraction as curious patrons in the rest rooms learned of what I had in the bowls. They started asking all sorts of questions about the game and I ended up giving an illustrated lecture in every men's washroom from Vancouver to Toronto. By the end of the flight the films were still OK, were thoroughly washed and were DEFINITELY ready for drying."

When Bob worked for Federal News Photos in Toronto, a press photo-agency , he was always given the task to replace blown electrical fuses, something that happened all to often at night when the offices would be thrown into pitch darkness. Fellow photographer, Bill Russell, hated to touch anything electrical and persistently declined when anything of that nature needed repair. One evening when the fuse blew, Bob chose to be stubborn and resolutely downed tools to force Bill to, once-and-for-all, face

reality and change the fuse. The electrical panel was housed in a small eerie closet and into this Bill gingerly stepped, lighting his way with matches and timorously fiddling with the errant fuse. It became quite a pantomime as each match burned low, scorching Bill's fingers, then much scrambling in the dark to light another and continue with the extraction. Of course, everyone relished his predicament. Suddenly Bob was inspired to fiendish devilment and at the precise moment that the new fuse was inserted into its socket Bob grabbed up his strobe flash and fired off a blast of light. Fuse and match flew into the air as a yelp burst from Bill; he was sure he had been electrocuted That fuse was the last he ever touched and guess who had to change them all from that time onwards?

A beer store clerk had been killed during a robbery in Toronto and the papers played the story for some time. It appeared to the police that it might have been an accidental shooting with a ricocheting bullet hitting the victim. The papers appealed to the gunman to give himself up. Phil Jones, reporter for the Globe & Mail, received an anonymous tip that the killer would meet him on a specific evening at Dufferin and St. Clair Avenue. Bob recalls, "At the appointed hour Phil, in his regulation reporter's raincoat, was waiting discreetly by the specified lamp-post. But mysteriously, the tip had been leaked to all the other papers and parading in the passing crowd were at least half a dozen of Toronto's recognizable press photographers. All were carrying shopping bags with their Speed Graphics and flash equipment hidden inside. I was determined to record this scenario somehow, so I hid my camera in a cardboard box and carried it to a vantage point on a streetcar safety island. I set the box on the ground, ostensibly to tie my shoelace, but uncovered a false panel and grabbed a time-exposure. Well, it turned out to be a false alarm and was, more likely, a prank by a fellow reporter. After several hours waiting and parading, we all adjourned to a restaurant to lower our disguises. That's when Phil admitted he enjoyed watching the antics of his fellow pressmen trying to be invisible. We all tripped back to the scene to restage and photograph our memorable adventure as under cover agents."

While on assignment in Europe, Bob got a rush message to join the Marilyn Bell crew at Calais, France, as she made ready to become the youngest person to swim the English Channel. Recalls Bob, "The swim was sponsored by the Toronto Telegram and I was received with cool reservation as most of my assignments, back home, identified me with the rival Toronto Star. On the morning of the swim, all our luggage was ferried out to the main boats. I stripped down to pants and shirt then sent my shoes, money and passport out with the bags. I was just starting to use a strobe flash and many feared a short circuit would surely electrocute me while wading in the water. But the kick-off went well as Marilyn headed out to deep water and I returned to the beach to await pickup by the last shuttle. All the boats gradually disappeared over the horizon and I finally realized that I had been forgotten or unceremoniously dumped. With no money and no passport I was in a real predicament. The hotel staff eventually took me into their care and made arrangements to find running shoes. All stores were closed for Sunday and they could provide only a pair that was a full size too small. In mid-afternoon just as I was heading for the ferry to England, a launch came skimming over the waters and landed at the beach. Dorothy Howarth, writer on the Telegram team, had been sent back for a jar of Lanolin grease to fend off the jelly-fish which were stinging Marilyn. I was only a secondary thought but was included on the return trip to the plodding swimmer. I finally joined the marathon swim when it was three quarters complete. In a way, I was lucky as most everyone was sea sick from the rolling channel waters and burned by the hot overhead sun. I didn't stay there long as they dispatched me to a stretch of Dover beach under the high chalk cliffs where the Captain predicted our young Canadian swimmer might land. Again, it became a waiting game as I watched the flotilla sweep back and forth with the flowing tides. But patience did pay off as Marilyn came crawling up the beach at my very feet. My new fangled strobe paid off handsomely as I quickly cranked off shot-after-shot while other photographers fumbled to reload their flash bulbs. It wasn't until I got back

to Canada that I saw the papers for the first time. As the forgotten photographer I had run off with the photo coverage; I had the start... enough of the middle... and a great finish."

"Press photography in the city can be boring at times, but you never know when you'll be thrust into the midst of an exciting news break. On a cold wintery Saturday, I was sent scurrying to a farm in the Caledon area where it was reported a youth was holding the police at bay with a loaded gun. It seems that the youth's parents attempted to sell a pet horse and the boy had chosen to protect his dearest friend. Radio reports described a berserk youth firing at the police. By the time I arrived, the squads of police who had unsuccessfully searched the house and barn had decided to play a different game. They departed leaving only one officer in the home with the parents. Star reporters soon invaded the home to interview the parents and enjoy the warmth of the fire. I joined them there but our solitude was upset when a reporter yelped, 'He's coming round the

back!' We all jumped to the window to see for ourselves and were surprised when the young man burst through the door at our backs, threatening us with his rifle. Reporter, Ron Laytner, skipped out the front door and ran half a mile to a gas station to phone in the latest development of the story. He made the last edition for the weekend with headlines that screamed of Star reporters being trapped by the armed and berserk youth. Meanwhile, the boy ordered everyone out of the house, so we quickly grabbed our gear and exited to the driveway. We dragged out our departure hoping to calm the youth and gain something for the paper. He seemed calm enough, so I asked if I could retrieve my fur hat from the house, since it was so bitterly cold. He agreed and as I headed into the house I quickly changed the lens on my camera to a telephoto and started knocking off shots showing the youth aiming the rifle at the officer, his parents and the reporters.

Meanwhile, Russell Cooper of the Toronto Telegram had been out in the barn, doing his own sleuthing and, at that very moment, snuck up from behind and overpowered the youth. I was out the door in a mad dash to record the policeman and the Tely reporter wrestling the youth into submission. In quick order the youth was bundled away, the story was over, and I was heading back to the darkroom to process my exclusive photos. When the Monday papers hit the streets, the Star's front page carried a king size photo of the youth being wrestled to the ground along with the story of Star reporters being threatened at gunpoint. The Tely lacked the dramatic picture coverage but trumpeted a bizarre headline across its front page: 'TELY SAVES STAR REPORTERS'. Someone at the Star must have felt that the Tely deserved to win full laurels in this particular battle and when the second edition hit the street, my picture was ALSO on the front page of the Tely and the irksome headline had been squelched. Some one, high up, must have sent the picture over as a token of barter. I will say that there was real danger during that confrontation as I recovered a live bullet in the snow where the struggle had ensued."

Scooping the opposition was sitting in the lap of the Tely when two bank robbers chose to come out of hiding to get a meal in a Markham restaurant. The Tely photographer, relaxing in the restaurant, recorded all the action as police pounced on the robbers and unloaded bundles of money from inside their shirts. Recalls Bob, "Assigned late to the story by the Star I was dismayed to hear that our side was scooped and it would take a miracle to produce equivalent coverage. At the police station the two arresting officers agreed to be photographed with all the money tumbling out of a box. With some coaxing, they went one step further and agreed to illustrate how they pulled the money from the robbers shirt with myself substituting for the criminal; another Star photographer took the exposure. Later on, we were able to grab shots of the captives as they were being led down a hall to an identification line-up. When processing the films I noticed that a photo of one of the robbers would fit exactly into the dummied up shot of me being searched by the police. We made two prints and easily stripped them together. Although no one ever admitted to fakery, the Star had the better set of pictures covering that particular news story."

"Somehow you remember stories, not by date, but by the new equipment you've started to use. I had just bought my first Hasselblad camera with a 240mm telephoto lens, when I was sent to Ottawa to cover the visit of President Eisenhower to Canada. I was in the side balcony of the House of Commons to photograph Mr. Eisenhower as he addressed the House. After the first five minutes there isn't much to record so I was searching for anything else of interest. Adorning the top of the walls is a sculpted frieze running around the whole room. At the far end of the Chamber, it changes into a hidden balcony, decorated with two giant winged-cherubs. There, in the arms of the carved innocents, were CIA bodyguards with high powered rifles. I swung round my Hasselblad with the telephoto and snapped off two exposures then returned before the other photographers caught on to my scoop. The Star ran two pictures across a page: Eisenhower speaking at the dais gesturing to the snipers and their guardian angels!"

GEORGE WOTTON

George Wotton of Charlottetown, Prince Edward Island, travelled extensively to photograph for that provincial government's Department of Information. On one occasion he was loaned to the Department of Tourism to promote 'Fly-In-Tours' to PEI from cities like Ottawa, Toronto and Montreal. A papier mâché costume of a huge red lobster was created which would fit an actor.

Recalls George, "We accompanied this walking crustacean to various tourism and business areas in the three cities where it greeted everyone and made official pronouncements. The aim was to achieve a shock effect by the arrival of our giant lobster, which was a much different tactic than our usual travel council visits. Our goal was to be remembered; but the results were often more than what we had anticipated. Office staff, deep in their thoughts, would be startled by this giant clawed apparition clambering through their doorway. On the street, people would put their head down and pay no attention or would deliberately move off the side walk to give us lots of room.

At the conclusion of our tour, we were staying in a hotel opposite the new City Hall in Toronto. They have a beautiful setting there, so I thought I would create some interesting pictures of our lobster crawling out of the reflecting pool in front of this famous landmark. The actor agreed so I loaded myself down with three cameras and headed over for full coverage.

The lobster was worked into a pose and I had just started taking pictures when in my viewfinder I saw a man lunge at my lobster. He was kicking and beating it mercilessly, so I was extremely concerned as the actor could not defend himself while confined inside the papier mâché device. I got between the two of them but found I was taking all the beating, hindered as I was by my cameras flying about my neck. My concern was mostly to save the costume from destruction. I got the actor back to his feet and when I turned around the berserk assailant had vanished. One moment there was mayhem, then there was serenity as if nothing had happened. We could only shake our heads and assume that the attacker was intent on saving the city from an invasion of giant lobsters. So we hastily retreated to the calm and safety of our P.E.I."

Mr. Wotton was assigned by the Prince Edward Island government to photograph a Royal Tour. "The most important event to be covered, as far as they were concerned, was a reception they sponsored for the Queen. All sorts of dignitaries and government leaders were to be present and it was planned to photograph each person as they passed through the reception line and were presented to the Queen. The international press would be on hand to photograph only the first VIP through the line, then they would depart. I made preparations for days, getting the equipment together and testing the flash units for fast recycling times to make sure I would get a picture of each and every person. I thought I had every angle covered.

As the reception line started, I held back, out of courtesy, while the press boys crowded in to get their shots. Then as they were ushered away I moved forward to start my shooting. But a big Mountie grabbed me and started shoving me out with the others. I protested that I was shooting for the government – but he just kept shouting, 'OUT! OUT! OUT...' This was the time when threats had been made against the Queen and the officer was of single mind in removing me from the scene. He forcibly ejected me from the hotel while others scrambled together my equipment and cases. Within 30 seconds I was dumped unceremoniously out on the hotel balcony with NOT ONE single picture taken. That was a time when courtesy didn't pay!"

WILLIAM TETLOW

Chasing after Queen Elizabeth or other Royals during their tours of Canada requires wit and enterprise to keep the flow of photographs moving fast to the media. FedNews was a small photo agency that stayed in existence by the staff's enterprise. They chased the Royal couple across Canada setting up portable darkrooms and making do with whatever facilities they found.

On one tour they had reached Victoria and were booked into the prestigious Empress Hotel which was the official press headquarters. Bill Tetlow had processed the day's negatives and needed to dry them in a very quick manner. He had a can of methylated spirits which would extract all water from the negatives in about a minute. Bill carried a tray and his wet negatives down to the lobby and took up a position amongst the luxurious palm trees. After soaking the negs in the spirits he drained each one then set fire to a bottom corner. The highly flammable liquid burst into flames and ran up the roll of film. You had to move quickly, grabbing the bottom and releasing the top, before you burned your fingers. So, there was Bill in this grand setting, burning up his films and creating a real sensation. The dowagers of Victoria were much disturbed during their afternoon tea by Bill's fiery performance.

On another Royal Tour, the Fednews team was bivouacked for the night in one tiny room in the Chateau Laurier in Ottawa. Security for the whole area was terribly tight. The Queen and her entourage having suites in the hotel, they were particularly worried about fire. Bill Tetlow decided to wash his shirt and spread it over a light fixture that stuck out from the wall. He put it there just as the lights were turned off and everyone climbed into bed. In the morning, with the rush to get ready, someone turned on the lights and soon there was a smell of smoke floating throughout the room. No one could figure out where it was coming from and were becoming concerned for their safety. Finally, Bill recognized that his shirt was scorching and he yanked it off the hot lamps. There was a frantic effort to get rid of the smoke by opening up all the windows but that wafted the smell out into the hallway. Our attention was diverted to fire sirens down in the street. Our news sense suggested we might soon be chasing a big fire in the vicinity. The next thing there was a rumble of people running up and down the hallway. It was firemen and hotel staff frantically sniffing the smoke and looking for a fire. Bill Tetlow peered out of the room assuring them, innocently,: 'Nothing here! Not in here!' Well, Bill still had to wear that shirt and covered up the burn mark with his jacket. The press corp got wind of the incident and all day kept ribbing him about his odd smelling 'perfume'!"

When Canadian paratroopers "invaded" the Canadian National Exhibition in 1952 by chuting directly into the summer show, Bill Tetlow decided he would like to join them, in the hopes of getting some first rate stunt pictures. His request was granted by the Army and so Bill was assigned to a squad of young paratroopers, who proceeded to tell him of the dangers and risks he was running. He said he thought he could manage all right but the soldiers continued with their warnings, in patronizing tones since Bill certainly wasn't any spring chicken.When the jump was over, the photographer was asked... "How did he like it?... Had he been scared?... Pretty tough wasn't it?" Bill quietly agreed. "I liked it better.... and I wasn't as scared, nor was it as tough as ARNHEM." A whole new generation of paratroopers had emerged since the famous Arnhem drop of the Second World War.

JAMES T. LYNCH

In December 1953, Jim (James Thomas) Lynch of Fednews in Toronto, was sent to cover the Bermuda Conference where Churchill met with Eisenhower and Laniel (of France) to discuss world policy on the unstable Korean armistice and changing European defense. All the big international wire services were there to blanket the event and had an elaborate system worked out to get the pictures to the world as fast as possible.

The first greetings would take place at the airport so the American press photographers hired a seaplane to zip them across the bay to Nassau where the darkrooms were located and the US Army Signal Corp had set up to transmit the wirephoto signals out to the world. Jimmy went down early to scout the situation and figure out a way to keep up to the efforts of the powerful moneyed international press. There was a dress rehearsal, the day before the arrival of Eisenhower, during which all the Bermuda constabulary secured the airport and lined the one road that led from the airport into the city. Jimmy hired a taxi and along the whole route stopped to talk with each officer-in-charge informing them he was from Canada and appealing to their British loyalties to help him scoop the Americans.

When Eisenhower arrived the next day the mad scramble was on to get the first pictures away. But when a U.S. President lands at an airport there is a mandatory one hour ban on all flying in the area. The edict was still in force so the seaplane carrying the American film was held up getting away. Jim jumped into his taxi and headed for Nassau. All along the way the taxi was recognized and given special clearance, urged on by the police officers waving them through with: "Go to it Canadian! I say old chap go to it – Scoop the Americans!"

So Jimmy was actually the first into Nassau and quickly processed his film in his portable darkroom. His first print was a bum print so he rushed off a second print which turned out OK. Then he dashed off to the transmitting station and was surprised to

find himself the first to show up. So he handed over his good print and the Signal Corp Sergeant marked up on the scheduling blackboard: 'Federal Newsphotos – Print #1' and then started wirephotoing the picture to the New York Times. Jimmy still couldn't figure out what was delaying the AP, UPI, and Acme photographers, so to keep the machine tied up he handed over his bum print and the duty officer by firm regulation marked the board: 'Federal Newsphotos – Print #2'. That was when the AP photographer came dashing in and protested that the two pictures were the very same. But the Army man said: 'I don't care. My orders are: 'FIRST COME – FIRST SERVE!' So Jimmy effectively delayed the opposition by another precious seven minutes.

As the good print came off the wirephoto Jimmy dashed to the airport and handed that original print to the pilot of a Pan-Am flight that was leaving for New York. He told the pilot that someone from the New York Times would pick it up at the other end. Jimmy phoned the Times and was paid a thousand dollars for getting the first original print to them. The Times rushed off a copy and a cut for the paper, then re-packaged it and rushed it out to Idlewild airport where it caught a flight to London, England and so was the first print to arrive there, too. That resulted in another cash scoop for Jimmy's enterprise.

Jimmy Lynch was off to Korea as a War Correspondent and was up near the front lines to get some coverage. He was ferried around in a jeep that was equipped with a Bren gun on the back but he himself only carried his cameras. He and the driver had taken refuge in a fox hole just at dusk when gunfire broke out resulting in a lot of smoke that made it impossible to see more than twenty feet.

Jimmy recalled hearing a helicopter coming over top of them and that was the last thing he remembered.... until he woke two days later in a MASH unit hospital. What had happened was the helicopter had dropped a Mobile Army Surgical Hospital (MASH) which is a collapsed tent with all the necessary hospital equipment, packaged as a two ton unit. It crashed down on top of the two men, breaking Jimmy's collar bone and knocking them unconscious. After two days he woke to find himself in the very MASH unit which had plummeted out of the sky and came close to ending his life.

There exists a mystery about a fur coat for the Queen. Here are the facts, revealed for the first time.

For one of the Royal Tours the national press corp, who travelled with the Royal couple across the country, thought it a nice gesture to make a gift of a Canadian fur coat to the Queen. The original intention was to collect enough money to cover the cost, but the fund never quite made it. The coat was actually given to her by the Mink Breeders Association of Canada. Paul Taillefer and Peter Debra made a presentation of the pelts when the press were invited to a special reception on board the Royal Yacht Britannia.

As Taillefer recalls that part of the story: "I took along a nice blue box that contained all the pelts for the coat. During the ceremony we joked about the pelts being 'genuine wild' Canadian mink skins. To this, Prince Philip burst out laughing while the Queen just kind of smiled. When leaving the Britannia and waiting for our taxi we absent-mindedly left the box on the dockside with all those pelts, worth thousands of dollars. Thank goodness the RCMP were on their toes about stray boxes being left around, unattended, and soon delivered them back to us. Well, the coat finally did get made and was shipped through to the Canadian High Commissioner in London who officially presented it to the Queen."

"But the odd part of the story is that we didn't ever raise the money to pay for the coat. Where we expected to collect thousands of dollars, we only collected a ridiculous $55.00. One day, just before Christmas, I was in Toronto talking with Jimmy Lynch of Fednews Photos. Our heads were together trying to figure out what to do with the little money that had been collected for the fund. We went for a walk up Yonge Street and that's when inspiration hit us. That downtown area was crowded with shoppers and every hundred yards there was a Salvation Army Xmas kettle. Well each one we passed some of the conscience money was dropped in. With every ten dollar donation there were lots of warm and gracious 'Thank-you's.'"

"So Your Highness, if you ever get to read this story –that is where your coat money went!"

BORIS SPREMO

If perseverance is the sign of a top professional press photographer then Boris Spremo MPA of Toronto, ONT., must be the perfect example. His tenacity to stay with an assignment until he gets "THE PICTURE" has won him over 200 awards.

Boris immigrated from Yugoslavia in 1957, accepting his first job as a dish washer in the basement of the Royal York Hotel in Toronto. Delivery boy, tobacco picker, a miner at Elliot Lake, all were interim jobs while he learned the English language and finally found a job as a darkroom technician. Boris got the bug for photography in his native Yugoslavia when he was presented with his first camera at the age of thirteen. He went on to take formal training as a cinematographer. Immigrating to Canada, it was hard scrimping to save enough for a 4x5 press camera which enabled him to shoot week-end weddings for a studio at $15.00 each; he sometimes photographed three in a day. Luck was with Boris when he covered a soccer game that turned into a riot. With only five sheets of film he got two action photos of the game and three riot shots. These served to introduce him to the Globe and Mail and within six months he was hired as a staff photographer. It's been excitement and success since then, spending four years with the Globe before transferring to the Toronto Star as one of their top photographers. Here are some of his experiences which show why he is looked upon as "THE BEST."

Boris was sent to Poland in 1980 for the dedication of a huge monument to those killed the previous year in a labour uprising in the Gdansk shipyards. Lech Walensa was to lead this biggest show of strength since the uprising by his Solidarity supporters. Everyone wanted pictures and interviews of Lech, but he had completely dropped out of sight to all the media. Rumors were rampant that the Russians might move into Poland. Lech was in hiding while the world held its breath. Three days before the event, everyone was desperate to get something meaningful. Recalls Boris, "I was in a cab in Gdansk, heading for a labour union meeting and was chatting with the driver about my Slavic background and working for a Canadian newspaper. In Polish he said, 'You should be photographing that man, the man on the sidewalk with the fur hat.' I asked who he was. 'That's Lech Walesa!' was the answer. I could hardly believe my eyes. With everyone searching for him, here he was right in front of me. We were caught in a traffic circle but I yelled, 'Stop let me out!' I was out the door before we could pull over and I jumped a safety rail, running as fast as I could go. I started shooting pictures from 20 feet away, in case Lech chose to slip into the crowd. He looked puzzled but smiled and asked what I was doing. 'I'm here to take your picture." And with that he wished me good luck and we parted. That was an exclusive photo which none of the media could believe I got just out on the street."

"When Pierre Trudeau was elected to office for the second time I knew, from past experience, that he would go to his office the day after the election. After dogging him for the last three days of the campaign, everyone else gave up, figuring he would be too tired to do anything. I arrived at his office at 9 AM and waited. Sure enough, at 1 PM he arrived all by himself. He asked, 'What's the big deal? You've got plenty of pictures.' I explained that I wanted something of his first day back at the office; so we went up and he started opening a pile of mail that had an elastic band around it. He wound the elastic around his fingers like a sling shot, found a paper clip and fired it at me, mischievously close to my head. I was on my hands and knees shooting from in front of the desk. As soon as I got THAT SHOT I said, thank you, and beat it out the door."

"On my way to the office one morning, I got a call on the radio that a DC-9 had crashed at Malton airport. The plane had run off the runway into a ravine, so I knew its location and parked near the Etobicoke Creek. In the distance I could see the fire trucks, so I grabbed my equipment and started off across the fields. At an eight foot fence I threw my bag over and climbed over myself. The grass was tall and wet with dew so I was soon soaked to the skin as I ran towards the action. I scrambled over a second eight foot fence, cutting my hand badly, and then was confronted by the creek itself. I started to wade in cold water up to my waist to get to the other side. That was when I was spotted by a policeman up on a hill who yelled, 'Get the H*** out of there!' But somehow I just couldn't see or hear him. I was finally within view of the plane so slapped a long lens on the camera and started banging off shots. The policeman finally confronted me and ordered me off the property. With that precious roll of film I beat a hasty retreat back through the water and over the two fences. We had the first published photos of the air crash which was a real scoop."

In 1968 Boris was assigned by the Star to cover the funeral of Bobby Kennedy at Arlington National Cemetery. He photographed the day's events then processed late into the night to meet the deadline back home. Early the next morning, he was back at the cemetery hoping to catch some of the family returning for a quieter moment. Boris recalls, "There must have been hundreds if not thousands of people waiting outside the gate to visit the grave site." At 9 AM a military policeman ordered all the press to leave as the family wanted privacy that morning. Everyone packed up and departed past the long line of waiting people. Boris put his equipment bag in his car, but slipped one camera under his jacket and joined the long line-up himself. The crowd inched slowly forward, finally circled the grave site and having paid their respects departed for home. Boris, to the contrary, rejoined the end of the line and went through the slow process again and again. After two hours, Ethel Kennedy arrived with her family and as she knelt at the grave side, Boris was able to step from the line and, like any amateur, snap off a few shots. The photo won Boris another award.

Recalling the wedding of Prince Charles and Lady Diana, Boris says, "A scaffold was built around the Queen Victoria monument, across from Buckingham Palace. Only pool photographers with special passes were allowed to use it and the best positions were secured on a first-come basis. Arriving in London just the day before the wedding, Boris had no time for security clearance nor to be issued a special location. "To get on the platform and be right in the middle facing the Palace, I arrived just after midnight. Security had not yet closed off the area. The wedding wasn't to start until 11 AM the next morning, so I had a long wait on my hands. I tried to pass the time by snoozing but was wakened by rain at 3 AM. It had been a warm day so I didn't bring anything to protect myself from the wet and cold. There was absolutely no shelter and I dare not leave as I would never get back through the security. All I could do was sit like a wet mouse, freezing and shivering. With day break, I tried drying off my clothes spreading many of them along the rails of the scaffold. Looking more like a backyard clothes line, it didn't quite match the resplendent Royal decorations. One half hour before the Queen's appearance, a policeman started counting those on the platform. There was supposed to be only seven photographers, so I was soon singled out and told to leave immediately. I pleaded that I had come all the way from Canada on this my first major assignment. If I failed, I would lose my job.... and how would my wife and four children make out after that. The policeman looked sad for some moments, then finally winked and told me to stay. After that close shave and the ten uncomfortable hours, the gamble paid off handsomely with excellent coverage of both the departure from the Palace and the return of the Royal wedding party."

In 1977 Margaret Trudeau's split with her husband, Pierre, was hot news and word got out that she was flying off some place with her children. Boris and a reporter headed for the airport to get on the same plane but were thwarted by security officers who found it imperative to have extra papers filled out for the camera equipment. The two journalists followed on the next flight to Boston and there began sleuthing out Margaret's final destination. "Boston is a very big city," recalls Boris, "so we assumed she would be located in one of the smaller surrounding towns. That, in itself, was an awesome job but with a road map and the help of telephone information we asked for numbers of any Sinclair residents [Margaret's maiden name]. By the third town we recognized a first name and knew we had our party [Margaret's sister] located forty miles away in Winchester. It was evening by the time we arrived; luckily, the curtains weren't drawn and we could see a family discussion under way by Margaret, her children, her sister, and her father. Rather than bother them at that delicate point, we decided to camp out in the car and make our approach the next morning. Periodically, I would check out the house to make sure that Margaret hadn't left, always taking along my camera with a long telephoto lens just in case I saw something worthwhile. Then it was back to the car for a snooze. I guess our activities must have raised suspicions with the neighbors because early in the morning we were suddenly surrounded by three police cruisers with lights all ablaze. We were ordered out of the car with our hands over our heads then spread eagled on the hood for a thorough search. All the time they were demanding where our shotgun was. It wasn't until one of the officers checked the car and came up with my camera and the telephoto lens that they realized what it was all about. They admonished us for not first checking in with them, because in a small town everyone knows everyone else. That's when Margaret came out, recognized us, and asked how we had found her there. I said, 'Margaret, even if you go to the moon. I'm going to find you!' We stayed around and later got a photo of Margaret stepping precariously over a low picket fence while balancing a tray of food. That was an exclusive photo for the Star which was picked up by hundreds of other publications. That one shot was well worth all the effort."

Boris's escapades haven't always been photographic. He recalls when he was a young immigrant from Yugoslavia and financially strapped. He owned but one suit of which he was very proud and reserved it exclusively for courting his girlfriend, Ika, who became the future Mrs. Spremo. They were sitting on a bench in High Park one evening when a little animal appeared at their feet. "Don't move," whispered Ika in a trembling voice. Not having been in Canada very long and unable to recognize our native animals Boris exclaimed, "Pussycat!" Ika protested, "NO... IT'S A SKUNK!"... "Pussycat," reiterated Boris and bent down with a "Coochie-Coo" to beckon it closer. Since Ika was still apprehensive he clapped his hands to frighten the furry creature away. The question of identity was immediately settled as the skunk let fly its pungent spray squarely on Boris. His one precious suit got the works. That ended the evening abruptly and Boris hurried home to change, tossing the clothes in a plastic bag. When Boris's room mate came home he started closing all the windows as he thought the pungent smell was coming from the street. The bag soon ended outside when the room mate found out the true story. Next day, Boris took the clothes to a Chinese laundry. With Boris's broken English he had a hard time explaining his problem. After some hand waving the lady finally opened up the bag and PHEW! She immediately rushed Boris and his bag out the store. So it finally came to pass that Boris had to bury his one good suit. He was devastated at its loss but he did gain Ika as his bride.

In the eyes of fellow photographers Boris Spremo is a legend in his own time. Stories of this Yugoslavian-born Canadian photographer will be around long after he has hung up his cameras for the last time. Ted Grant witnessed this event during one of the many Royal Tours by Queen Elizabeth II. Her Majesty recognizes Boris from his assignments covering Royal family activities but she remembers him best from Canada's EXPO 67. An opportunity for photographers to mingle with the Royal party allowed Boris to add to his personal photo collection showing him "in the company with famous persons". During a lull in the proceedings he took a chance and stepped beside the Queen, handed his camera to another photographer and in his Yugoslavian-accented English said, "TAKE PICTURE... BORIS AND QUINN." Her Majesty smiled... Boris smiled... the camera clicked.

PAUL TAILLEFER

Paul Taillefer worked a lifetime on the Montreal Star before its untimely closing. Paul can regale you for days with stories of his adventures and mishaps. Some of the more interesting times happened during Royal Tours and here is a small sampling.

Paul recalls, "Princess Margaret lost her famous gold cigarette holder off the back of the train while touring across the Canadian Prairies. The press heard about it and made it into a big story. Hundreds of citizens along the line scoured the brush and grasslands to find the royal souvenir. Duncan McPherson, cartoonist for the Toronto Star, wrapped up the event by drawing a lone cowboy riding down the track with a jaunty gold cigarette holder poised in his mouth. At the end of the tour the press held a little reception for Margaret and broke the ice by presenting her with the cartoon plus one of her favorite gin and tonics. To show she was aware of the antics that the Press had lived through during the tour she asked if we would sing the official 'Royal Tour Song'. Out of boredom, this was a ditty created during one of the tours which the national press continues to sing while chasing Royal Cavalcades. It has been passed down, from tour to tour, and is sung to the tune of an old Sunday school song. It goes: 'When this Royal Tour is over, Oh, how happy we will be. No more waiting at the airport, no more dusty roads for me." It runs on for three verses and ends up with: 'We will tell the old Staff Sergeant. To stick his passes up his ass!' Well, for the dignity of the occasion we made a slight change and ended the serenade with: 'to throw the passes on the grass!' 'OH!' piped the Princess, 'that's not the way I HEARD you guys sing it.' Apparently, she really knew the words."

"At every stopping point on a Royal tour, the press sees hundreds and sometimes thousands of little girls dressed in Brownie (girl guide) uniforms. With bored minds it was bantered about the press bus that a conspiracy was afoot in which the same little girls were trucked from place-to-place to line the roads and pathways for the Royal entourage. 'Brownies' are like bunting that decorates every Royal Tour. On the 1959 Royal Tour, the press corps decided to form their own Brownie pack. So, in one of the Prairie cities we had our bus pull out of the Royal cavalcade, much to the consternation of the police escorts, and stopped at the front door of the local Hudson Bay store. Angela Burke of the Toronto Star dashed off to buy all the Brownie berets she could get her hands on. The amazed HB clerk rounded up some 55 tams. That night we held a party on the train to mark the end of the Prairie tour. An invitation was extended to the Royal couple and word came back that Prince Philip would attend. We even arranged for a car to bring him the whole five car lengths up to our press area where he would be met by our official greeter. But he slipped one over on us by walking through the train and joining the back of the waiting crowd who were all facing the other entrance. Suddenly we heard, 'Would somebody care to get me a scotch and soda?' It was Prince Philip announcing his arrival. When everyone turned around he saw us dressed in our official Brownie berets. He, too, was soon inducted into our group with his own tam. The party reached great heights of frivolity that night with the Prince being dressed in a Mountie uniform, presented with a set of RCMP spurs and dubbed 'Sir Phil, Mountie Extra-ordinaire'. Some of Royal Ladies-in-Waiting also attended the party and they were presented with packages of Brownie cake mix which we offered as evidence of the conspiracy to create instant-brownies (girls) at all the tour stops. The Ladies instantly took to testing our theory by mixing the powder with scotch. Then they had their burly Scotland Yard bodyguard, Kelly, hold me down while they test fed me the mixture. Well, the next morning Frank Grant, Jim Lynch and myself were sitting on the curb as the Queen and Prince Philip came out to get in their car. Prince Philip turned and asked, 'How do your heads feel this morning?' Frank Grant retorted, 'Not very well, sir. And you?' At that the Queen gave the Prince the dirtiest look the world has ever seen."

"On the last night of the '59 tour, we threw another doozer of a party in the Lord Nelson Hotel in Halifax. It started off on one of the lower floors but when Frank Grant led us in a Kangaroo jump, the manager sent the hotel detectives to quiet us down. Each time this happened we had the Prince's personal bodyguard talk to them. He would say, 'I'm Kelly of the Yard.' The police always acquiesced but asked us to please tone it down. When their visits got repetitive we moved the party up another floor and started all over again. Eventually, we ran out of floors but discovered a fire ladder and a hatchway that led to the hotel roof. In the midst of an impenetrable Halifax fog we continued to carouse to the wee small hours of the morning. Frank Kelly, the Scotland Yard detective assigned to protect the Royal couple, had thoroughly become one-of-the-boys. So during that evening's festivities he was made a member of the Boston Police with a badge offered by Walter Green, the AP photographer from Boston. I presented him with a red French Canadian toque while the girls wrote across the front of his shirt 'Kelly The Great'. Jimmy Lynch presented him with a bottle of scotch shaped like a camera. The drinking glasses were disguised as lens caps while the cork stopper looked like a winding knob. Kelly slept it off in my room that night and the next morning we arrived at the Lt.-Governor's residence for the start of that day's activities. Well, who should come out of the door, first, but Prince Philip. He eyed the grey state of our faces and asked Kelly about relinquishing his status with Scotland Yard to join the Boston Police and then said he was quite curious to see Kelly's shirt. Evidently, he knew everything that happened at the party"

Everything seemed to happen on that tour. We were touring the Ontario Midlands in a motorcade, then were to transfer to a train. With the schedule running late, the engineer was eager to keep to his timetable. We all understood the signal that two blasts of the whistle meant the press were to get on board, while a single whistle meant the Queen was boarding the train. Our transport was trapped at the end of the long motorcade while the Royal couple exited their limousine, made their fairwells, and headed for the train. From the whistle blasts we realized we were about to be left behind, so everyone piled off the bus and headed for the shortest route to our section of the train. Some 35 photographers and reporters –men with heavy movie equipment, women with skirts and high heels. We all spotted the same lane way leading through a beautifully manicured garden next to the rail line. The garden

owner was peacefully sitting there, drinking beer and couldn't have cared less about the Queen, when we charged through like a herd of stampeding buffalo. He watched in dismay as the news hounds destroyed his garden, hurdled his back fence then scuttled through a gully up to the train. The Vice President of Air Canada saw all this from the train and likened it to the Calgary Stampede. That tour was completed in 45 days. With such a fast pace of whistle stops we had to jump off the train before it had stopped, in order to be in position when the Queen made her disembarkation. A CBC-TV cine photographer with heavy camera gear jumped off early and slammed into a railway switch at the side of the track. We had to ship him off to the hospital. That was the 1959 tour when the Queen became pregnant... we weren't responsible for that!"

"Success at covering a news event can hang on the whim of fate. I was covering the Springhill mine disaster in New Brunswick and after four endless days I crashed into a deep sleep. When I came to, they had rescued the last survivor out of the mine, alive and I had missed the whole event. I was in a panic how to cover myself so I rushed to the hospital and questioned a nurse. She explained, 'They are all gone.'... 'Well,' I pleaded, 'who was the last guy out? Where does he live?'... She was finishing her shift so offered to drop me off at the man's home. There I found him, still black with coal dust, with two daughters who had arrived from Montreal and Toronto – a great tie-in for our paper. I took one shot of them together and rushed off to Amherst to process and wirephoto to Montreal. As the transmission finished I heard my editor yell, 'Great shot – front page!' They had held up the last edition for my photo. With audacity I asked if they wanted any more pictures – I didn't want them to know I had missed everything and only had that ONE shot. I breathed a sigh of relief when they said they had all they needed."

"Remember the big fire at La Grande River in Quebec? A union worker went crazy and punctured the gasoline tanks, then set fire to everything. The company wouldn't allow us to fly into the project but we heard workers were being moved to Matagami. So we headed there and started making the rounds of the three taverns in town figuring it was the best way to start. The stringer from the Toronto Telegram suggested that someone must have taken pictures of the fires, so I started asking around and this one guy said, 'Oh yes, I've got two Polaroid shots.' I could have screamed with glee and ordered up beers for the whole gang. I asked how much he wanted for the pictures but he said, 'Just pay a round of beers.' These were Polaroid colour, and with the dull weather the pictures were beautiful. I put them on the wirephoto machine just in time for the final edition. The editors were delighted."

"We were in Quebec City for the Cardinal Villeneuve funeral at the old Basilica and I climbed up to the balcony to take a time exposure of the overall scene. This was before television and there was absolutely no light in the place... just deep gloom. So I did several time exposures hoping to get something on the film. Then veteran cine photographer, Roy Tash of Associated Screen News, showed up with his movie camera and did the same thing giving a five second exposure for each and every frame. Since it takes sixteen frames just to produce one second of movie action he painstakingly counted off: 101 - 102 - 103 - 104 - 105, then advanced to the next frame and repeated again 101 - 102 - 103 - 104 - 105. The ceremony was four hours long and hardly anyone moved; so he had plenty of time to build up his footage, inch by inch. I went to the movie house the following week to assure myself of the results. And there I saw the whole Basilica lit up like a modern television studio. Time exposures for movies – frame by frame. That, to me, was fantastic. But you could always rely on Roy Tash to come through!"

LORNE BAMFORD

As a young man during World War Two, Lorne Bamford of London, Ont., assisted a photographer to shoot the interior of an armament factory making gun barrels. There were lathes stretched as far as the eye could see for some three city blocks. The only place to get an overall view was up in the Supervisor's cabin that was suspended from the roof fifty feet in the air. The Supervisor had a clear view and could look out over the shop to see if anyone was goofing off.

"We set up the 8x10 camera," says Lorne, "shooting through a porthole. For illumination we used a Victor flash gun packed with flash powder and held it out a side window during the exposure. 'Watch this!' the photographer said mischievously as he made the first picture. The flash went off with a tremendous white light that carried for hundreds of feet. But it also erupted with an almighty BANG and everyone thought the place had blown up. It scared about every worker in the plant as they dropped tools or just about fainted on the spot. I'm sure some of the foremen had bladder problems at that moment. We laughed hysterically and enjoyed our little joke."

"Completing the job, we packed up the equipment and were just leaving when the Superintendent of the plant stopped us and asked, 'Had a lot of fun boys?' We agreed, yes, and said it had been really worth it. The Super said, 'Before you leave you better take a look back up there' and he pointed to an enormous black mark on the side of the cabin where we had held the flash out the window. 'MY GUYS', continued the Super, 'are going to have a lot of fun watching you clean that up!' "

"Well, we spent the rest of that afternoon at the top of a couple very wobbly ladders, – hanging on for dear life, while we scrubbed away our little joke."

LARRY BOCCIOLETTI

Flashbulbs, although they were received as a blessing by photographers, also brought surprise and heartache to many who used them. Much later the changeover to electronic (strobe) flash had its own dangers.

Larry Boccioletti originally comes from the Welland, Ont., area where he had a studio. He was assigned by the Toronto Telegram to help cover a Royal Tour of Niagara Falls and was one of fifty photographers that were jammed into a designated area where Her Majesty was to inspect the famous Flower Garden. As Larry recalls the scene, "The Queen was strolling towards us when Peter Tenszen, my competition from the Star, asked if I had an extra flash bulb as he had run out. I tossed him a #22 which he fumbled and let fall to the ground. He inserted the bulb, anyway, and fired off the shot as the Queen was about five feet away. The bulb exploded with a shower of glass and she gave him a real dirty scowl, then proceeded on. That evening when the papers came out, they ran stories about how a photographer had annoyed the Queen. I was quite put out by all the fuss; it was MY flash bulb but he got all the publicity."

"I hired a young lad as an apprentice and he looked after all my equipment. I dashed out one day to cover a fast breaking story for the Toronto Telegram. A robber had taken a hostage in Hamilton, forced him to drive to Welland then murdered him. I was told to wait outside the local funeral home and grab a shot of the victim's wife as she left. There were about seven other photographers waiting as well and as she came out faced a barrage of flash bulbs. The other photographers were using bulky press cameras and only got one or two shots while I proudly had a Rolleiflex with a brand new Braun Hobby Strobe Flash and was able to crank off five shots, shooting from the hip. I was quite satisfied with myself, particularly when several of the regular pressmen asked if they could buy one of my shots if their's didn't turn out. It was at that moment I was asked if I always replaced my lens cap that fast after every shoot. I looked down at my camera and with a sinking feeling saw the shiny cover fastened to the lenses. My apprentice had dutifully put the lens cap on and I hadn't noticed it. I took it off and threw it across the street in a rage. Needless to say, I had no pictures, just a blank roll of film. My buddy photographers had a great belly laugh out of it and never let me forget as whenever we met they would enquire, most courteously, about my lens cap."

"I got into photography when I was smitten by a Cine Kodak 8mm movie camera. It took months to scrape up the 70 dollars to finally take full possession. That was when the dealer told me there was no film available because there was a war on! I soon realized I couldn't make any money, so I decided to buy a still camera and sell prints. I bought an Argus C3 from Warner Drugs in St. Catharines. I was assured it was easy to operate and would make good pictures. At $105 dollars I had to do the whole lay-away bit again. Finally it was paid for and I was handed the camera with a roll of film and instructions to set the shutter at 100th of a second at f8. It was also suggested I buy some #11 flash bulbs in case I wanted to do some night shooting. I proudly hung the camera around my neck and wandered around the city until darkness fell."

"As luck would have it, a spectacular fire broke out in a shoe store on the main street and I was on the spot. I cranked off the twelve shots, using up all my bulbs, then ran a few blocks to the local St. Catharines Standard hoping to make a sale. Staff photographer, Don Sinclair, said he already had some shots but offered to process the film in case I had something better. Here I was, my first day with the camera and I was about to make my first big sale. How great!

But talk about shock and disappointment... the film was completely blank! Mr. Warner was not aware that the C3 is only synchronized for flash at 1/50th of a second, not the 1/100th as he had suggested. I found that out by finally reading the manual. So my first effort with flashbulbs was a complete bust."

Now that flashbulbs are considered a collector's item, Larry searches out residual supplies to sell them to movie producers who are shooting scenes with press photographers in action. Larry adds a new twist to the flashbulb saga. "I was in Los Angeles and was given a tour of one of the big prop houses for the movie industry. I noticed an employee packing several Speed Graphics, obviously being shipped out on a rental. When I asked my host about flashbulbs, he said they were becoming scarce and offered to buy as many as I could supply since he had twenty press cameras on the go.

He was also interested in flash guns that would fire the #5 bayonet base bulbs. Since he paid a good price for the shipment of bulbs I decided to run some ads in the used camera magazines and was amazed by the response. I had letters and phone calls from all over the States and made many purchases so that I soon had an inventory of some 3000 bulbs in my backyard shed."

"I shipped off twenty flashguns with a nice markup in US Dollars and envisioned a hefty profit on the demand for bulbs to keep those units supplied. After a month there was no sign of an order so I phoned down to the guy to see what the situation was. Much to my chagrin, the client had modified the guns by putting electronic components inside the barrel with a strobe flash tube mounted in the reflector. Thus he eliminated the need for the scarce and expensive flashbulbs."

"The bottom line is: I now have a load and a half of flashbulbs for sale. If lightning ever strikes my tool shed, those bulbs will illuminate Toronto for miles and miles around."

ROBERT E. PATCHETT

Bob Patchett MPA HLM of Hamilton, Ont., broke into photography in the 1950's working for Ron Nelson of London. "We were using the biggest #50 flash bulbs to photograph a massed choir for the Messiah concert in an arena," say Bob. "There were three assistants spaced out around the arena, each with a flash extension to attend to. It was our job after each exposure to bring the lamp down and replace the burned bulb with a fresh one then run it up again. We couldn't see the photographer but knew that we had about 15 seconds before he would take the next shot. We got the first shot taken and I brought down the reflector. I was slowed up fumbling to get the new bulb into its socket when suddenly Mr. Nelson fired the second shot. There I was, bulb in hand, when it went off. Boy was that hot... it burned itself right into my skin and I couldn't let go. That was one job I will never forget."

GEORGE W. JAMES

George James MPA of Chatham, Ont., recalls his first newspaper photography experience in 1930. Working out of Leamington, as a reporter for the Windsor Star, his camera was a folding Kodak Brownie with a simple lens and shutter. The Star's legendary Horace Wild provided George with the camera plus a home-made flash gun and two ounces of flash powder. The gun consisted of a gas-stove lighter (flint rubbing on steel) mounted on a six inch handle to which was soldered the shiny lid of a Keene's mustard tin. The tin provided a convenient saucer to hold the flash powder. "How much to use?" That was answered by Horace as: "Oh! just enough!" The picture was taken by squeezing a cable release to open the camera shutter, then in the other hand squeezing the gas lighter held high above the head. A spark from the flint-igniter would fire the flash powder. This rough and ready method produced pictures that were regularly run in the Star. The flash also produced a big cloud of acrid smoke that left subjects and photographer coughing their lungs out. George recalls, "The chorus line for a local-talent musical was practicing in a church basement when I was called upon to take their publicity picture. The larger-than-normal group took more space and required me to stand well back. So I figured more light would be needed and shook out extra powder; it must have been a bit too much because when I took the picture there was quite an explosion. The girls screamed and ran for cover, bystanders swore the ceiling lifted perceptibly, the solder on my flash gun melted and the mustard-tin lid fell in a heat-curled ball on the floor... but I had the picture. Luckily, I was able to get the local tinsmith to solder another lid in place, so I was soon back in business shooting smaller groups this time!"

JOSEPH W. H. STONE Sr.

Joe W. H. Stone Sr. SPA,HLM of Fredericton, New Brunswick tells of the 1930's when he was working for the Climo Studios in Saint John. "One Easter," says Joe, "we were asked to photograph the inside of a church, festooned with a great array of white lilies around the altar. Looking it over, we decided that we had better use flash powder to get the necessary illumination. Since we were running a bit low we borrowed some powder from another photographer by the name of Lou Harrison; but we hadn't figured that he followed a different formula in which he used a base of black gun powder. We went into the church, loaded up a big shot and fired it off. Looking up a huge cloud of sooty smoke was ascending into the rafters of the church. We fled out of there in a hurry just as the soot started settling out onto the pews. The congregation was arriving for the services and we grimaced at the thought of what was going to happen to all their pastel coloured Easter outfits. There would surely be a lot of black bottoms and ruined hats by the end of the service."

GILBERT A. MILNE

Gib Milne MPA of Toronto, Ont., remembers when he was requested to photograph Gordon Sinclair of radio station CFRB and the flash bulb exploded. "That was a common occurrence before the bulbs were covered with a plastic safety coating; they would go off with quite a loud bang. Luckily Sinclair wasn't hurt by the flying glass but it scared everyone. It was the first bulb I had reached for after a previous job in a brewery. That job had me shooting over an open vat containing some 25 thousand gallons of beer to illustrate the foam and fermentation process. I shudder to think of the mess I would have inflicted if, by chance, my bulb had exploded into all that beer."

ANDRE AMYOT

André Amyot MPA HLM of Longueuil, Quebec describes how: "The Olympic Stadium is used in summer for baseball while in winter they hold big trade shows there. At this particular exhibition there was everything to do with 'agriculture'; they bring in all the animals: cows, horses, dogs and cats. In the equipment section they were just introducing electronic machines to read the bar codes on packaging. There was quite a display with six or seven of them lined up, all working marvelously picking out the codes and magically providing the prices and descriptive data; the crowds that gathered were awed by the up-to-date technology."

"I was hired by a large food chain to photograph the people around the machines. There were so many people around the first machine I used the wide angle lens and blasted away with my strobe flash... wacko! wacko! For some unknown reason the machine stopped working and the technician couldn't figure what was wrong. So I moved on to another machine to get the action and the interested spectators; I took a shot and that machine stopped working too! I tried to shoot FOUR of these machines before it finally dawned on me that I was probably causing the failures. I wasn't aware of it, but these were the first generation of optical scanners and, without realizing it, my flash was hitting the sensors and burning out their circuits. The technicians were all over the machines trying to find the problem and restart them."

"When I realized it might be me who had made such a shamble of their expensive machines, I changed over and shot the rest of the photographs by available light.... then slipped quietly away!"

EVERETT ROSEBOROUGH

Ev Roseborough of Toronto, Ont., tells of the time he and assistant, Bill "Willy" Morchen, were photographing a choir from a vantage point in the balcony of a church. They had taken the first shot using the largest #75 flash bulbs, screwed into the receptacles of a big tungsten light reflector; it grouped a number of bulbs together, rather than just one. Firing of the bulbs was accomplished by plugging into the house 110 volt-current. After the first exposure, Ev changed the film holder while Willy started to replace the flash bulbs. But they forgot to pull the plug from the wall socket, so when the assistant put in the first fresh bulb, it went off directly into his face. Willy was momentarily stunned, and with his back to the edge of the balcony teetered backwards over the low guard rail. Ev, surprised by the flash, turned just in time to see his companion desperately flailing his arms and heading to certain doom below. With instant reaction and a life saving lunge, Ev caught a patch of clothing to drag his friend back to safety.

MAURICE J. (SLIM) BENT

Slim Bent of Toronto, Ont., had a hair raising experience with flash powder, to say the least. "The device I had to fire it with," says Slim, "was a little tray on a handle with a lighted wax match at one end and a quantity of powder located at the other end. The trick was to tip the tray forward to run the powder into the flame of the match. I held it over my head and tried it out but nothing happened. I shook it well... still nothing happened. I brought it down to the level of my face to see what was the problem and that was when it went off... AND SO DID MY EYEBROWS!"

"Now you'd think once would be enough, but on another occasion I picked up a Speed Graphic camera with its flash gun and an extension flash, both of which were loaded with flash bulbs. I tried to gather up everything with one hand and must have pressed the trigger, because suddenly two #22 flashbulbs went off into my face. For the next half hour I was wandering around blind as a bat."

Slim had the task to photograph 400 banquet guests at a large Toronto hotel. "I had the 8x10 camera set up and ready. It took ten of the big #50 flashbulbs, well spaced out, to light the ballroom. I coaxed the crowd into a pose and fired the shot; then, to my horror, saw that I had forgotten to pull the dark slide from the film holder. The photo was ruined... so I quickly yelled, 'Hold everything I want to take another.' Luckily we had enough extra bulbs so my assistant and I ran around madly replacing a full set of ten bulbs; I made darn sure that the slide was out for the second shot. In those days that is what you called a 'back-up' when you went out on a job with 20 big flash bulbs and two sheets of film."

A photographer who worked with Slim was photographing a large banquet and chose to pre-wire his flashbulbs into the ballroom chandeliers. Each bulb had a black paper placed behind it so that the light would not flare back into the camera lens. Unfortunately, the photographer left no space between paper and bulb; so when he took the exposure the papers caught fire from the intense heat and showered the guests with flaming debris. It didn't go well with the formally dressed guests who scattered to get out of the way!

JOHN H. BOYD

Back in 1923 when an elaborate junction of five streetcar lines was nearing completion in Toronto, press photography was still young. Film speed and flash weren't what they are to-day so ingenuity was necessary to overcome challenging situations. The ceremony for driving the "last spike" was not to be missed by the newspapers but a problem arose when the event was scheduled to happen at night.

To John Boyd MPA HLM, staff photographer for the Globe & Mail, that meant a lot more flash powder was needed to illuminate the expansive scene. John coaxed the other press photographers to pool their quotas of powder while he built a super-sized reflector in which the powder would be fired. On the night of the event all photographers gathered on a high vantage point overlooking the scene and arranged their 5x7 and 4x5 view cameras mounted on tripods. Each photographer added his supply of powder to the big curved metal contraption that John had created as a flash-pan.

At the arranged moment in the ceremonies, the dignitaries and workers posed rigidly for the official photograph. John gave the signal to remove lens caps and fired off the shot. KA-BOOM! went the flash and everything became brilliant daylight. What a stupendous explosion... the buildings shook... the ground trembled... the pan took off like a bird, flying end-over-end while surprised photographers jumped for cover.

When the smoke and commotion had cleared it was realized nobody had recorded the picture as every camera was shaken by the very explosion which provided the light. There wasn't enough powder left, nor nerve, for a second try.

WILMOT BLACKHALL

Wilmot Blackhall SPA of Lindsay, Ont., explains his accompanying portrait by the following story: "My most interesting photographic request was to judge a photo contest at a nudist colony. During the proceedings one resident, dressed only in his shoes, offered to buy my Hasselblad for $25. Not withstanding this staggering offer I pointed out to him that he obviously had no money on him. Later, we all got together for a sumptuous banquet where only yours truly was dressed for dinner."

"When I was at engineering school the lab boys found a box of flash bulbs, and since I was the only one interested in taking pictures, I was given the whole batch to take home. They had a screw type base and were full of an aluminum foil. I did some tests by screwing a bulb into my bedroom lamp, arranged a little table top setting before my camera and then pulled the chain on the bedroom lamp to fire the flash for the exposure. It made a brilliant flash but blew out the fuse in the basement. We had to call the hydro company to come and put in new cartridge fuse. I didn't dare tell my parents what I had done.

I put one in my Dad's reading lamp. His favorite time just after supper was to sit in his big chair and read the newspaper. He always sat down and reached over to pull the chain to put on the light. This time there was a terrific flash so he called my Mother over to ask what kind of bulbs she was buying as the one in the lamp was so black he couldn't read with it. I figured I had better explain to him that I was testing some photographic lamps; I never did get any pictures with them.

In those days we had flash sheets which looked like the cardboard dividers you have in Shredded Wheat and were about the same consistency. I had an envelope with six sheets with which I was going to take some pictures of our wiener roast at Rouge River. I was elected to search for wood and while I was away somebody found the envelope on the seat of my car and decided to use the paper to start the fire. Suddenly there was this tremendous burst of light as all my flash sheets went off at once. Nobody could see for a while and there was so much smoke the property owners almost called the fire department. I didn't get any pictures that time either!"

"Being interested in nature photography, I decided one day to photograph a colony of ants. I fixed up my super macro equipment and got right down on my hands and knees to photograph the little pests. A full hour later I struggled to stand up rubbing my sore knees and straightened my aching back. But I knew it was worth it as I was sure I had the winning 'slides-of-the-month'. I had recorded them painstakingly from all angles and in a variety of lighting. Starting to rewind the film, I suddenly realized how loose the camera was. I soon discovered that I had meticulously shot 36 exposures with my wife's camera which was an identical model to mine. Unfortunately, her camera was empty of film and my whole effort was down the drain!"

Wilmot continues, "While visiting a family friend, I noticed she kept shouting at me. I was puzzled but didn't say anything to her about it. After some time, she said: 'I'm sorry to see you are getting deaf'. She was staring intently at my shirt pocket and I realized my Weston exposure meter must have looked like a hearing aid case!"

SANDY BARRIE

Here are a few stories from Sandy Barrie of Queensland, Australia which have an earlier perspective in time.

Sandy is a portrait photographer in Brisbane and is interested in the photographic history of the late 1800's. Mr. Barrie has built up an enviable collection of old cameras along with the stories of photographers and their business'. Nineteenth century photographers had a much harder time to record their images. The wet-plate process required guncotton to be dissolved in ether for coating their glass plates. Working under candle light it could be a highly volatile process which often led to spectacular accidents.

Julius Stecher suffered the ultimate effects of the explosive power of flash powder when he was blown to bits near Ipswich in 1913. Police reported that his wagon, equipment and horses were "spread for an acre". Although dynamite was first suspected, it was theorized that a fire in the darkroom-wagon may have set off a flask of powder.

Here's a different type of flash that proved to be most embarrassing to Sandy. The moral of the story is –Never, never, try out a new suit on one of your wedding assignments. "On this particular job, my bride had no voice while the groom was deaf. Many guests spoke in sign language, so those who could hear communicated my instructions to the wedding party. Mostly, I used charades to relay instructions for all the hand positioning so I was quite agile with my body language. We had a beautiful landscaping setting with a waterfall. Everything was going well, but oddly the bride and groom started "talking" and making funny gestures with their hands. All the time there was much smiling which gradually spread amongst the other bridal members. It took a few minutes to register with me that nylon zippers are notorious for coming undone and mine had chosen to do it at a most inappropriate moment. I was the center of attraction with my fly wide open. I found it most embarrassing and insist now on all metal zippers!"

ALBERT GILBERT

Albert Gilbert CM F/PPOC SPA HLM of Toronto, Ont., having attained innumerable honours and titles as one of Canada's leading portrait photographers, received high accolade from his country with his appointment to the Order of Canada. Lecturing throughout the world, Mr. Gilbert is cited as an ambassador of goodwill through his contributions to the field of photography.

The memories of photographing world leaders, dignitaries and the 'beautiful people' are all diminished when Al reminisces about the children who have visited his studio. Mr. Gilbert recalls a perky eight year old girl who came to him and said: "I've looked at all the studios and I've chosen you. I'd like a portrait of myself and my two year old brother as an anniversary present for my mother." Al was intrigued by the youngster's self confidence. "I can pay for it!" she added, "I've got eighteen dollars but I can't let you have it all at once. I'll pay you two dollars a week, and you have to promise one thing -on the anniversary day I would like it in your window, just like the other big ones." Al had been completely won over and said, "That's fine, you've got yourself a deal! But how are we going to get your little brother here?" "Oh!" she said, "I'll take him for a walk." Al asked for the name of the little girl's school teacher and verified the facts to assure everything was OK. "On the shooting day I met the child and her brother at a corner near their home. There was a park across the road which we used as a location for the portrait. We finished the picture and put it in the window and on the appointed day the little girl brought her mother and father to see the big surprise. They stared at the window, in utter disbelief, with tears in their eyes. I later got a thank-you letter from the little girl and also one from the mother. I learned they were quite a poor family and we have been friends ever since. I gave them the l6X20 portrait for $l8.00. The little girl, true to her word, came regularly to pay $2 every week, which she earned from her paper route."

"Another memory," says Al. "I got a call from a client who wanted to have her thirteen year old son photographed at home.

She warned that the boy just could not stay still, so if I didn't have patience then not to bother as she felt I never would be able to get him. 'Fine!' I said, 'let's set an appointment.' When I arrived at the house, the kid was pinching his sister and teasing her with all sorts of names. I finally got him set in a pose then headed back to the camera for the shot... and he's gone. I get him back again, get all set up and command: 'Stay there for a minute 'til I get your picture.' He's gone in a flash. I cornered him the third time and now HE lectured ME. 'You know Mr. Gilbert if you'd work a bit faster you would make a lot more money!' "

"Through my son, Michael, I've learned much about the history of photography. His penchant for collecting early cameras, prints and memorabilia has made me aware of the old processes and the early masters of photography. That knowledge has proven its worth. I went to Mexico to give a lecture and on the Sunday morning, the wife of my host, Hector Herrera, asked if I would like to visit the local thieves' market. It covers some ten city blocks with everyone spreading their wares on the ground. In the very first stall there was a framed picture on the floor. The glass was broken and filthy with dirt but where one of the pieces of glass was missing, I could tell it was a platinum print. Trying to clean off some of the grime I asked Mrs. Herrera to find out how much the vendor wanted for the 'dirty picture'. I thought I could read something like 'Weston 1921'. He mentioned that it was by a famous American photographer and wanted the equivalent of $30. 'Let's pay him,' I said. 'No! no!' Mrs. Herrera protested, 'you have to argue with him. He won't like it if you don't haggle.' But the vendor was firm and I finally bought the picture for the thirty dollars. We took it home and underneath the glass found a portrait of a young woman. It had a penciled inscription: 'To the maestro', then some love words and a signature: 'Tina Madotti'. The picture, itself, was signed by Edward Weston and dated 1921. The next day, the newspapers were running stories to mark the anniversary of the Mexican revolution. Like a bolt out of the blue, the story gave enough details to piece together the history of my picture. Tina Madotti was a Mexican revolutionist who became the mistress of Edward Weston. She was a photographer, in her own right, and there are many books about her. Hector, my host, has been choking ever since his refusal to go to the market; little wonder, since we can now value the picture to a similar Weston print that sold in New York for over $100,000."

Disasters? Yes, Al has had his share! "Back in the old days," recalls Al, "when we were using 8x10 film, our studio was kept hopping on Saturdays shooting wedding groups -one after another. Ukrainian wedding parties of 30 and 40 people would crowd into the studio to have their photographs taken. I only had ten holders which would be sent downstairs for processing They were immediately reloaded and sent back up. I had an assistant in the darkroom to develop the film right away. We had to rush through 100 to 400 thank-you cards, per wedding, for delivery to the reception by the very same day. This particular day, I sent down my holders to be processed and the guy didn't come back up. Finally I yelled down the stairs: 'What the h*** is the trouble, I need those holders.' A moanful voice floated up, 'Your going to kill me. I made new developer, –it was too hot and has ruined all the films. The emulsion has just slid off to the bottom of the tank!'... I sure had a lot of reshooting to do. Luckily, most of the wedding party was still there."

Al had to take a photograph in the Toronto Stock Exchange for an annual report. "We were to shoot from the second floor spectators room to show two executives looking out on the main trading floor. The two areas have different types of lighting - tungsten and fluorescent. With light stands we wedged a 4x6 foot panel up against the ceiling to block the fluorescent lights above our subjects, standing at the window's edge. This enabled us to balance the type of lighting. Right in the middle of the shoot the scrim and stands came loose toppling right out of the window and crashing

20 feet to the Traders floor with a loud BANG! It wasn't too busy at that moment so, when those stands hit the floor, you should have

heard the yells. Luckily, nobody was underneath to get hurt. I cleared out of there fast sending an assistant down to pick up the equipment."

"If you've ever tried to photograph visiting VIP's you know how it can be a real pain in the butt. You have to be up in a secured area two hours in advance. With the Prime Minister of Israel, Levi Eshkol, they set aside a series of rooms and I was given one in which to work. They move the Prime Minister from room to room all the way down the hallway giving only five minutes to each person, whether its for an interview or for a photograph. There's the Toronto Star in one room, the Sun in another, the Globe, TV and radio etc and its a real production line, running like clockwork. When Eshkol flew into Toronto in the morning, I was at the airport to snap pictures which I rush processed and used to locate eye glass frames that matched the Prime Minister's own heavy glassed spectacles. His glasses were so thick I knew I would never be able to see his eyes... while my borrowed frames had no glass in them. I put up an appropriate blue background and when he arrived I showed him the picture from that morning; he willingly changed glasses and did the shoot. When he passed away, the Israeli government looked through all the pictures taken of him and chose my portrait to use on a commemorative stamp in 1970. When they asked to use it, I shipped them the negative as a gift and have been in friendly contact ever since."

"Then, when David Ben Gurion was here, the Consulate called and said: 'If you want to take his picture better get down to the Royal York Hotel fast.' So I grabbed my camera and some lights. Every floor down there was cordoned off by RCMP and bolstered by Israeli security. Since no one had cleared me ahead of time, the security people gave me a serious hassle asking what I was doing there, who was I? All the Press boys were sitting on their heels, waiting. They took me off to a separate room and I was getting worried. But there was the chap from the Israel Information Services whom I had been corresponding with for over 15 years. As soon as they mentioned my name he asked: 'You're Gilbert?' And immediately he straightened everything out. It proves that friendships, even through correspondence, can be helpful at times. I was given the green light and ushered into a room where 20 people were in the midst of a high level meeting; I was told to 'just snap pictures' but I protested that I didn't take pictures like that. I wanted a proper portrait. When Ben Gurion arrived, accompanied by his wife, I asked him to pose, but his wife interrupted as to why I was bothering the old man. I replied that I had been waiting for years to photograph him; at that Ben Gurion resolved the whole problem by asking: 'How many pictures do you want to take?'... I replied, 'Four!'... He said, 'You can take FIVE!'... He was that kind of guy."

"Over the years I've had a number of assistants so I was bound to have my share of problems with some of them. One chap who was shooting weddings for me got seriously into the drink. The father of the bride got up to toast a very close associate, one of the top comedians of the day, who had flown up from New York just for the wedding. The father wanted to introduce this special friend for the honour bestowed to him and his daughter. So, they pulled open the curtain and who dances across the stage but my inebriated assistant. That was the end of him! Another time, I had a big tall guy working for me who got into an argument with the caterer at a place where we did a tremendous number of weddings. Something was said by the caterer and my photographer lifted him up off the floor by his neck and jammed him against the wall. Those things aren't good for business at all."

"I went to New York to do some location portraits for Kodak. We were to shoot Wilber Scott at NBC but it turned out they were on strike, at the time, and we knew we couldn't get our equipment through the parading strikers. Besides, the Iran problem was about to break open and all the studios and newsrooms were keyed for that event; so they wouldn't let us get near the sets. I, therefore, had a real problem on my hands with 20 people in tow: Kodak people, public relations and art directors –but no place to shoot the picture. So I called a musician acquaintance of mine, Jack Lawrence who's written a number of famous songs, to see if he could suggest a location. Without hesitation he invited me to make use of his apartment which is in the middle of downtown Manhattan; it is one of the most magnificent suites you have ever seen and was featured in Architectural Digest. So my reputation which was on the brink of failure, suddenly shone like glory when we walked into this beautiful setting and were given free access to the whole two floors. So that is where we shot Wilber Scott. Then we had to shoot Spencer Christian at ABC and they gave me a room that had nothing on the walls. It was an empty reception room that offered no decor, so we had to steal furniture all over the building in order to create our own setting. With my experience in overcoming the challenges on location I usually can work around any problem. I've always been an innovator and don't wait for trends to develop."

Al is noted for his power napping and the effect it has on him. Gail Gilbert knows that she can let Al turn on his favorite TV sports program because five minutes later, he will be sound asleep; then she can turn to her own program. Assistant David Lewis tells of the time in Chicago, after a day-long shoot for an annual report, the crew had their supper and returned to the hotel exhausted. Everyone drifted off to bed but Al was 'paralyzed' in front of the TV - power napping. After half an hour he got up, showered, shaved and dressed for the day's activities. Then he walked over to the window and wondered what all the cars were doing in the street at six in the morning. He thought he had slept all night but, in fact, he had only napped 20 minutes. He repeated the same thing in Vancouver and also in Boston, ever eager to be off to his next assignment –but each time twelve hours too early.

M. JAMES MATHIESON

Jim Mathieson MPA HLM of Calgary, Alberta, recounts the time a lady came in to have her passport taken. He started to photograph her in the usual way but the lady protested, "You're doing the wrong side... you should be photographing the back of my head... the way it appears on the passport application." She was obviously referring to the blank image on the form that looks like a silhouette.

MARIANNE KOVACS

Marianne Kovacs of Kingsville, Ont., vividly remembers her first days working for a studio in Leamington. Her boss was late in returning from an assignment while a passport sitting was due at any moment. Luckily, the studio was still set up from a previous portrait; it just required changing a canvas background that was suspended by hooks to the motorized backgrounds. "I thought it would be a big help if I got everything ready, so I hit the switch to lower the proper passport background. Immediately, the canvas dislodged from its hooks and started falling towards me. Before I could grab it, the canvas hit the hairlight which tipped over and fell on a big soft-light box which in turn fell over onto a background light. It was like falling dominoes in all directions and an utter panic for me! I didn't know what to grab first, they were falling so fast, while at the same time the background continued to unroll. I felt devastated when it all came to a stop. It was only my second day on the job and everything was in a shambles; I was ready to quit on the spot and go home. Then and there, I learned to keep my fingers out of anything that did not concern me."

TERRY HRYNYK

Terry Hrynyk also recalls his first day working for Fry's Photo Shop in Gravenhurst, Ont. where he took a phone call. "This is Beavercreek," said a gruff voice, "We have some fellows for you to photograph. Can we bring them in?" I said, "Sure!" and immediately prepared the studio, setting up a canvas backdrop, a background light and a light for the hair. I worked out my lighting ratios so everything was just right when the fellows came in and I was ready to take the best portraits of my life. That was when I learned that 'Beavercreek' is a minimal security institution and these were to be mug-shots, complete with numbers in front of them. But if I may say so, they WERE the most beautiful portraits that had ever been done for the institution!"

FRED MEULEMEESTER

Can a client pull a prank on a photographer? "Possibly so," says Fred Meulemeester MPA of Tillsonburg, Ont., "We were pho-

tographing a six months old baby and the mother had requested that we take a special shot in the nude. To create a setting we had decided to put the baby girl in a porcelain wash bowl. To prevent her getting a chill we put a blanket in the bottom to sit on. When we completed the shot and lifted the baby out we discovered she had diddled in the blanket and left quite a puddle there. I threw the blanket to one side and carried on with other props. Later, I had some objects which I wanted to cover so I grabbed for the blanket, forgetting about the earlier 'wet' incident. To fluff it up I gave the blanket a couple hardy snaps. I really made the ends crack and each time I got a face full of wet diddle. You'd think I would have woken up with the first wet spray; but I did it twice before reality caught up to my senses. It ran down my face and my glasses, it was all over my suit, even the walls and the ceiling were dripping. It took some courage and time to get back to the photography. The baby's mother came back a year later to update the portraits and wryly asked if I still remembered the sitting. How could I ever forget it!"

ANDRE PIERRE LEDUC

Andre Leduc MPA of Toronto, Ont., remembers when a young couple came to his studio for an engagement portrait. "It was quite obvious they were very much in love. As soon as I went under the focussing cloth to compose the picture they started to kiss and cuddle. But when I popped my head out, they stopped and everything was normal. Once more, I went under the cloth and the same love scene started all over again with added vigor. Looking at the ground glass image was like watching a TV love scene. I found it darn difficult to keep a straight face. I finally did get the portrait taken and I'm sure my subjects never realized I could see them the whole time!"

DOUGLAS J. SPILLANE

Doug Spillane MPA, formerly of Stratford, Ont., recalls his first year photographing the Stratford Festival. "In l960, I had to photograph the very first set of actors for the Stratford Theater and Christopher Plummer was one of them. At first, he would not follow my instructions and often told me simply to 'go to hell'. It developed into quite a banter with each challenging the other. With a huge stage sword, a prop from King John, he threatened to cut off my head. I challenged him with: 'You try it and I'll drive you into the ground with my Speed Graphic. He came at me with the sword but I was given a big hug instead; from then onwards the photo sessions progressed nicely. That was my start in theatrical photography. Director Michael Langham was the one who got me assigned to the Stratford company and from 1960 to 1970, I was the only photographer doing everything for them. Michael and I continued the tradition of insults –most vengefully, with tirades running on for some time. He would describe my photos as snaps while I called his plays -skits; but no one else knew it was only a sham. So, we would be screaming and ranting while the staff was scared stiff we would tear each other apart. But, it was all a pretense and a tension release. Michael Langham was the greatest guy there."

DAVID JAMES ENTWISTLE

David Entwistle MPA SPA of Waterloo, Ont., wanted to buy a 30mm lens for his Hasselblad camera. "I was quite shocked at their expensive price; besides I really needed a new camera body before fantasizing about a high priced lens. I was browsing through a magazine and spotted an ad for a complete Hasselblad outfit which included the 30mm fish eye lens. I hoped the seller might offer it separately so I made the call. In our conversation I got the feeling the equipment might be old and too unreliable to use on my assignments. A week later the same gentleman phoned to ask if I was still interested and invited me down to inspect the equipment. Although still skeptical, Jackie and I drove two and a half hours down to the address and found ourselves on the grounds of a beautiful mansion on the edge of a lake. We were given a wonderful family welcome, toured the house which was dripping with antiques and Group-of-Seven artwork.

During tea, our host brought in two Hasselblad cases with ten lenses ranging from 30 to 500 mm. There were filters, close up attachments, extension bellows, two Hasselblad bodies. You name it, it was there! I had not come to buy all this brand new equipment, I only hoped for the 30 mm lens. The gentleman explained that in his retirement he had planned to do a lot of great photography but found he hadn't enough time and preferred to travel with his wife. The equipment had remained unused. Previously I had worked out a rough estimate for the items listed in the ad, basing it on rock bottom prices for used cameras. I explained that I had come for only one lens but I could not let all this lovely equipment go by and brashly offered the nineteen thousand that I had scribbled on my little piece of paper. He said 'YES!'... I couldn't believe my ears. Why was I so blessed. My benefactor's wife then explained that her husband had put the ad in the magazine but they had left the very next day for California. The phone probably rang off the hook and nobody was there. I explained that I didn't have the money handy and would have to make some bank transfers before I could write out a cheque. But my host suggested I take the gear with me to test it and even offered to finance me if I had problems raising the money! 'You give me a cheque dated for a month today and take the equipment home with you,' was his suggestion. The deal was struck, I signed some papers and off Jackie and I went with the equipment. It was like heading off on a second honeymoon!"

"I had a bridal party to shoot that was staying at the Valhalla Inn in Kitchener. I chose an area just outside the ballroom for our photography because of the abundance of light and its beautiful setting. First to be photographed was the bride by herself. Then the bridesmaids and maid of honour were to come down from the eighth floor where they were dressing. The bridesmaids arrived OK but the maid of honour, who was last to follow, got stuck in the elevator. Of all people to get stuck, she was claustrophobic and unfortunately the repair man was some 35 minutes away. So all panic let loose. We couldn't shoot any of the photos that involved her. Finally, we had to leave for the church with the young lady still stuck in the elevator. At the church we delayed as long as possible and took more photos. The bride was just about to go down the aisle at which point you could hear a pin drop. In the distance we heard a telephone ring. The minister came out and announced to everyone that the maid of honour had been released and was on her way –so would we all hang on a little longer. I snapped a fabulous picture outside the church of the bride and the maid of honour, with tears streaming down their cheeks, hugging each other. From then on everything went ahead as planned. I think the moral of the story is: Never give up, invariably something will happen to brighten up the day."

David and his wife, Jackie, boarded a plane heading for Calgary and found the first class section cordoned off for Bette Midler and her band. "When we arrived in Calgary we had to wait while they were allowed off the plane first; everybody else was kept waiting. We finally got into the airport to find that Bette Midler and the band were scattered around the airport, buying magazines and shopping. Well, we recognized her and, of course, wanted to get an autograph so started searching for a pen, but we couldn't find one. We went crazy looking for a pen. We went through our bags, we searched everything: pockets, camera bags, luggage but finally gave up the search and the quest for her autograph. We got into the elevator which decided to go down instead of up. The door opened at the next floor and who is standing waiting to get on but Bette Midler. We joked and invited her on board but she refused. We rode up to our floor, got out and waited. She came up on the next elevator so we bantered and laughed with her some more. We really lamented we didn't get her autograph. But can you believe that while all this was happening, I had a 35mm camera on my shoulder and Jackie had her video camera. With all the excitement we never once thought to use them to record an even better memento of the occasion. That's a photographer for you!

"How about passing up an award winning picture before your very eyes. I was checking out the Elora Gorge as a possible setting for family photographs. We had just had thunder storms and I chose the Sunday evening to ride out and check for sites. Needless to say, my daughter had borrowed my car which had my equipment in the trunk. I was forced to take my son's car and was sitting there minding my own business enjoying the beautiful evening . I happened to look off to the right and there were seven teenage Mennonite girls, walking down the gorge, daintily lifting the hems of their dresses from the wet grass; four were in blue, two in purple and one in black. A shaft of sun light spotlighting them from the back; it was absolutely beautiful... a fantastic picture... and I had no camera. Ironically, all around me were tourists with cameras... and not one of them saw that fabulous picture of the seven Mennonite girls."

"Don't underestimate the kindness of your clients." says David. "I had just commenced some prebridal portraits when the bride's father popped his head in the door and said I had a flat tire. It started to rain with a vengeance so I figured I would rely on a taxi for transportation. I finished shooting and headed out to move the car but to my surprise, found that the bride's father and brother, in all that terrible weather, had changed the tire for me and had even stored the flat wheel in the trunk. Now, I thought that was really generous and completely unexpected from a client."

GEORGE W. JAMES

George James MPA of Chatham, Ont., wrote: "I made quite an attractive portrait of my wife, Marjory, and hung it proudly in our living room. My Mother came upon it during a visit and studied it for the longest while. She finally remarked to Marjory, 'Is that a photograph... OR did George take it?' Only an Irish sense of humour held Marjory from making any comment. Later, when I started my studio in Chatham, Mother must have overcome her inhibition about my abilities as she was one of my first customers. As to the portrait of my wife, it was successfully hung in the first OSP Print competition that I ever entered in 1958. It also became part of the retrospective exhibit I held at the Chatham-Kent Museum in 1992. Not bad mileage for the 'picture that George made'. EH!"

MARK LAURIE

Mark Laurie MPA of Calgary, Alberta specializes in nude and boudoir photography for which he is in great demand. Combining with artist, Tim Hammell, their finished artpieces portray their clients in fantasy settings of the 25th Century. Mark's photography sensitively captures his subjects emotions. "Our situation is different than other photographers," say Mark, "in that their sitters have clothes on, while in my situation the model is nude. We have insights into the lives of our sitters which other photographers may never experience. Not all sitters arrive ready to throw off their clothes; different reasons cause them to seek my special brand of photography."

"We had a lady in her forties arrive for a portrait which was to be presented to her husband. She was extremely nervous and when she came out of the dressing room was clutching her robe tightly to her throat. She backed away from me across the studio and with eyes wide explained, 'I've never done this kind of thing before, so don't you laugh.' It was up to me to replace her uneasiness with the emotion of love for her husband."

"We get quite different reactions when we project previews of the sittings. One lady brought in her husband for the selection of the final pictures. He was a rancher, hard as nails and like a character out of a western novel. His wife was everything to him. We project the proofs onto a wall to 4 by 5 ft in size, the images dissolving into each other so that it becomes quite a show. The lady brought along a special piece of music by which they had met, fallen in love and been married to. He was unaware of what was going to happen and when we projected these incredible pictures of his wife along with their favorite music, he started to cry. Of course, that isn't something a hard-bitten ranchers does, so he tried to stop... but it wouldn't work. He pretended it was a runny nose, but that didn't work either. He finally gave in, his eyes welled up... and he cried; he was so touched by the whole presentation. The lady told me later about the aftermath of the viewing

session. They had come from out-of-town leaving her mother back at the ranch to do the baby sitting. He was so excited by the photographs he wanted to stop over at a hotel for the night. The wife disagreed saying they must head home to relieve the Mom from baby sitting. But they came to a compromise whereby they would

stop at every second motel on the way home, once they had left the city. 'You know,' said the wife, 'I had no idea how many motels there are from here to our ranch!' "

"With some portraits it takes more time for them to work their magic. One time I photographed a mother with her twelve year old daughter. Being a single she felt the daughter was about to embark on her terrible teens and feared that times would get difficult when she had to be a tough parent. At that point they were very close, so I concentrated on capturing that emotional context. She bought a large size print, bigger than she could really afford; but the emotional sensitivity was such that she felt it was necessary. Several years later we met again and she explained that whatever she had paid for the photograph, it wasn't enough! She recounted that the daughter wanted to do something with her crowd of friends which was just not permissible. They had a horrible row with a division between them that would never be bridged. The mother fled into the kitchen... she could see her losing her daughter. Their strong bonds were collapsing. As a single mother this was very scary for her. The daughter was left in the living room, glaring with hate at the picture taken years before. An impenetrable gulf of some fifteen minutes passed while the mother tried to regain her composure and decide on what to do next. A voice from the living room broke the silence. 'Mom, we still love each other, don't we?' They rushed into each others arms and were able to work out a compromise, something that neither one was really happy with, but at least, both could live with. There was now a greater strength in their relationship that never existed before... all because the daughter recognized the love in that photograph. It seems unbelievable that a portrait could have made so much difference."

"I remember another client who was married for a second time with a nine year old son by the first marriage. She wasn't sure how the new husband would take to our type of photography, but, as it turned out, he doted on her and thought she was spectacular. He was completely awed by our preview presentation and ordered up two 30 by 40 canvas prints and an album. When the price came to two thousand dollars I expected him to pare down the order. His wife snuggled up to him and said, 'I don't think I'm worth $2,000!' The husband asked the step-son if he thought his Mom was worth it and the kid said, 'You bet.. every penny and more!' He looked at his wife and replied, 'See, both men agree; this is what we are going to get!' You could see this incredible glow of pride come over her face; he thought so much of her that the money wasn't a problem. There is a special little footnote to this story which is kind of cute. The boy had been promised burgers after the visit to our studio and he was hinting to get going. The dad said, 'You know, Billy, that money for your Mom's portrait was all we had. Now we can't afford to go out for burgers.' You could see the dismay on the boy's face and he probably was thinking: 'Maybe mom should have been worth about $9.50 less!'"

"Some of our clients go to extreme lengths to extend their fantasy. The wife of a prominent person in our city created a scenario to entice her husband on his birthday to see the previews of her secret portrait. He was a James Bond freak so she told him to wear his James Bond tuxedo for their dinner celebration that evening with his sister. So he put it on and was waiting to be picked up at his office by 5.30pm. At 5.40pm his phone rang and his wife in a mysterious voice answered that his sister wasn't coming and she wasn't either. There was a message now waiting in his own car, and then she hung up. He was apprehensive because, several birthdays earlier she had hired a stripper who dropped into his office on the 30th floor - a totally glassed-in office, and did a complete routine for him. In the car he found a cassette tape, a glass, wine, a water pistol and a rose. He was informed that he was to be James Bond for the evening and was on the trail of art thieves who were stealing paintings of women. He followed the driving instructions that led him through the city to a phone booth where there was a secret number taped under the phone. He phoned and said: 'This is James Bond, agent 007. Women have nice fannies.' That was his pass word. The wife didn't say anything except give the address and hung up. This gentleman now made his way to our studio and got out of his car with the rose in his lapel, the leaking water pistol in his pocket and his James Bond Tuxedo. I answered the door and you could tell from the look on his face that he was wondering if he had the right address. He says, 'I'm James Bond, agent 007. Women have nice fannies! Again it was the pass word. He followed me down the stairs into the darkened studio and I guided him to a chair. He had no hint of what was about to happen, so I hit the tape deck starting the music for James Bond's 'For your eyes only' and commenced the slide show with the dissolve units. The first image that popped up was one of his wife sitting in a chair in a dress. Its a fairly plain dress but I'm sure it had some special meaning to them. As he was viewing this 4 ft by 5 ft image the second image dissolved to the screen. She was still in the same position –but without clothes; so it appeared her clothes dissolved. Then a wine glass was presented to him from behind and, as he sat up straight, his head bumped into an exposed breast. She had been hiding downstairs and had slipped out of her garments to present him with his glass of wine. She whispered, 'Happy Birthday, dear. I hope you enjoy it, James!' She then sat opposite him drinking from a glass of wine. He was incoherent for an hour! All he could say was, 'This is incredible... truly awesome!' He would look at her then back to the pictures on the screen. For an hour he was in seventh heaven."

"We sometimes try different effects and for one client we did a variation on body sculpture. We had the model stand in a hole cut into the middle of a table, so that it looked like she was a living sculpture. We then covered her with wet clay which had to be kept moist otherwise it would peel off and look horrible. We continually had to spray water onto the model; the water was kept hot but by the time it hit her body it was quite cool. She had beautiful white teeth and when she smiled the effect of mud and teeth was awesome."

"We photographed another young lady decorated with body makeup and props to make her into a fox –from head to toe. When we had finished the studio shooting we climbed into the van and headed out to a park with a sunset that was conducive to the photography. I was quite surprised at the number of people still there and told my model to think that it was a costume she was wearing... NOT that she was totally nude. We sauntered to the middle of the field and started the photography. An old man, 20 ft away, shook his head, thinking it must be a punk rocker costume. After a couple rolls of film we headed back to the van. A couple of kids, driving by in a car, squealed their brakes and backed up! We, unconcernedly, walked to my van."

"We were photographing a girl, one time, on top of a Lamborghini. They are fairly expensive cars and the man who owned it was concerned because we wanted the lady standing on the roof with high heels and not a stitch on. At one point we had her on the roof doing the splits and, for some reason that totally alludes me, the car owner made a crude comment. She started to bounce her splits on the roof of the car at which the owner went white. 'Oh!' he moaned, 'I'm sorry, I'm sorry, don't bounce.' You have to keep in mind that this car is made of aeroplane metal. If you bounce it and it dents, it will cost from 5 to l0 thousand dollars to replace the part. It was, to say the least, an interesting job."

"A lot of couples are now coming in, for nude portrayals; particularly those involved in body building programs. We had one girl who was so smooth in getting her boyfriend to join her in a picture session. He knew she was having nude photographs taken and had volunteered to carry in a heavy box. He thought it was equipment but it actually was full of rocks. At the studio she complimented him on how good he looked in his suit. She suggested that she slip into one of her slinky dresses and do a photograph of the two of them together. He agreed. Then she mentioned she had some of their fitness gear with her so why not slip into some body building outfits? He agreed. Then she suggested taking the shirts off and he thought that was a great idea too. Well pretty soon she had him down to his buff skin and we were doing the body sculpture portraits. Sometime later we had a display in the lobby of the building where he worked. He happened to pass by with his secretary and stopped to point proudly at his photograph saying: 'See that! Those are MY BUNS!' "

"We often get different reactions when we display our award winning portraits. Although we get many compliments for the sculpted nudes, a picture of an expectant mother often proves quite controversial. It shows a mother exposing her full tummy with two other children, 5 and 7, feeling for the beat of the unborn child. It is a beautiful picture and I adore it because of its sensitivity. I watched as a mother and daughter stood debating for some 20 minutes over its values and acceptability."

"We were photographing a mother and daughter with the child just at the stage where she wasn't quite talking and wasn't potty trained. The tot wandered to another part of the studio and a couple minutes later we heard: 'OOOH wet!' and of course she was pee'ing. We laughed about it and the mother commented that it could have been worse. We no sooner finished laughing when we spotted a little mound at the far side of the studio... and indeed it WAS worse!"

RONALD and ELEANOR MILLER

Ron Miller MPA and his wife Eleanor are now retired after operating their portrait studio in Toronto for some 25 years. At times, they had to work with pretty uncooperative subjects but as Eleanor explains, "When photographing children Ron set the pose and watched for the right expression while I teamed up with him to make the kids relax and laugh. It didn't matter if they fussed or cried at the beginning, by the time the sitting was over I had gotten through to them. I remember a two year old child where I started into

my routine but after a supreme effort I was still drawing a complete blank. The child would not pay any attention to me at all. Jokingly, I said to the mother: 'My goodness! I don't know what's wrong. Are you sure he can see me?' I did it as an off-hand remark but I guess the mother thought about it seriously enough to take the child to a doctor. On examination it was discovered that the little boy had a progressive disease which was gradually blinding him. The child had, for some time, been relying solely on his hearing to do everything. An operation was quickly performed to save the remaining sight. The mother told us that shortly after the operation she approached her son for the very first time with open arms and got absolutely no response. Fear struck her deeply that the surgery had been a failure. She had no idea what to do next..... 'Honey Bear!' she cooed. And at those precious words the boy's face lit up with smiles of recognition. She realized her son had never seen her before, knowing only a blurred image and a mother's soft voice. 'Honey Bear' was the signal to the boy that THIS was his mother. Three years later the boy returned for a new portrait, this time wearing thick glasses... but he could see!"

Eleanor remembers booking a sitting for a family photograph. The father commented about an odd thing that his son had said. "My ten year old asked if I had lived in the olden days when the world was only black & white. I explained that the world has always been in colour. 'No!' said the child, 'in the olden days, when the old photos and the movies were only in BLACK AND WHITE.'"

Eleanor used all sorts of tricks to get the tiny sitters into the right mood. Following the teachings of a Convention speaker, Eleanor told an uncooperative child that she was going to hit Mr. Miller with a rolled up newspaper when he wasn't looking. The four year old brightened to the idea. Eleanor sensing success quipped: "I'll hit him on the head, OK?"... "NAH!" exclaimed the child, "hit him in the balls, it hurts more there."

JOSEPH and LOUISE SIMONE

Joseph and Louise Simone MPA of Montreal, Quebec are a charming couple who have endeared themselves to both their customers and their fellow photographers throughout Canada and America. Louise recalls an incident when they were photographing a love-story portrait of a young engaged couple in a local park. "I asked the young lady to stretch out on the grass and brace herself on her hands so that she could snuggle close to her husband-to-be. Unfortunately, a dog had relieved himself there and she put her hand into what she shouldn't have put her hand into. It was most distressing to everyone and we hurriedly cleaned her hand the best that we could. It was hard to get everyone back into the love mood. We continued on, and in one of the poses we directed our young lady to motion towards her fiance with a caress of her hand on his cheek. It looked oh so romantic... but he reared back quickly and exclaimed, 'Oh! you smell so bad!' The mood was lost and that ended the picture taking. Now, every time we see them, we have a good laugh at this story; it is a hard one not to forget."

"We have a sad story about this little family that came to our studio and asked for a very special family portrait. We didn't know the man was so sick at the time, but we are always determined to make each sitting the best possible. We did a really good picture for them and they were so happy with the results. The mother picked up the proofs and took them to a hospital in Toronto. She placed an order but we were surprised when her brother phoned suddenly and said the finished print had to be ready by that very afternoon. The prints were not completely finished but something inside told us we should finish them for 3 o'clock. Usually, I wouldn't do that as the customer will wait another day for the finished work, in the specified time that I say. But in this case, I had a feeling I must deliver the work in that moment. When the brother of the lady came to pick up the prints, he

explained to Joseph that the father had died and they were taking his body to Italy for burial. We were both crying at this sad news. The lady placed a large order afterwards, as everyone wanted pictures that captured the memory of them still together as a close family. That relationship was captured in the picture and it was as if the father was

there again. It made us mindful and caring with every portrait sitting that we undertake. We must never permit ourselves not to be 'present-of-spirit' when doing a portrait."

Both Joseph and Louise are kept busy giving lectures and demonstrations to fellow photographers in order to pass on their knowledge and expertise. Louise tells this cute story about her husband. "At one of the speaking engagements Joseph had a really bad cold and he ducked backstage to blow his nose. He forgot that he still had the tiny microphone pinned to his lapel; so when he started blowing his nose this terrible honking noise came blasting out over the audience. Well, everybody was hearing THAT NOSE so I rushed back in a panic to stop him. Realizing what had happened, Joseph returned to the audience still with the handkerchief in his hand. He asked the laughing crowd, 'Does anyone want to know about Soft Focus? THIS is the only one I'm using today!' " [This obviously is an in-joke for photographers.]

GRAHAM BAILLEY

Graham Bailley MPA of Thornhill, Ont., vividly remembers a wedding where he was setting up a large wedding group. "As I added more people I had to back away further and further. What I didn't notice was the prickly privet hedge that ran around the side walk outside the church. I crouched down for a lower angle shot of the group and sat right on the bush. It was a spiked bush with two inch thorns and I got a seat full of them. The bridal party understood exactly what had happened when they saw me dancing wildly around rubbing my stinging derriere. It broke up the whole wedding party."

Graham remembers a tedious portrait sitting of a little boy during which he wasn't achieving appropriate expressions. Graham's perseverance came to an abrupt standstill against the child's stubbornness when the two and a half year old angel looked him straight in the eye and said, "Fuck Off!" "But somehow I must have captured something of his personality," says Graham, "as the parents ended up ordering a 20x24 print."

IAN RANSBERRY

Ian Ransberry MPA from St. Catharines, Ont., was invited to lecture at a seminar of photographers in Thunder Bay. The following day, Bruce Cameron CPA SPA took a camera group out on a shoot in Sibley Provincial Park. Recalls Ian, "There was a fresh four inch snow fall which encouraged us to shoot beautiful scenics all day long. As we were returning at twilight, a fox emerged from the brush by the side of the road. We stopped the van and from twenty feet away got some shots. We did a quick look through the truck

for anything left over from lunch which we could throw out to the fox and keep it from running away. But everything had been eaten, so in desperation we were throwing rolled up napkins to entice the fox to come closer. I had a better idea and threw my business card case which is of brown leather, thinking that it would contrast against the snow. The fox immediately grabbed it up and ran off into the bush. So I gave chase while everyone was yelling to watch myself as the fox might be rabid. About a quarter of a mile through the bush I came across a strange pattern of footprints that circled the mushed up remains of my card case... he had eaten some but, at least, had left half of it. But I still came out on top when one of my shots of the fox proved to be a prize winner and was made into a limited edition print which was sold through the Kiwanis Club as a fund raising project.

EVERETT ROSEBOROUGH

Ev Roseborough is the elder statesman of Canadian professional photographers. He first joined Eaton's advertising department in Toronto as a 15 year old junior artist for the summer of 1927. His dablings in photography led him to set up the first Eaton's commercial photo studio in 1933 and eventually establish his own studio, servicing commercial and advertising accounts. Ev gained prominence as photography became the prime illustration for catalogues and magazines replacing drawn artwork.

This is one of Ev's favourite stories and is about Walter Smith, the manager of the Eaton's portrait studio which was located on the 3rd floor of the old Yonge Street store. This stocky, jovial Englishman had learned his craft in England and Ev owes much to him as a guiding mentor. 'Smitty', as he was known to the staff, had been apprenticed to a haberdasher upon leaving school. The dusting wasn't too bad a task but the counting of celluloid collars and collar buttons did irk him, particularly when working out the stock in pounds, shillings and pence on a per gross basis.

Small wonder this young man should venture to apply for a more interesting position in a photographic emporium a few doors down the street. There he spent many months cleaning glass, drying prints and spotting before he finally was given a photo assignment to do by himself; a small wonder indeed.

A Mrs. Allingham wished to have a photograph taken in her home of her husband who had been an invalid for years. Smitty packed up his plate-holders, tripod and Thornton-Pickard half-plate camera and set off for the far end of town. Arriving at the house he set down his gear and was about to seize the knocker when the door suddenly flung open and there, before him, stood the proprietor of the local undertaking establishment. Replete in frock coat, he motioned to our apprentice to enter. "Mrs. Allingham does not have a portrait of her late husband," said the

undertaker as he picked up the camera case and withdrew into the house with a bewildered Smitty following behind.

The late gentleman lay peacefully in state in a small parlor, a vase of roses on the casket. "Mrs. Allingham would like it full face; you and I can tip the casket on end to make it easier. Take hold, sonny!" said the frock-coat, removing the vase. Smitty hesitated, first taking a minute to fasten the camera to the tripod, despite his shaking hands. Measuring out the flash-powder proved to be far more difficult, if not nearly impossible. The undertaker was getting impatient by the lack of assistance from the young photographer. Henry Allingham, possibly due to inactivity and the prescription of stout for his ailment had been a man of considerable weight. Smitty manfully grasped the handle on the box and with much grunting and straining the two managed to stand it upright against the wall. This casket had been the only one available with sufficient length but it had taken the embalmer considerable effort to confine the Allingham girth into so narrow a box.

With a remark about Mr. Allingham's upright character, the undertaker bade Smitty a good morning and admonished as he left, "Be sure to open the eyes!" The shaking Smitty focussed the camera carefully, eye to eye with his departed subject, then fastened the plate-holder and held high his flash holder for the exposure. BOOM!... Everything happened at once! At the instant of the flash the long suffering latch on the casket finally yielded to the weight of its occupant. The lid flew open and the body swished out to straddle the legs of the tripod and the feet of the now-petrified photographer.

With one mighty 'Whoop', Smitty grabbed up his gear and was out the door. He legged it down the street, never stopping 'til he burst through the studio door. "I never did find out," says Ev, "whether the photograph was ever delivered. But I did receive a warning from Smitty to the effect that: 'This studio (Eaton's) does not photograph stiffs... ever!'"

"Some years later, I got a phone call from the Executive Office. The sister of R.Y. Eaton, President of the company, had just passed away in Oakville. 'Just some slides to send to the folks in Ireland,' R.Y. said. When I mentioned the call to Smitty, he just looked at me and said, 'YOU look after it!'"

HUGH ROBERTSON

Hugh Robertson MPA of Panda Studios in Toronto, Ont., tells of this episode which happened so long ago that he hates to tell the number of years since its happening. His two children were four and five years old when, one Saturday, he had the task of baby-sit-

ting them and at the same time driving to Collingwood to photograph a house. "Back in those days," recalls Hugh, "everything was done with black and white film on an 8x10 camera. We made a fun day of the trip, taking the photographs, having lunch and starting the drive back home. About three quarters of the way back, the kids were amusing themselves in the back seat when I heard the distinctive sound of a film holder being dropped on top of another. 'What are you two kids doing?' I questioned, 'Oh,' said one of the kids, 'we're looking at these things. There's all sorts of funny stuff in here.' With that, a tiny hand reached over the back of the seat and dropped a flurry of 8x10 film beside me. They had opened most of the holders and delighted themselves by collecting all the films in a pile; they had half of the holders unloaded. So, I had to turn the car around and go back to reshoot all the photography again. That's a baby sitting job I will always remember!"

PAUL and ANNE PEDERSEN

Paul Pedersen of North Bay, Ont., and his wife, Anne, were photographing a wedding together. "On this particular occasion it paid to have two photographers. I began the coverage by photographing the groom at the hotel where he was dressing. The room was an absolute mess as most hotel rooms get before such a function. The next to last shot was a portrait by window light with the groom holding the ring. With that done, I placed the ring on a table and went on with the final portrait. Then I headed off to the church for the ceremonies. Just as the procession was forming to go down the aisle, the best man came to me and asked: 'Where did the ring go?' He hadn't picked it up from the table. I left Anne to carry on with the wedding coverage while I dashed back to the hotel and got the hotel manager to open up the room. The ring wasn't where it was supposed to be, so I got down on my hands and knees and searched all over the floor. I removed the furniture... everything! I checked with staff to see if anyone had been in to clean the room? No! So then I got a rug rake, moved all the furniture to one side and thoroughly raked the rug... but still NO RING. To this day, no one has found the ring. But there is a satisfactory ending to the story. One of the mothers in the bridal party was wearing two wedding bands. The bride cheerfully accepted one of them as her wedding ring, knowing of its personal family history!"

Anne, recalls a gem of life when she was to photograph a little boy in her studio. "I was going to take a high key portrait so had arranged the white background paper sweeping down the wall and across the floor. I led the little boy into the studio and asked him to sit with me in the middle of the paper. 'Oh!' he questioned, 'Should I take off my pants?' I was quite perplexed by the query, wondering what he might do if he did. His mother came to the rescue by explaining that her son had been visiting the doctor's office for the last few weeks. Every time he was hoisted onto the examination table, which was covered with paper, he was requested to take off his pants. So, it was obvious to him such a big sheet of paper required the same courtesy."

Paul remembers, "When I was living in Parry Sound, I was asked to shoot a publicity photo of a popular rock band. The only problem was that the photo had to be done after their last performance which ended at one o'clock in the morning. They had a name similar to 'Street Noise' and the photo had to reflect that character. So how was I to accomplish that at 1 AM in the morning? I took them down to the center of town to do an available light shot on the main drag, thus tying in with their name. I found I didn't have the intensity of light that I needed, so in desperation used my car headlights to illuminate the area. I backed my van across the street and shone the lights on the appropriate spot. No sooner had I accomplished this when two police cars came screeching around the corner and poured out a squad of menacing gendarmes to surround us. It took some fast talking to calm their threats and show my innocence. They pointed out that I had made a very poor choice of location when I backed my van up to the front door of the Toronto Dominion bank! The people in the apartments above the local stores were sure that a bank-bust was in progress and had squealed on me. It was a most unusual evening and one I won't forget."

ROBERT E. PATCHETT

Here is a warm and heartening story from Robert Patchett MPA HLM of Hamilton, Ont., that recalls the joys of children and Christmas; it happened back in the days when Bob had a studio in Port Credit (now Mississauga). Every Christmas he had the commission to run Santa Claus photo stations in three different shopping centers. Each location had a team of three people dressed as elves to take the photos and promote the sales. "We always seemed to have problems with our Santas," recalls Bob. "One Santa was found drunk in the dressing room, -so guess who had to jump in and replace him at the last moment. If a Santa didn't show up or wasn't performing then I would have to dash up from the studio and fill the part. Of all the things that happened I remember the number of kids who wet me. It is quite a sensation to feel that warm wetness seep through your suit and then run down a leg into your sock. I very quickly learned to put several layers of toweling inside the outfit to take care of that problem. So give hearty thanks to the next Santa you see bouncing a child on his knee and wish him a Merry (dry) Christmas!"

WILLIAM MEEKINS

This endearing story comes from William Meekins of Newmarket, Ontario. "I had an appointment to photograph two small children in their home, a baby boy and a five year old girl. When I rang the bell the door was immediately opened by the little girl who must have been anxiously awaiting my arrival. The mother was busy in another room getting the baby ready. 'Mummy,' bellowed the little tyke, 'the flasher's here!' I was taken aback by this bold introduction and the embarrassed mother took great pains to explain her daughter's remark. The night before she had prepared her daughter for the visit of the photographer, describing the camera, the backgrounds, and the exposure flashes. All the child could remember was the flashes so it became the appropriate word for my introduction."

William puts a lot of tender-loving-care into his portrait sittings and it pays off in different ways. After finishing a location shoot of a family, Bill was packing his equipment to leave. The little girl ran up to him, threw her arms around him and said, "I love you MISTER MAN." Such is the impression he has with children.

Mr. Meekins was photographing a Catholic wedding where a four year old boy was sitting with his father in the front pew. During the blessing services the priest raised the chalice above his head and the altar boy rung a bell. The little boy had followed everything with great intensity and as the priest raised the chalice, he joyfully yelled out: "CHEERS!"

At another wedding a little eighteen month old girl was sitting with her mother. At the point where the priest announced, "And now we will hear the word of God," the little girl chirped... "UH O-O-OH!"

WILLIAM E. HART

Bill Hart CPA, of Rothesay, New Brunswick has a favourite story which he calls "Ralph's Revenge". It goes this way. "Our studio is in a renovated CN Railroad station but many of the portraits are photographed in our one acre PhotoPark adjacent to the building. One beautiful August day a local family arrived for a long anticipated portrait sitting. It was to be a surprise for the father so there was Mom, three children, a four year old golden lab and a very disgruntled eight-year-old cat named Ralph."

"They had dressed in their finest with the mother in a fine off-white silk suit and the children well co-ordinated in their costumes. It was going to be a lovely environmental shoot so we moved out to the Park and took a few photos by a rustic fence then moved over to a large overhanging tree in the center of the field. The PhotoPark is bordered by the main CN rail line to Montreal with traffic mostly slow lumbering freights and a few speeding Via passenger trains. You could spot them coming by their distant whistle then they would fly past with a clatter of the wheels and the roar of the diesel. On our way to the tree, I heard the distant whistle and warned the mother and kids to watch for the train. The dog was on his leash while the cat was tethered with its Rhinestone studded collar.

The train whizzed by and we marvelled at its speed and the desire to go travelling some day. When the train had passed we returned to our task of taking more portraits. I looked at my group and saw Mom in her white silk suit holding a beautiful rhinestone leash but NO Ralph! The cat had slipped his collar and escaped without us seeing the escape. We immediately started a search in all directions, the mother, the children, the dog and me. After thirty minutes – no Ralph, an hour later of desperate searching and calling and STILL no Ralph. I had to go back into the studio for another appointment but kept checking the progress from time to time. Finally after two hours I happened to look out just as the mother came stumbling out of the brush, her white suit all dirty

and torn, her perfect makeup all smeared, her coiffed hair askew and Ralph, the cat, firmly clenched under her arm. The lady walked up to her car, opened the door, threw Ralph into the back seat, settled the kids and slammed the door in disgust. As she backed out to leave, I could see Ralph sitting proudly in the back window preening his paws as if nothing had happened. He gave me a look as if to say, "Hey, I'm a cat, I do what I want....!"

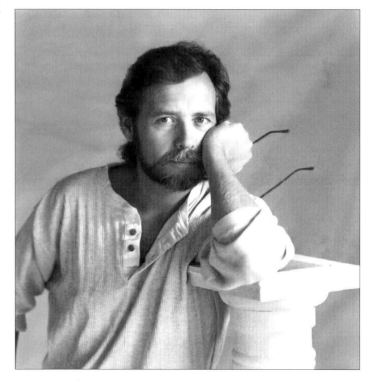

" I love to photograph children and enjoy talking with them, before we do the pictures, to let the children become adjusted to their strange surroundings. I was to photograph three year old Justin as I had portrayed his sister, Jaimee, when she was the same age. I asked Justin how he was and if he had brought his happy face. I started asking what he had done all week and he described going to a friend's birthday party, their new dog and having gone to the zoo.

That was the perfect moment for me to launch into my routine where I imitate all the sounds that the animals make. He told me about the lion, the sheep, the duck and the elephant, so I find myself, barking, meowing, quacking and I am rather proud of my elephant impression. I said, 'Justin, I can be like an elephant. Do you remember what an elephant looks like? He looked up with his big brown eyes, took a breath and blurted enthusiastically, "An elephant has a big penis!' I looked at the Mom, sitting next to him on the bench, totally shocked at her son's observation, and offered: 'How 'bout a duck?'"

"I used to photograph for a small town newspaper which entailed attending lots of socials, quilts and anniversaries. But one day there was a fire in the back room of the local convenience store with flames shooting through the roof. The local volunteer fire department mustered to the scene and eventually got everything under control. Since the fire was on the main street and the water hydrant was next to the funeral home on the other side of the road, the boys had to run the hoses across the street to hook up to the pumper. They placed wooden timbers along side the hoses so that the traffic, heading for the post office, could still continue to use the street."

"One of the firemen was stationed next to these boards to guide the cars so that they wouldn't miss and thus damage the hoses. A brown Ford approached the boards with a local lady driving ever so cautiously past all the excitement. She started to drive over the boards but was slightly to one side, so the volunteer yelled for her to "back up" and try again. The lady put her car into reverse then slowly backed up ....and continued to do so, until she reached the funeral home down the street where she entered their driveway, reversed, and came back out onto the street facing the other way. We expected her to make her safe getaway. But no! Now she backed the car tediously towards us and made it successfully over the boards. Having done this she continued down the street, entered the post office lot, did a reverse and finally headed out of town. It was the longest ten minutes I ever experienced."

"The fire was soon put out, the hoses and boards put away and our small town was soon back to its normal peacefulness."

Now the following has a different twist to a fireman story. –

DOUGLAS A. GROSE

Douglas A. Grose of Ottawa, Ont., was hired to photograph a wedding starting with group portraits at his studio then to the church for the ceremony. "Unfortunately, the groom arrived an hour late putting our whole schedule under a lot of pressure. The first pose was a large group with eighteen adults. I was in the midst of composing the group when suddenly the building's fire alarm began ringing. The bell was right in my camera room, so it was so loud you couldn't hear a person shout. That put the whole party into a panic and many wanted to escape the building immediately. The bride was now crying, with two strikes against her wedding. The best man went off to search the other two floors in our building for signs of fire while I made an attempt to quieten the bell by jamming it with a pair of pliers. It worked temporarily so we continued with the photography. Next came the sound of sirens and four large fire trucks roared up to the front of our building! A dozen firemen with helmets, boots and heavy axes barged into the already crowded camera room and my bride went again into a crying fit. I thought it would make a great photograph but she couldn't see the humour and refused to be photographed with the firemen. Eventually, the alarm switch was shut off, the firemen left and peace was restored to complete the photography. Thank goodness we weren't scheduled for a boudoir sitting that day!"

Doug spoke too soon and several months after moving into a new studio he was shooting a revealing and sensitive boudoir portrait when someone enter the front door. "It was a big burly fireman complete with hip boots and helmet; this time they were looking for leaking gas. Once again I explained that he couldn't enter the studio during a shoot and he went away protesting. Every five minutes there was another fireman and my sitter was wondering what was going on. Finally the Chief, himself, shows up at the door yelling, 'What the *** are you doing to my men? I'm supposed to check this building out and you are NOT stopping me!' So I had to run back and get the sitter to put on a wrap. The Chief walked in and saw our setting; he turned red with embarrassment and made a quick exit. FINALLY there were no further disturbances and I completed my boudoir sitting."

CRAIG MINIELLY

Craig Minielly CPA of Oakville, Ont., was assigned by the local newspaper to get interesting animal photographs at a mall where they had a petting zoo. "I was trying to photograph a mother cougar with her little cub and was finding it a bit difficult shooting through the bars. The attendant recognized my problem and figured I needed a close-up shot if it was going to be used in the newspaper. So I was allowed inside the cage and I was getting some great shots of the mom and the cub when I saw this blur. The next instant, I found I was flat on my back with this cougar standing over me, her hot breath and sharp fangs thrust into my face. She had me pinned down with a big paw on each shoulder. The hair on my head must have stood rigid as I knew I was going to be her next dinner. Then she gave me a big sand-papery lick to my face. Was this in preparation for the first taste? The attendant brought relief to my suffering with a, 'Hey, she likes you'! Evidently I was of the right flavour."

ROGER J. SANDS

Roger Sands MPA of Smiths Falls, Ont., tells the story of how he got a picture of a five legged horse. "I was hired to photograph the horse trials near St. Lazare in Quebec. We spent the day shooting steed after steed jumping a fence in the ring. And every so often, I would have to run over to the presentation circle to shoot the winner of each division. The most important division of the day was being covered by The Sports Network and it ran late into the afternoon with the light fading fast. The TSN crew was anxious to leave and I, also, had a long drive home. But we all had to wait for this last winner presentation. Finally, the results were announced and the champions were lined up for parading. The slow pace of waiting and presentation created a problem. Second to last in the line up was an attractive mare followed by a Bermuda stallion called Amigo. By the time Amigo reached the presentation area he had been thoroughly aroused by the female in front of him and was really 'up' for the occasion. The TSN crew didn't know whether to laugh or cry while I could hardly hold my camera steady, I was laughing so hard. Luckily, the prize included a large blanket which was strategically draped over the horse. But if you examined the picture closely you could still tell that a five-legged stallion had won the event."

Roger recalls, "I was photographing a wedding last Spring with a French-English mix of families. I got the bride's family arranged in a group, about seventeen in all. They were all French speaking and I had to leave it to my wife to do the communicating. As I completed the group I asked my wife in a fairly loud voice, 'How do you say smile, in French?' Without missing a beat, the whole group yelled... 'SEX!'... So now you know how to say smile in French!"

EDITH VANDERKLOOT

Edith VanderKloot now of Calgary, Alberta, had a special request from an engaged couple to be photographed different to their city-dwelling character. "I suggested they be photographed with cows out in the country. The bride laughed at the idea, but

thought it would be a fun thing to do; so I made arrangements with a neighbouring farmer to use his field and his cows. My city couple arrived wearing white sneakers and were not prepared for the damp field and the large 'meadow muffins' which are so common to cow pastures and must be avoided with care. The girl was quite apprehensive about the cows which, out of pure curiosity, were crowding about us. Cows are harmless but the young lady panicked and dashed for the car. In her mad run she forgot to watch where she stepped and meadow-muffin-material was thoroughly glued to her like clods of gumbo. It took a lot of persuasion, after that mess, to get her back into the field. But we were finally successful and took some great photos. The finished enlargement was displayed at the wedding banquet and showed the couple with three cows that had slipped in behind them. They had been completely unaware that the cows had moved in so close. The bridal party added to the theme by displaying a large stuffed cow at the head table."

"One day I looked out my studio window," says Edith, "and was surprised to see a man waving my garden shovel in a very menacing manner. On checking, he advised me not to come out... and at that moment a big black bull went galloping through the space between my house and our neighbours with two men in hot pursuit. Intrigued I dashed to get a camera to take pictures but as

Murphy's Law would have it... not ONE camera was loaded with film! Why does it take so long to load up when your in a panic situation? With the camera finally ready, I dashed out the door at the other side of the house but almost got trampled as the bull raced by. Wow, I thought its just perfect for some action shots! But it proved to be the wrong door to leave by, because I completely forgot that is where my four dogs reside and they were out the door in a shot adding to the pandemonium. Fearing the bull might get chased onto the highway or my dogs might get hurt I had now to set aside my quest for pictures and go screaming after the dogs. I had to literally drag each one back into the workshop. Successful at that, I ran for the road still hoping to capture at least something of the action. But by now, the bull was away in the distance, the two farmers still chasing after him. Everything was too far away to get that ONE great action photo!"

"I had a request to photograph a very pricey llama for a catalogue. I asked if it was to be done indoors or outdoors, but I was assured the animal was well behaved and house trained so I wouldn't have to worry about "accidents" in the studio. I worried about everything on this job, even whether I could get it through the door to the studio. The day finally arrived and the llama proved to be my own height, had lovely soft b&w fur and big round eyes which constantly moved with alertness. Although the trainer had tested the animal in her own kitchen the night before, the llama proved to be very frisky in my studio and just would not stand still on the background material. As soon as I took the first strobe-flash shot the animal darted right out of the studio and was pressing up against the front door trying to get out. We coaxed her back a number of times, repeatedly trying to ease her into the middle of the background and not have the trainer show in the photo. But all our efforts seemed useless and to no avail. Finally I called in my husband to see if he had any clue how to overcome the problem. He thought it all simply funny and casually whistled at the animal. Lo and behold the llama froze on the spot, lifted her head and stared in the direction of the noise. Paul whistled again, the llama reacted in the same way and I got the perfect shot for the catalogue.

ALICE HILL

Alice Hill CRA of Thunder Bay, Ont., remembers a particularly cold winter day for the portraits that her husband, Dennis Hill MPA was shooting, rather than for the frigid minus 40 degree weather. "Dennis was shooting a family portrait that included two pets -one a very small dog and the other a young highly strung Doberman. After a series of pictures the Doberman looked like it was going to fall asleep, so Dennis suggested the owner walk the dog through to the front area to relax it and get a change of pace. They no sooner had left the shooting area when we heard a terrible crashing of glass. We rushed to the front to find a gaping hole where the bottom half of our door had existed. The dog had seen something interesting outside and had charged after it... right through the glass. Icy cold air was blowing into the reception area but everyone was in a panic to catch the dog. It was a prize dog and surely would have been injured going through that plate glass. We gave chase and found him trotting up and down the main street, investigating everything and everyone. The dog was checked out by a vet who couldn't find anything wrong –no cuts, no bruises, no swelling! We were relieved to hear it but were left with the problem of fixing our broken door. On Saturdays you can never find a glass repair place open, so we had to resort to boarding up the hole until the following Monday."

"Well, that is only part of the story," continues Alice. "Dennis likes to work alone when he is in the studio shooting and didn't see a small detail that almost led to disaster. When the proofs came back every shot of the male Doberman showed his private parts which indicated an ever increasing level of sexual arousal. It would have been most embarrassing in the final print. Of course, the enlargements made it even more prominent so they had to be delicately retouched and corrected. That wasn't any great problem for me as it is all in a day's work. But THEN the client came back and ordered 50 Christmas cards of the very same image. Now, it isn't normal to retouch such cards but in this case I had to retouch 50 Doberman activated sex organs. To get through the job I kept telling myself... 'I'm glad the client didn't order a hundred!' "

Alice relates a personal story of how family pets can touch our lives. "My Mother had a lung disorder and she was in and out of the hospital many times. This particular time she was very bad and it had resulted in surgery to relieve the problem. She was moved to intensive care and wasn't responding very well. The nurses could not get her to start the physical therapy she was required to do; I guess she had given up hope of recovery. My sister and I were constant visitors and realized that something special had to be done. Now, my mother was a dog lover all her life and, at the time, she had a big collie dog and a little Lhasa Apso, a cute curly haired terrier. We decided we must take "Pokey" to see Mom. We wrapped her in a blanket and went up in the elevator, then slipped stealthily down the corridor. You would think the dog knew what was happening as it didn't make a sound nor make any fuss at all. My mother was lying there with all these wires, tubes and breathing apparatus coming out of her. She didn't stir. We put Pokey on the end of the bed and she immediately flattened herself on the covers as if to be inconspicuous. Then with her paws extended she crept forward to touch my mother. Pokey gave a couple licks to Mom who immediately opened her eyes, saw her beloved little friend and started to cry. When she cried she started to cough, and when she coughed she started to breathe better. It was a miracle that turned her around. It gave Mom the needed will to live and I'm glad to say she lived for many more years to come."

G. KEN BELL

Ken Bell MPA SPA HLM, formerly of Toronto, Ont., began his photography career in 1931 and, since those early days, has traversed many fields of professional photography including commercial, advertising, magazine and military. Adding to this varied list he's led photo safaris to exotic countries and travelled the world collecting material for his many books. Here are some of his interesting experiences.

"When I had a studio on Avenue Road on the second floor, we were to shoot an ad showing a salesman standing in a sinking boat before a sunset. Being winter we were forced to create the set in the studio. We cut the bottom off an old boat to make it look half-sunk then built a shallow pool in the studio using sand bags and a heavy sheet of clear plastic. It covered practically the whole studio floor with just enough space around the edges for the camera and lights. A hose from the kitchen took a day to fill the pool to a depth of four inches... that was a tremendous amount of water. I kept checking it and called a halt when I realized that we could see the actual floor through the water. So we had to drain it all out and that took another half day. The painter was called back, this time to paint the floor with a mirror image of the sunset which he had created on the wall behind the set... really a hand created reflection. Then back with the clear plastic, removing every wrinkle, as we filled the pool to its full depth. I set the boat and the male model into position and shot 8x10 colour using tungsten lighting. To break unwanted reflections on the surface of the water I had assistants in the corners rippling the water with paddles. Only after the completion of the assignment did we calculate the weight of the water and then realized the awesome risks we had taken since the building was so old and creaky. The weight could have broken through the floor plunging everything into the premises below where David Smith, the famous couturier had his store. We shuddered to think of the destruction we could have caused to his designer garments worth hundreds of thousands of dollars. David, incidentally, was also our landlord and he had a fit when we later told him the story!

"Despite four trips to Africa to collect photographs for a book about Cardinal Léger and his work with handicapped children, the publisher still wanted more B&W photographs. Stopping off at Montreal to pick up the Cardinal, I was notified the trip was cancelled. All my preparations, inoculations and shifting of assignments went down the drain. The trip was reset, again, for that fall. During the summer I took a short holiday and tore the ligaments in my knee which I was told definitely required an operation. But since the Africa trip was again at hand, I refused and was given elastic bandages with which to bind the joint. I plane-hopped to Yaounde, the capitol of Cameroon, but my bag with clothes and extra lenses never arrived. We still got the necessary pictures of Cardinal Léger for the book and had time for some extra photography. While concentrating on a photograph, in the centre of town, I walked into a pot-hole. Of course it had to be the injured leg that went into the hole and in trying to save the knee I broke the ankle. At the Mission they did the best they could by taping up the leg from ankle to knee like a stiff peg.

The Mission Brothers were going to transport a little boy back to his home village so rather than sit around with my pains, I accompanied them on their little trip. On our way we saw a swath of ants migrating across the road. It looked just like a wide strip of black tar, it was so solidly packed with ants. I had to take pictures and got so involved photographing them that I backed off into the grass to get a better view. I felt something under my pant leg and that was when I noticed I was standing with my dear injured leg right in the middle of the seething mass of ants. They were killer ants and were ravenously chewing through the bandages. Everyone was frantically beating and picking the ants off me. I got a few bites but was lucky the bandages protected me so well. Further along on our trip, we got stuck some ten kilometers from our destination. There I was, sloshing around in the mud, trying to heave the car out of the rut with one good leg. Finally we got it out and resorted to having local natives carry the boy to his home while we returned to our base. The following day I was to fly out to Nairobi but missed the plane by some 23 hours, having misread the time-table. The next flight wasn't for another six days. With so much time to kill they offered to operate on me in the local hospital but I still chose to wait 'til I got back to my own doctor. You know, despite all those problems, it was the greatest trip of my life... I love Africa!"

Ken transferred his photographic expertise to the Canadian Army during World War Two applying his magazine experience in the public relations area. When he was so successful at getting Army photos published in the Canadian media, Ottawa was reluctant to let him go overseas. He eventually went to England and joined the Normandy D-Day invasion when Canadian troops landed on Juno Beach. When a German bomber attacked their landing craft Ken's natural instinct was to stand up for pictures, but his Brigade Major pulled him down reminding him that he was now in a 'real' war and wasn't there to take pretty pictures. During the push to capture Caen the date of August 16, 1944 and the time of 2.30 in the afternoon is burned into Ken's memory. Ted Pritchard was driving him up a dusty road when they stopped to photograph a wave of Lancaster bombers as they swept overhead heading towards the enemy. Looking back they saw clouds of dust and smoke rising into the air. That was a sure sign bombs had been dropped early so everyone piled into the jeeps and started back to investigate. "As we were driving we saw the next wave of bombers heading in. It was a really beautiful sight but they seemed to be hesitating while shifting their final aim point as they came nearer. Suddenly I saw the bomb bay doors opening and we knew they were going to drop their loads early, far short of the enemy positions. We screeched to a halt right beside a deep quarry and if you can imagine running down a shear incline, well we did it as fast as we could drop and headed for caves on the far side. We could actually hear the whistle of the bombs on their way down so it was in the final seconds that we reached the safety of the cave. We felt the blast pull our ribs apart. We were lucky to reach only the mouth as we later found other men huddled at the back of the cave - crushed to death by the concussive impact of the explosions."

Ken recorded the conquest through France, Belgium and Holland. His military connection continued, retiring as Honorary Lieut-Colonel of the

Royal Regiment of Canada. Ken produced a series of books on anniversary visits to the war zones and a history of the Royal Canadian Regiment.

"In collecting photographs for 'The 100 Years of the RCR' I accompanied NATO troops on a winter exercise in Norway. I flew with the troops by helicopter up into the mountains to land behind the enemy. Busily shooting through the front window, I missed the first landing when the troops piled out and in no time we were airborne again. Back again with a second flight I charged out with the rest of them. Spotting more 'copters coming in, I crouched up for photos and was nearly decapitated. I had forgotten about my helicopter as it took off sideways. The skiis clipped my parka and tore off my toque. If I had been standing I would be dead for sure. That was too close!"

"I was equipped with army gear but had refused a respirator as it impaired my photography. After the drop the troops moved off to attack the enemy. Suddenly I smelled something; to simulate battle, they were firing grenades with gas and I was in its very midst without a respirator. I could not breathe and was coughing madly, it was terrible. I got away into fresh air and started being sick. These army guys of 20 and 21 can take it, but I'm much older. Boy, was I down in the dumps! I said to myself that I'd had enough and decided to walk back to the base. I figured I just had to keep descending until I hit a road. There I was struggling through the snow in my heavy boots and parka, feeling sorry, and mad at missing the final assault. An hour later I was still trudging along and going around a hair pin turn when suddenly I heard shooting and a commotion. There, right before me, the troops were crossing the road and I, of all things, was in the middle of the assault. It could not have been better for photography since I was on the leading edge of activity, whereas I would normally have been way back in the rear. I got great shots for the book. Later, I was told search parties were scouring the mountains for me, but I had been busy photographing the action."

GENE HORBATIUK

Gene Horbatiuk of Mississauga worked at Photo Engravers in Toronto, Ont., creating fashion photographs for the Simpson-Sears catalogues. "We were on location in Florida, shooting a fashion assignment with a van full of clothing, four lovely models, a stylist, a camera assistant plus other crew members. We couldn't get the van close to the actual shoot site and had parked it a distance away. It was up to the stylist to run back to the van for more clothing as the photography progressed. Somebody must have spotted our stylist with her arms loaded and reported to the police that clothing was being stolen from a parked vehicle. Well, it was quite a surprise when two burly guys burst through the bushes with guns drawn and we immediately thought it was a robbery. We all stopped in our tracks and didn't move until we found, to our relief, that they were plain clothes policemen."

BILL DAVIS

Bill Davis in Thunder Bay, Ont., had a co-op student working for him as a temporary assistant. "I was teaching her the rudiments of cameras and the business of photography. We were scheduled to do a business portrait and I had chosen to use a 35mm Nikon. In the studio I have my Speedatron strobe flash plugged directly into the wall outlet. I said to the student, 'Here's the end of the sync cord, go plug it in.' So she plugged it in while I started setting up the sitter. All of a sudden my camera went BANG in my hands and smoke billowed up all over the place. I hadn't been specific enough with my instructions and my young assistant had plugged the sync cord directly into the 110 volt wall outlet instead of into the strobe pack. So my little Nikon camera got the jolt of its life and blew apart. The repair technicians said there wasn't anything they could do... the camera was finished! Thank goodness it wasn't my Hasselblad!"

GEORGE HUNTER

George Hunter of Mississauga, Ont., has photographed across the full width and breadth of Canada to portray its beauty, natural resources and industrial achievements. His photographs have illustrated calendars, magazines and corporate brochures for decades. George relates an assignment that wasn't quite an average day.

"It was late afternoon on a gorgeous fall day in 1982 when we arrived back at the Val d'Or Airport in our U-drive car. My assistant and I lamented having been underground in a gold mine during such a beautiful day 'on the surface' which is the term used by miners when referring to the outdoors. Little did we know that the photographs we made that day were within seconds of being our very last. Both film and photographers came close to the brink of fiery incineration in a plane crash."

"We had been flown to Val d'Or early in the day by a mining company, in a chartered Piper Navajo, to make photographs underground, while the two executives who accompanied us held meetings in town. While waiting for the execs to show we engaged in idle chatter with the pilot who was the most bored looking individual we had seen in a long time. He had spent the day, mumping around the airport, waiting to haul us back to Toronto."

"Being a flyer, myself, I asked this jaded pilot what 'alternate' he was filing for Toronto (i.e. alternate airport in the event the destination becomes closed in by bad weather). He replied that it was Ottawa because of a weather system to the west of Toronto and he wanted to stay well to the east, if worse came to worst. I expressed that Ottawa was certainly a distant airport from Toronto and inquired whether the aircraft carried enough fuel for such a long backhaul. The pilot replied, 'Sure - and an extra hour on top of that.' Such is mandatory for twin-engine planes, so it was quite reassuring to know."

"The executives arrived and we packed into the plane. I grabbed the back seat and soon fell asleep. I awakened with a start when the left engine sputtered and quit. Not to worry - we were near Toronto and a Navajo flies quite O.K. on one engine. But moments later, the pilot started screaming into his radio, 'Mayday! Mayday! Mayday!' as the right engine quit and there was this terrible silence... then another series of pathetic Mayday's."

"Damn, I thought, why didn't I get a step ladder and dipstick back at Val d'Or and check the tanks, myself... and surely if I had taken the co-pilot's seat, I would have read the fuel gauges and started asking questions. I should have been suspicious of the pilot's self-assured attitude. Two engine failures within minutes is too much of a co-incidence. The plane couldn't have been refuelled, at all, after arriving in Val d'Or. I recalled the fiery crash, the previous week, of an American business jet that ran out of fuel two miles short of Pearson International airport, taking the lives of all on board. The cockpit door was open so I was able to see Pearson International Airport away in the distance through the front windshield. We were about 20,000 feet up and twenty miles north of the field - over the built-up area near Heart Lake where there is no place to make a forced landing."

"I must say one thing for the pilot: he knew how to trim up the plane for the best gliding ratio. But a twin Navajo does not glide like a Piper Cub. I've made power-off landings in single-engine aircraft but I always selected the appropriate distance from the landing strip before cutting power. On this descent, we had no such choice and the sink rate was much greater than a Cessna 180."

"You don't think of death at a time like that, although there is a terrible sinking feeling in the bottom of your stomach. You know darn well the pilot can't make the airport but hope for a one-in-a-million chance to survive the inevitable crash landing some where in Brampton. We were nearing the ground faster than we were approaching the runway; buildings and trees were reaching up to us with the runway just too far away. We all sat on the front two inches of our seats as if to coax a few extra metres out of the glide; yet were ready to fold into the crash position at the last moment. But with inches to spare, five guys thanked their lucky stars as the aircraft skimmed the fence beside Dixie Road. We just made it onto the first metres of Runway 15. Fire trucks, ambulances and RCMP cars raced alongside as the plane rolled to a stop on the foamed runway."

"The emergency vehicles departed, leaving one RCMP car at the nose of the Navajo and another alongside the door. I don't know what they were worried about - the plane couldn't go any-where. There wasn't enough fuel in the tanks to fill a cigarette lighter. They kept us waiting on board for an hour on the closed down runway, before finally allowing us to deplane. A Board of Enquiry had been assembled and when the door was opened, the pilot was escorted away. We never did hear the result of the enquiry but did learn that the pilot wasn't flying any more. As to the mining company they chose, thereafter, to fly charter aircraft using two pilots."

"My final thoughts were: 'What a terrible way to end such a beautiful day' - being safely on the ground suddenly made it more beautiful than ever. Incidentally, I never go to horror movies - too many frightful things happen to a photographer in real life."

George Hunter's photo assignments cover the world and he brings to light this story how he narrowly missed spending the rest of his life trapped in a remote dark jungle in West Africa. Recalls George, "I was in the city of Monrovia to photograph mines, rubber plantations and an explosives plant in Liberia. I took a morning off to scout around and make background shots in town. I photographed street scenes, open markets, store fronts, etc., – general atmosphere subjects."

"The manager of the explosives plant and his family were from Montreal and I was a guest in their home at Robertsfield, the main airport of Liberia, with a housing compound for foreigners. When I returned to the house in the evening my host, Jim, exclaimed, 'Man, oh, man – were you ever lucky this morning.' I responded, 'What's the matter? Nothing happened to me this morning that I can remember.' 'Oh no!' was the reply, 'You were almost a goner.' 'How come – what, – where? I don't understand, please explain.'"

"As Jim poured me a double Scotch which he said I needed and I was doubly lucky to be able to enjoy at this point in my young life. He began to explain: 'Remember those three bare-chested little girls you were photographing on the street down-town? Well the younger girls were showing off their elder sister in order to find her a husband. According to tribal custom, the first man who so much as touches the prospective bride, automatically becomes the bridegroom – right then and there – bang – whammo! The father was patrolling the far side of the street to keep an eye on the trio.' 'How did you know about me photographing the girls?' I stammered incredulously. 'When your friend, Karibaforce (the company driver), dropped you off early this morning he came back to the compound to take me to work and then returned to town to find you. He saw you taking pictures in the street and was not far away from the tribal overseer who almost became your father-in-law.' 'What's the big deal?' I questioned skeptically. 'What if I had touched this 'beauty' on the shoulder to direct her which way to look as photographers often do – no tribes-person would have anything to do with me, a foreigner, as a prospective bridegroom for a native girl!' 'Oh, no – you were just so very lucky you didn't touch her on the shoulder,' Jim replied. 'You'd be surprised how quickly you would have been swept away. First of all, after selling your cameras (a pair of Hasselblads and a Nikon) and your clothes, except for your shorts, the father and his nearby tribesmen friends would have hauled you out to their village in the distant back-country jungle where they have a thatched or galvanized-tin shack set up for the 'groom' – which would be you – and they would spend maybe two weeks 'tribalizing' you, including scribing your face with tribal sciatic cuts, for example, and many other 'formalities' too horrible to contemplate. They don't have electricity or communications out there, so you wouldn't be able to get in touch with us or anyone else.' "

"I continued my plea for information, 'What about Karibaforce – wouldn't he have rescued me?' 'No way!' was the reply, 'The girls and their father were from another tribe and he would have been afraid to do anything. He wouldn't know where they took you. He wouldn't have bothered to tell anyone until he came back to the office to bring me home just now. It would all happen so fast you wouldn't have known what hit you. That's how desperate the fathers are to find husbands to take daughters off their hands. Enjoy your Scotch. You are lucky you are not out there being deep-etched at this moment.' "

"I guess the lesson here is not to go shooting pix in the streets until you know something of the customs in the land you are visiting. I have always depended on luck, and I hope it will stay with me at least another ten or twenty years of making photographs in foreign lands."

GEORGE DUNBAR

George Dunbar CPA was an industrial photographer for IBM in Toronto and recalls the day he decided to build himself a pin-hole-camera. He obtained a mailing tube, closed off one of the ends with a piece of black paper and pierced a fine hole in it as a lens. Then he loaded the other end and sealed it over with more black paper to keep out all the light at that end. He took his new creation down to the shipping doors where he laid the tube across a steel drum and pointed it out the door. He commenced the exposure and figured he would return in ten minutes. But first to arrive on the scene, was a caretaker who came by to sweep and clear away the trash. George just happened to return as the caretaker picked up the tube and was examining it with suspicion. George, of course, yelled at the man, "Put down my camera!" The caretaker, in disbelief, eyed both the mail-

ing tube and George. He finally shook his head and walked away muttering, "Sure, sure... anything you say, sir!"

MALAK

Malak OC MPA of Ottawa, Ont., is readily identified for his gorgeous photographs of our nation's capital, festooned in tulips. On a par with this world renown for flower pictures is Malak's high reputation for industrial, commercial, pictorial and artistic photo subjects, built up over fifty years of award winning professional photography.

"In the Fall of 1945, the FDC which preceded the National Capital Commission found itself overwhelmed with great quantities of tulip bulbs sent as a thank-you gift by Queen Juliana of the Netherlands. Short of space to plant them, they turned their thoughts towards Parliament Hill. But to do that, they needed the approval of Prime Minister MacKenzie King who promptly vetoed the idea on the grounds that flowers would take away the dignity of the Peace Tower. As the story goes, the resourceful gardeners of the Federal District Commission waited until the Prime Minister went out of town on an official visit. Then the crews quickly planted thousands of bulbs at the base of the Peace Tower. On his return the Prime Minister never suspected anything unusual. The following Spring, Parliament Hill erupted with a spectacular and unforgettable sight of masses of colourful tulips. The gardeners anxiously awaited the Prime Minister's verdict... his pleasure or his wrath. But they were surprised as the Prime Minister expressed his unbounded enjoyment. At heart, he loved flowers and gladly allowed me to take his picture with the tulips. That picture and others I took in the Spring of 1946 were published widely throughout Canada and many other countries. As a result the Associated Bulb Growers of Holland were favourably impressed and appointed me their official photographer in North America. That assignment lasted over forty years. Eight years ago I finally resigned the account to devote my attention to other fields of photography and to publishing books."

"For Canada's Centennial I carried out a special photograph of 'The Charge' which is the most spectacular part of the RCMP Musical Ride. To do that I arranged with the Superintendent to stage The Charge in a different location in order to minimize the density of the curtain of dust raised by the horses. I set my camera within a few feet of the finish line and waited. The Charge started but something unusual seemed to be happening; the riders were having great difficulty controlling the horses. At the finish line they had to fiercely rein in the horses to stop them. The pictures were great but they could have cost me my life. I found out later that the horses were confused, due to the changed location and could easily have kept on going through the finish line to crush the photographer and his camera. When I went to thank the

Superintendent I noticed his face had lost some of its healthy colour. He simply said, 'Now you know how good we are.' He naturally was referring to the discipline of his men and their ability to stop the horses to spare my life; I could not agree more."

"While photographing the Aluminum industry in Kitimat, B.C. I found myself on the floor of the huge plant waiting for giant pots of hot (8000 degree F) aluminum to be poured into molds and formed into ingots. Before starting I was warned not to move from the spot where I was standing because there were many pots cooking under the floor around me. However, in the excitement of picture taking I forgot my instructions and moved to another spot for a different angle. It could have been the last picture of my life as I stood right on top of a hot melting pot. Fortunately, that was the only one that was tapped several days earlier and had formed a thick crust on top, solid enough, to carry my weight. No one expected to see even a trace of me or my cameras."

"With hair raising assignments like these it is nice to come home to the lady who runs the business, my wife Barbara. She is a combination of secretary, darkroom technician, book-keeper and librarian. I credit much of the success of the photographs, housed now in the vast library of my studio, to her sincere support and honest criticism."

"Shooting the Spring log drive, north of Ottawa, there was a huge log jam on a lake formed behind a dam. To get the logs moving, lumberjacks had to push many of the logs out of the channel. In order to capture the action I needed a high angle. So I decided to place a step ladder on the floating logs near the edge of the dam and had two men hold the ladder while I started taking pictures. Everything went well for the first few minutes but then suddenly the logs parted and the ladder and photographer disappeared into the water. My lumberjacks could only see two hands above the water, each holding a Rolleiflex camera. I was glad to be pulled out but much happier when I found the cameras remained perfectly dry."

"During the construction of the Canadian Museum of Civilization in Hull, there were numerous delays and I found myself on a tight schedule and deadline to produce the necessary photographs for the official opening brochure. Most important and still missing was the exterior view of the finished building. When the crucial moment arrived, I climbed a stepladder and anxiously awaited the passing of the clouds. Meantime, I heard a voice below asking to talk to me and said he was an admirer of my work. Deeply involved in my photography, I politely asked the gentleman to go away until I finished my work. To my horror, I discovered the person I had dismissed was none other than the famous architect of the museum, Mr. Douglas Cardinal, whom I had been anxiously waiting to meet for months."

Malak, 81 years young, is the brother of the world renowned portraitist Yousuf Karsh. His famous brother once made this statement, "When people ask me if Malak is my brother, I am most happy to say, rather, that I am HIS brother."

GILES RIVEST

Giles Rivest MPA of Chambly, Quebec recalls when he was shooting a medical brochure for a large company in Montreal. "One of the doctors was giving a slide show the next day and asked if I could take some photos for him of eyes that are used in transplants. The eyes were kept in jars and the technician nonchalantly asked, 'What colour would you like? Brown? Green? Blue?' I selected a jar and proceeded with the photography, but I must say it was not done with pleasure. I was quite shaken by the crowd of ghoulish eyes staring up from the bottom of the jar!"

Another unnerving assignment was Giles first commercial job. He was requested by a family to photograph their father who had died. "I had to shoot at the funeral home after closing hours where I was all by myself with four bodies laid out in their coffins. To add to the eerie scene, there was a big storm outside with lots of thunder and lightning. In those days I was scared of dead people... today I'm more scared of the living!"

TOM and JEAN-PIERRE BOCHSLER

Tom Bochsler MPA is Hamilton's most noted commercial and advertising photographer. He is part of a photographic family with the line continuing by his son, John.

Tom was accompanied by John to an industrial assignment. He recalls, "We had taken quite a load of light stands, heavy cases, power packs and all sorts of equipment to cover the job. At 7 o'clock when we finished we were tired and not too careful how we loaded everything into the van. The last item to go in was a big light stand sitting on top of the load. Over the years I've carried a fire extinguisher which I keep in a milk crate along with other utility items. As we drove out onto the road I heard a loud clunk as the heavy stand rolled off the top of the pile... and then was followed by an eerie hissing and gushing sound. Before we could realize what was happening the whole van filled with fire extinguisher powder. The falling stand had activated my 2 lb fire extinguisher causing it to empty completely. John and I jumped out of the van with the stuff chasing after us. We opened the back gate to a fog of overpowering powder and had to wait some time for it to settle. While suffering this predicament, the client left the plant and drove right past us; he never stopped to see if we needed any help. You can't imagine how thorough that spray can be until you've experienced it yourself. It got inside every one of the photo cases. At the studio, luckily we have an air compressor, so we blasted everything with air and vacuumed every nook and cranny.... but it still didn't clean away the residue thoroughly. If we turned on the car heater fan, it would blow white dust all over us. So I resorted to taking the van into a car wash and they did a super job, even used high pressure air. They admitted they had never faced a problem like that before. As a result I haven't carried a fire extinguisher since!"

Tom had quite an experience with a #50 flash bulb while photographing 300 people at a Christmas banquet. "The year was 1957," recalls Tom, "and I was using a 4X5 Speed Graphic with a wide angle lens. Although there was some electronic flash available at the time, it was too low powered so I resorted to the trusted flash bulb. After focussing with the ground glass, I didn't close the shutter as there was no sync coupling on the lens. As I inserted the flash bulb into its socket it lit up in my hand, burning my thumb and finger quite severely. As if that wasn't bad enough the bulb flew out of my hand, bounced over the side of the balcony and dropped some 15 feet onto a lady's plate of chicken with a PLOP! She screamed and everyone got excited. I ran down expecting to see someone injured and fully expected an angry husband to hit me. Cuddling my burned fingers gingerly, I managed to blurt out my explanation and offer an apology then finally went to the hotel housekeeper for medical attention. From then on I always used a thick leather glove when handling flash bulbs... just in case!"

"For many years, during the 50's to early 70's I was the official PR photographer for the Hamilton Tiger Cat Football Club. Each year, I had the team photograph to shoot and it was usually done just before a home game, so little time was available to complete it. On this particular occasion I arranged the location behind the stadium with benches for the front three rows and then some tables for the very back row to stand on. I was putting the final touches to the massive group when suddenly the whole back row disappeared as one. The tables had collapsed under the weight of eight big linemen. Fortunately, no one was hurt and after some humorous jibes they were regrouped for the picture and then sent off to win the game. After that close call I did consider an increase in my liability insurance!"

Tom recalls the time his son, John, went up to shoot aerials in a helicopter. "I sent my son-in-law, Don, along for the ride and to change film in the cameras. With the number of assignments and with the locations almost side-by-side, extra cameras were needed to keep the shoot moving as rapidly as possible and thus reduce the expensive flying time. So Don was hunched over reloading film while the copter was circling round and round. With so much motion Don's stomach went woozy and he started to bring up. In a panic he looked for something to be sick in but there was nothing handy. In desperation he grabbed for the nearest thing.... the camera bag! Well that really finished off that bag, so from then on we have always made sure to carry a special 'barf' bag (not camera) on aerial assignments!"

Tom was shooting industrial pictures in a nuclear products lab in Ottawa. The area has very high safety standards against contamination. Everyone wears a film badge to monitor any trace of radiation when working near radioactive areas or products. After a session in the lab you have to be tested by placing your feet on sensors and your two hands into pockets which are sensors as well. When the system is activated, it counts to see if your radiation is higher than normal. Tom recalls, "On my departure I went through the procedure and a little picture came up saying that my left hand was contaminated. My guide said that sometimes it didn't work right, so try it again. It gave me the same reading, so they brought in a man called a "Surveyor" who took me to a more sensitive unit and scanned my hand. He zeroed in on my watch which is over 30 years old and has a luminous dial painted with radium salts. It caused a little bit of a stir and it was suggested that I don't wear the watch to bed, even with the little bit of radiation it gives off. I was reminded of workers who painted aircraft dials with this luminous paint. Those who licked their brushes absorbed the radium and often died from cancer. But I have no concern, I've been in nuclear plants for over 20 years and, even though I've picked up some radiation on my shoes, its been easily removed."

John Bochsler MPA remembers one of the first jobs when he accompanied his dad down into a mine. "We had to travel quite a distance underground to reach the location of a heavy mining truck that carried ore to the conveyer belts. We were assigned to photograph the truck for the manufacturer. The art director wanted a low angle shot on 4x5 transparency, so that meant grovelling down in the muck and getting really dirty. Except for the lights on our hats it was pitch black, but that was to our benefit as we decided to paint the scene with a hand held Metz strobe flash while the camera lens was left open to accumulate all the exposures. We had popped off so many flashes while testing the scene with Polaroid that we were running out of strobe power. I had worked out a path and sequence where I lit the equipment and then the rock background. I had about a dozen flashes to make each time while my dad worked the camera, covering the lens between exposures. The lights of the mining vehicle were also turned on for a short period of time by the operator as he sat on the vehicle. Since I was fumbling my way around in the dark between exposures, my dad came up with the idea to cover the lens after each flash sequence and then have the operator turn on the machine's headlights to aid me to find my next spot and to adjust the flash aperture. The teamwork worked well and we came up with a prize winning photograph."

ALAIN BOILY

Alain Boily MPA of Charlottetown, Prince Edward Island, survived an unforgettable moment. "As a young photographer in the Canadian Air Force, I was assigned to photograph a group of paratroopers from the Search & Rescue wing who were practicing their jumping techniques. We were using a "Buffalo" aircraft that is

equipped with a rear loading ramp. When we reached the proper altitude they opened the rear ramp so the jumpers could go directly out the back. I donned a safety harness with about 15 feet of harness which would allow me freedom to move about while the team made their jump. The jumpmaster helped me on with the harness and I eased out to the very end of the ramp so that I could get a clear angle of the action. I kept clicking away until all the jumpers were away. Then I turned around to get back to safety and that was when I noticed the jumpmaster standing holding the end of the harness... looking at it, then looking at me; he hadn't secured the harness to the airframe. My hands suddenly wanted to tear into the metal ramp for a life grip. I could have been the first photographer to jump from an aircraft without a parachute. Needless to say, the jumpmaster was obligated to buy the beer that night!"

"There were two little boys who I always photographed for their family Christmas card. The mother always left the assignment to the very last moment and she was determined that they should be in an outside setting. We're talking the first week of December when it was fairly cold and desolate, but we found a good location with evergreen trees beside a running brook. I set the two boys to playing by the waters edge with a stern warning not to get too close or too daring. I went over to the far side of the stream to shoot the picture from a different angle. The boys responded quite well and I was concentrating on the composition when suddenly I lost my footing. Like a ski race gone wrong, I slithered down the muddy bank and splashed into the water... camera, tripod and all. I pushed the camera up over my head as the icy waters reached to my chest. I still remember to this day, the look on the boys' faces - their eyes were as big as 'toonies'. That is the moment I should have clicked the shutter but I was too darned co-o-o-old! I got back out and finished the sitting in very quick time with no problems from the boys after that."

RICHARD D. BELL

Richard Bell MPA of Toronto, Ont., proves through his experiences that shooting location and action photography is not always easy and by no means safe. Take the situation when a lion attacked him. Rick was shooting fashion pictures at the African Lion Safari when a big lioness, de-clawed and on a chain took a dislike to his Hasselblad and charged him. "I was battered and tossed about, like a cat playing with a mouse."

"In covering winter sports I like to locate where I'm going to get the best action photos," says Rick. "Shooting car racing-on-ice I picked an outside corner behind a snow barrier. One of the cars couldn't make the turn and came crashing into the safety snowbank; a blast of hardened snow hit me with such force that I was thrown 20 feet backwards. That same day I was shooting the snowmobile races and was following one racer in my camera finder. He came up along the ridge of the snow bank, teetering on the edge, and I realized he was coming straight at me. I dove for the snow but received a set of track marks across my back and my head. The racer... he just kept on going."

"When shooting the Benson & Hedges professional ski races, I made the front page of the Toronto Globe and Mail but not the way I would have wanted to. I was shooting with the other photographers at the first bump. It was a dual slalom race as Harold Stouffer faced off against Jean Claude Killey. Everything was tense as they were in the quarter finals. I was following Stouffer through my viewfinder and realized that he had come through the gate, incorrectly, and was way off course... heading straight for me. Everything happened so fast; he tried to jump over me but one ski sliced across my ear while the other caught underneath my arm. I was hit smack in the chest and went sailing down the slope for the next 3 or 4 gates. The Globe & Mail ran THEIR photographer's sequence showing me dragged along with my head caught in the skiers crotch. That's how I made the front page!"

"I've been to the Arctic a number of times shooting for various companies; travel is most often by helicopter. On one flight I climbed in and was just setting up my equipment when the pilot took off. The tail went up first as we rose 30 feet into the air, then we came crashing down, breaking one of the landing struts. 'Oh shoot!' yelled the pilot, 'that's the second time this week.' I immediately chided him for taking me up in an unsafe helicopter. 'Oh,' he said indignantly, 'it doesn't happen THAT often!' "

"I accompanied a ski team throughout British Columbia to locate new training grounds for the Canadian National Ski Team; I had been a professional ski instructor for seven years. The party consisted of avalanche and ski development experts with myself as the photographer. I am trained on the pack snows of Eastern Canada but it was a real challenge to master the deep powder snows in the B.C. mountains. You drop off 10-30 foot cliffs and sweep through chest deep snow. A helicopter took us to the starting point at the 10-12 thousand foot level where the lower oxygen brings on fatigue in no time. On top of that, I had to carry a 30 pound pack of cameras. Being the 'hotshot skier from the East' I certainly wanted to prove myself, but got into trouble right off the bat by getting buried into a drift, so deep, that my poles couldn't touch anything beneath me. Two guys had to come back and dig me out for 20 minutes. We set off again and my companion-guide went to one side of a large rock while I chose the other side. As I skimmed past the rock, the ground disappeared completely as I sailed out over a cliff edge and saw what looked like a thousand foot drop to the mountain side below. I managed to turn inwards and slide back into the mountain face coming to an abrupt stop, standing upright in another snow bank.

Then suddenly, I was hit by a cascade of snow from above, and as I recovered from that jolt, I discovered myself hanging upside down. I was suspended at the top of an avalanche-trough with my skis bolted into the snow, holding me back from a thousand foot run to the bottom. I could see mad scrambling at the base with the helicopter taking off. Evidently they expected me to pull down an avalanche on top of them and they were getting away fast. I used my poles to bend up and try to get my feet free. I got one ski loose and was working on the other when the whole shelf of snow broke loose in what is called a slab avalanche. This was now a life and death situation and, if I didn't get clear, I would be rolled up and buried in tons of snow. I worked frantically to get on my feet as the slab and I headed down the mountain. I knew if I could right myself I could rely on my skiing ability to get out of the danger zone. Finally I pulled the other ski loose and rolled over on my shoulder. I felt the skis grip the snow and so raced ahead and out of the path of the avalanche. By the time I hit the bottom, my legs were shaking so much and I was so-o-o exhausted, I just dropped onto the ground. The helicopter was radioed back and they loaded me in like a sack of old potatoes. With wry humour they ordered, 'OK, let's head for the next ski run!' "

After a strenuous assignment, Rick unloaded his cameras from around his neck and placed them on top of his car, until he could pack them away properly. Being exhausted he sat in the car for a spell to collect his wits, then drove away. As he was heading along the Queen Elizabeth highway a trucker started honking madly and waving him to stop. Rick felt his car was running OK and couldn't figure what the trouble was. It was only when he pulled over to check the car that he found his cameras wedged in the roof rack and luckily were still intact. Now that should be the perfect lesson to any photographer but a few years later, having finished another job, Rick unloaded his gear putting the cameras on the front hood of his car and drove away. He was suddenly alarmed to see his Nikon cameras dancing merrily on the hood before his eyes. "Not again!" he screamed. "If I brake too fast they will slide off and hit the ground." So he eased slowly to a standstill, fearing disaster at any moment, and was finally reunited with his precious cameras!

"I had an assignment years ago where I travelled to several prisons in Ontario. One cold November day I had to photograph in the psychiatric wing of one of the prisons. We had to take some shots out on the roof and one thing I always do is check the lock on the exit door to see that I can get back in. I was talking with the client as our crew exited onto the roof... and we all forgot about the door. Then suddenly, we both remembered and made a mad grab for the door... but it was too late and it slammed in our face. Being a prison, the door locks from both the inside and the outside. It was darn cool in my casual clothes with the winds whipping up the white caps on the lake beside the building. We figured we had better find a way to get help, so started waving to staff members as they arrived for a 3.30 shift change. Six of us were frantically waving but everyone ignored us and just went into the building. No one paid any attention at all. After a good 25 minutes it was really getting cold. Then we spotted one of the female kitchen staff out having a smoke. She glanced at us as we were waving and yelling, but she probably thought we were inmates making advances at her. Finally she disappeared but came out with someone else. As she pointed to the roof you could almost hear her say: 'Doesn't that look like the Building Manager? The other person nodded but they still didn't comprehend why we were on the roof and why all the waving. Well, finally they got help and after an hour of freezing, the door was opened. I can't describe how relieved I was to get back into a prison!"

FRED BIRD

It takes a special expertise to produce photographs of succulent food. Fred Bird of Toronto Ont., is the creator of many of the colour illustrations for Canadian Living and in advertising posters and billboards.

Fred says ice cream has always been a nightmare to record. "I remember when regulations required us to use the real thing and that forced us to bring in tons of dry ice plus a half dozen freezers to store a truck load of the product. The food stylists spent hours grooming and forming each dish, then freezing the final masterpieces. On shoot days, visitors to the studio would instantly salivate when they saw all that ice cream and decorative condiments. A designer friend of mine could smell his favourite food from the other side of the city and always happened to drop in on the right shooting days. His timing was perfect and he had an appetite that would rival a bear. Food literally disappeared when he was around so that, on more than one occasion, our best creation was destroyed before we had a chance to photograph it. My assignment was a cover shot for Canadian Living featuring two ice cream cones. We had experimented with a simulated ice cream made of shortening and icing-sugar and were giving it a try for this particular cover shot. Food stylist, Olga Truchan who pioneered this amazing substance, had prepared a dozen mouth watering cones and had them displayed on the kitchen counter when 'guess who?' walked in. While Olga was tending to our set, my friend couldn't resist temptation. The first gulp of the goodies was quite a shock to him. But still his cravings urged him on to a second bite... that was the clincher! Finally his brain caught up to his taste buds and registered... TILT! He suddenly dropped everything, sped off to the washroom and lost his 'composure' (to say the least)... and then quietly left the studio. Now, when he comes to visit he stays well clear of the kitchen!"

"On another occasion a grocery chain assigned us to a series of posters of their no-name products. In our fourth day of the shoot, we constructed a 'country' set consisting of earthy tiles, barn boards, lots of props and eight beautiful pies. The barn boards were built up on bricks to elevate the pies at different levels. My assistant and I had sweated out the morning arranging the set and positioning the pies. The client arrived at noon to OK the shot and was curious for a close inspection. We warned him to watch for the lights and stands BUT failed to point out how precarious the barn boards were set up. As he manoevered for a different viewpoint, he stepped on the end of one protruding board which immediately reacted like a teeter totter. The set burst in all directions as two of the pies catapulted into orbit. The first pie hit the client just

below the knee while the second struck him square on the chin. Luckily they weren't in hard serving dishes otherwise he could have been hurt. Still, his feelings were quite bruised with embarrassment... while we were left to clear up the mess and restart from scratch!"

DOUGLAS R. JAMIESON

Doug Jamieson MPA of Oakville, Ont., followed his father, Ross, into the family photography business; his dad retired in 1966. There are many memories from the two Jamiesons which Doug recalls with pain and laughter.

"When my parents were first married," recounts Doug, "my Dad photographed wedding groups in the living room of our house. It was the custom for my Mom to show the bride and groom to the washroom to check their hair. This one time, she sent a wedding couple in and noticed it was taking an awful long time for them to come out. Finally she threw open the door and had the surprise of her life. The couple was in the process of consummating their new marriage!"

"My Dad did a lot of passports and one day this man came in who couldn't speak any English. He was ushered to the dressing room but was confused what to do, so Dad indicated to go in and check his hair. The man didn't come out, so finally Dad looked in and found he had taken all his clothes off. As a new immigrant he had been through so many medical examinations that he automatically assumed he was required to take his clothes off... again!"

"One of our local industries was having a dinner dance at the Casa Loma so we had to string big #50 flashbulbs around the main ballroom to shoot a picture at the stroke of midnight. My Dad set the camera for the correct view, left the shutter open and when he put in the first bulb it went off in his hand. Those #50's would just fry you and your skin would peel for about a month afterwards. Despite incredible pain he pressed on as the deadline was approaching. I was sent out to the car for extra equipment and at seventeen and just learning, I was rushing like mad trying to be of help. I grabbed the stuff, stuck it under my arm and while leaning on the car with one hand I kicked the door shut... 'BANG' - right onto my thumb! I had to drop all the equipment before I could open the door to get my thumb out. So here we were trying to get this picture, me with a squashed thumb and my Dad with a fried hand. I don't know how we got through it but the picture did come out!"

Doug recalls a job he did for a wallpaper company. "The designers wanted to use a photograph with a ratio of 18" wide by 24" high to fit the paper. One of the designers had a collection of antique containers like old Quaker Oats packages etc. They wanted to include delicatessen items so I shopped around for an assortment of fancy foods, chocolate bars and teas, all in metal containers. I built a wooden frame on the studio floor and tediously arranged the items in it, turning them at different angles then building them up to a common level with styrofoam. Numerous test polaroids were cut and lapped together to check against objectionable patterns showing up such as bright yellow mustard tins creating a line down the wall. I slaved over the project the whole day - up and down the ladder to check the view in the ground glass and bending over the frame for hours. I thought I had it pretty well finished, and since the designer was coming in the next morning for the final check, I left everything standing and went home. When I arrived at 9 am the next morning I found that a mouse had gotten into the studio during the night, walked over the whole set-up and out of the selection of candies, biscuits and scrumptious delicacies it had chosen to eat a solitary chocolate bar out of the very center. It could have spent the whole night tasting and destroying everything but chose only this one item. Fortunately, I had a second chocolate bar so I just picked the one out and replaced it with the new one. The designer arrived and said, 'Fine...go with it!' Incidentally, the company loved the story when they heard about the "gourmet mouse".

"When I was first starting in photography, I had a Saturday morning assignment to shoot interiors of a warehouse when no workers would be around. Once let inside by the client, I was left alone to complete the photos and then I could let myself out. The instructions were to climb up on an overhead crane at each end of the building to get the pictures. I had to climb about 20 feet up a vertical ladder that was attached to the wall and do it while carrying a 4x5 camera, a tripod and camera case . You never make two trips so there I was struggling up with one hand and the equipment in the other. I finally made it to the top where I then had to walk over the length of the crane to get into the operator's cab. I made my first picture and meticulously retraced my steps back down to the ground. This is strenuous work and I was beginning to get out of puff. So then I had the other end to do and it was the same 20 foot ladder situation again. Part way up, I had quite a nasty surprise. The metal plugs, securing the ladder to the wall, were loose and the closer I got to the top, the more the heaving and hauling was pulling the ladder out of its moorings. Each time I grabbed for the next rung up, the bolts would yank back and forth from their holes. I feared the whole thing would peel away from the wall like a nightmare out of a slapstick movie. Harold Lloyd clinging to the sides of Manhatten skyscrapers in the old silent films had nothing on me. I still went on, testing my fate with each new rung, and happily made the top where I completed the shot, then realized I could not get down. In no way was I going to try that ladder again and there wouldn't be anybody around 'til Monday morning. I figured I could most likely get down without the equipment, but shortness of energy and nerve dampened my feelings for anything outlandish or daring. As it turned out luck was with me, for there lying on the floor of the cab was a coil of wire. I tied it around the tripod and case and lowered them down as far as the wire could go. It was still about 10 feet off the ground. I scrambled down the ladder to safety then climb up on boxes to disconnect my equipment."

"The trouble with photography is you get so enthusiastic that you don't realize when you're putting yourself in danger. I had a job for a company that was shipping huge quarried rocks to Buffalo to be used for improvement of the harbour facilities. I took a lot of photos as they loaded these chunks of armor stone onto a barge, ready to float down the Erie Canal to their destination. As a finish they wanted a shot of the loaded barge coming down the canal itself. So I drove ahead and found a bridge that crossed over the canal. The barge would be coming by in one minute, so I was under some pressure to be ready for its arrival. I looked over the side of the bridge and discovered that a big pipe also stretched across the canal and blocked the view. Still, I thought, that pipe is the place to be. I could hear the barge coming ever closer by the blasts of his

warning horn. So I decided to climb out on the pipe and ran to the end of the bridge, leapt over a little wire fence and, in the process, was smacked in the nose by my Hasselblad as it swung up and hit

me in the face. My eyes filled with tears and my nose started running blood, but I still had to scramble through the bushes beside the canal to find the pipe. I finally found a safety mesh to keep kids off but it was ripped open, so I worked my way through the hole and walked out onto the pipe to finally get the photographs as the barge made its pass. Then it suddenly dawned on me... 'How did I get out here?' This was a round tube of slippery steel about six feet in diameter. It curved off to a straight drop into the water with no safety nets or hand rails... and I had just walked out there standing upright. I had my Hasselblad in my hands, blood all over my shirt, my face starting to swell and now I felt like I was stranded on a tight rope over Niagara Falls. So I hooked the camera under my armpit and on hands and knees crawled, ever so gingerly, back to safety. Everyone thought I was crazy... and I thought so too!"

"I was to photograph the President of a sugar company in Montreal so I took a morning flight, grabbed a cab to the company and had the job finished by 11am. It had all been a hectic pace and, once more, I headed for the airport for my return flight at 1 pm. When I struggled up with my equipment the passenger agent said, 'If you rush you will catch your flight.' I rebelled and thought, 'I've been running all day so I'll just check my equipment through and have a quiet lunch and catch the next flight home. When I returned from lunch I found that the flight had been cancelled, so that meant I had to wait another hour. They even had the nerve to cancel the next flight too! I wasted the whole darn day waiting to fly home. So much for taking a leisurely lunch!"

"A number of years ago we worked on a project that involved taking photographs of the Stanley Cup. Oh! what history is wrapped up in that 100 year old trophy - 35 pounds of silver plate, 4 feet high, with the inscribed names of all the great teams and heroes of Canadian professional hockey. Gretsky's name is on it - I saw it and I touched it. The cup was brought to our studio in a large padded case by the Director of Security from the Hockey Hall of Fame. He had to be with the cup at all times. The client and art Director flew in for the appointed day so it was like having an important celebrity in the studio. Walls of reflecting white paper surrounded the set which featured the cup on a deep blue background with sparkling stars to emphasis the beauty and shine of the surface. It looked awesome! My wife dropped into the studio with our nine year old son and two of his buddies. They were allowed to peek into the setup while the security chief swung into a little talk about the amount of silver and the insurance coverage for the cup.

My wife and I were aglow with pride being able to provide our son with an unforgettable memory, being in the very room and touching the legendary Stanley Cup. The next morning at breakfast it was still on our minds as my son asked, 'Dad, do you still have that trophy at the studio?' I replied that it went back to the Hall when we were finished shooting. He looked thoughtful then blew us away with: 'What was that thing, anyway...?' "

W. BRUCE POLDON

Bruce Poldon HON MPA, now retired to Islington, Ont., served as a Technical Representative for Kodak Canada practically all his business years during which he was posted to different parts of the country. "By the time I got to know Charles E. Stride in New Westminster, British Columbia, he was eighty years old and had given up portraiture. He was by then a B&W photo-finisher with a huge gas-fired dryer, a large sorting table (where the final prints and negatives were assembled into envelopes) and several sheet fed Apac printers in the darkroom. This, of course, was the days before the arrival of colour which drove everyone to roll printing and continuous process machines. Charlie enjoyed telling about the olden days and how he had survived sixty years in business at the same location. The stairs up from 657 Columbia Street to the top floor seemed exceptionally long and not at all enticing to prospective customers. When he first rented there, he joined three other photographic studios stretched out along the hallway; Charlie was allocated the room at the very far end. Mr. Stride still saw potential in his remote location despite all the competing signage which patrons had to pass before arriving at his studio. There were glorious and elaborate signs for this studio and that studio while away in the distance Charlie mounted his own small, almost unreadable, sign -'Stride Studio'. But above it he placed a large bold sign emblazoned: 'MAIN ENTRANCE'. It brought customers past every other door and, some 60 years later, Charles Stride was the only photographer still in business!"

SHERMAN HINES

Sherman Hines MPA began his photographic career in Halifax as a portrait and industrial photographer. He amassed a long list of awards before changing direction for his business in '82. He turned his talents to stock and landscape photography which has led to the publication of some 21 photo books covering much of Canada. He opened his own publishing firm to facilitate a growing list of future books.

Sherman recalls back to his studio days in the Maritimes. "I used to do thousands of graduate photographs and got a little bored doing the same job. The students came into the studio on an assembly line basis every fifteen minutes and I would take four shots and then they would leave. One day, just at lunch time, I got a phone call at the reception desk. Someone came in while I was on the phone, diverted my attention and then invited me out to lunch. I had unfortunately forgotten about a poor student I had left on my posing stool. She sat for the next hour waiting for me to return from that phone call. Returning from lunch, I discovered my error and had to think fast. Approaching her I said, 'I hope you didn't mind, that was a very important long distance call but I finally got rid of them. NOW, I'll finish your portrait. She never knew I went to lunch... at least, so I thought."

"I was putting up a new background drape in the studio when the next student-sitter arrived and caught me at the top of the ladder adjusting the heavy folds. She looked at me and asked, 'Is the photographer here?' Jokingly I said, 'No, he's gone to lunch but I'll look after you. I've been working on these drapes all morning and I've seen what Mr. Hines does. All he does is fix up your hood and gown like this, (at that I adjusted her hood and gown) and he invites you to sit on the stool.' She was quite amused but hesitant, saying that she could wait for the photographer. But since she was here I offered to proceed with the sitting. I continued with my charade giving a running commentary as to how MR. HINES moves the lights... MR. HINES adjusts them this way... MR. HINES says OK, smile! By

this time she was blown away that the drapery man would dare to take her portrait. I took the usual four poses then ushered her out the door assuring her that they would be as good as MR. HINES photos. To this day I'm sure she believes that the drapery man took her graduation portraits."

"My life has proven to be much more interesting since those studio days. My cameras have taken me into odd and challenging situations as I've crossed the country time and again recording the scenery and the people. I was travelling through British Columbia to collect photographs of logging activities for my B.C. book. I was following the inland water-

ways up around Prince Rupert. Arriving at one of the camps, the loggers figured here was a city slicker with a fancy camera who would be fair game for anything that would break the boredom of their camp existence. Throughout my stay they repeatedly asked if I would like to try on the big cork boots that they run the logs with and also would I like to try my hand at standing on a floating log. I turned their offers aside by saying that it looked too dangerous to me since I was from the city, while they were very capable of walking around on the logs. For two days they kept chiding me as they were determined to see this city slicker fall in the water. Finally when all my pictures were finished I gave into their pressures and asked if they really wanted me to get on the log. They eagerly said yes, so I agreed that to-day was the day to meet the challenge. Word spread fast and a crowd gathered to see the yokel meet his fate. They outfitted me with the boots and a pike pole with which to balance myself. We were up on the deck of the little tug-boat so they suggested I climb down the ladder to reach the logs. To rebuff my challengers, I spurned them aside saying, 'That is the way you guys do it. All you can do is run around on the logs and that is what everybody can do. I intend to polevault off the deck of the boat to the logs below.' They declared that I would surely kill myself. So I laid into them even more so, pointing out they would have to hold themselves responsible if I got killed because they had been chiding me so incessantly. 'Not only that,' I added, 'I'll go up to the Captains cabin and jump from there." Well, by this time they were ready to make funeral arrangements for me. So I climbed to the top of the boat, poised for a moment and took off into the void. There, off McDonald Bay, about a 100 miles south of Prince Rupert, my spiked boots went slicing through the air ahead of me... and I landed squarely on the top of one of those big Douglas fir logs. I threw away the safety pole and for the next five minutes gave them my best impressions of how a city-slicker can roll a log. What they didn't know was I had been a pole vault champion in high school and had won the Nova Scotia Log Rolling Championship, Junior Grade. So I left them totally astounded and applauding because I had put one over on THEM. I picked up the pike pole and challenged them to go off the deck, but it ended there as none would do it."

PETER DENNIS PATES

Peter Pates MPA, of Waterloo, Ont., received a call one day from London, and got into a conversation for some twenty minutes. "The gentleman finally mentioned that he was phoning from London, England, not London, Ontario as I had assumed. He gave me an advertising assignment involving school children and the ecology of trees. The directions gave the location as being in ALMA but with my English background and my clients accent, I interpreted it as being AYLMER. So for the day of the shoot I travelled to AYLMER but soon found I was at the wrong spot. I should have been at ALMA, which is completely in the other direction some two hours away. So panic set in and I phoned my contact, apologizing for my big mistake and said I would be there as soon as possible. They obviously saw the funny side of it and proceeded to laugh. They agreed to wait until I got there, three hours later, with the rain pouring down. But we successfully got our picture coverage with the kids happy... the client happy... and me happy to keep ALMA under my hat!"

BILL YUKKA

Bill Yukka of Etobicoke, Ont., was assigned to photograph a VIP reception on the top floor of a tall Toronto building. He arrived early and as he entered the elevator a foreign speaking gentleman joined him. "The elevator only went up so far and then stopped. Luckily, I found someone who told us the elevators to the top floor only operated from 6pm onwards. It was still only 5.30 so we became quite friendly in the extra half hour as we chatted away. Finally, the elevator came to life and took us the rest of the way to the top floor. I was quite surprised at the fuss made of my new found friend, and it turned out he was the Ambassador from Morocco. Feeling giddy at the chummy way I had talked with him and the topics we had discussed, I was afraid I might not be able to cover the assignment comfortably. But the ambassador eased the pain by asking me to join in the party and enjoy the food."

STIRLING WARD

Stirling Ward MPA SPA of Vancouver, British Columbia tells these stories of his life as a west coast advertising photographer.

"The Royal Bank was changing its signage atop their skyscraper building in downtown Vancouver. They brought in a giant Sikorsky helicopter -a flying crane to transport the heavyweight sign. A video crew would record the event while I would get some dramatic aerials for Royal Bank publicity. All the streets in the downtown area were closed off for the Sunday morning event with special permission being given by the Ministry of Transport to fly so low to the buildings. The Sikorsky took off from the downtown heliport to initiate the construction changes, followed by the video crew in another helicopter to cover the first phase of the project. When they returned, the video crew got out and my assistant and I got in. While I was putting on my headset and stowing my cameras, the video photographer who is a good friend of mine, strapped me in. It is not a conventional seat belt but is a harness on the end of a long lead that is attached inside the helicopter. It enables the photographer to stand outside on the rail to shoot clear vertical views.

So we went up and got some fantastic shots, hanging out of the helicopter while doing a complete 360 degree fly-around. The Sikorsky dropped the sign into position and I got the worker on the roof securing it into place. The views were absolutely spectacular with some shots looking straight down into the canyon core. It was a great assignment and I was riding high with exhilaration as we landed at the pad again. I turned to unstrap myself and that was when a cold chill ran through my body. You are always protected by a secondary safety unit that goes through a ring and clips on. Its got an unusual catch. As I reached to take it off I realized that the safety hadn't been done up at all and I knew I quite easily could have ended up as a blotch on the downtown pavement!"

"We were doing some editorial illustrations creating an oriental setting. The last shot involved an opium couch which we accessorized with a number of decorator items borrowed from a lady who travels all over the world collecting authentic material. Our shot included an oriental figurine that contained burning incense. As we were gradually building up the set we were feeling very tired and were working slower and slower. The smoke from the god-figure was filling the room and the longer we worked the more tired we became. We had to drag ourselves to finally finish the shot. When we returned the props to our benevolent lady we mentioned about the incense and the tiredness. She was very much amused by the problem and explained, 'That is special incense used to sedate snakes! So now I know how it works on humans!' "

"I was asked to shoot for a manufacturer of corrugated metals. They had a roof installation of which they wanted some pattern shots taken. It was quite a climb to the top of a crane which, itself, was on top of a high rise building. When I reached the crane operator, I then had to go out on a catwalk with no hand rails. Of course the best vantage point was at the far end of the catwalk. By the time I reached the end of the walkway, I was crawling on my hands and knees dragging my camera bag. I thought it was a great shot for the wide angle and as I looked through the camera everything seemed to jump away another 200 feet. I was immediately disoriented and got quite dizzy. In a panic I grabbed for the catwalk and clung on for dear life. The crane operator was having a real hoot watching me –the brave photographer, hanging on for grim life. With no safety belt, I gradually worked my way back to safety, – but what a price for perfection.”

“We scouted out a tranquil site for an advertisement that was located beside a pond. The concept we were to follow was 'passing our knowledge from one generation on to the next generation' and 'for each generation to enjoy time with their family'. We made arrangements with the park commission to have the area for ourselves when we would shoot in mid morning. The weather turned out perfect. The models arrived -a grandfather, his son and a grand child. The stylist, the client and the art director were on hand, plus a few noisy black crows sitting in the trees. We positioned the grandfather on the grass with the father and then his son. It was all nicely back lit with my assistant holding a reflector to soften the shadow side. Every one was ecstatic the way it was all coming together. It was looking so great! The stylist went forward for one final touch up and, just at that moment, one of the crows flew down and dive bombed the set dropping its bird dirt amongst everyone. One of the models thought the make-up stylist had dropped something on them and there was a sudden change to our tranquility when they realized what really had splattered all over them. That crow must have waited all morning to dump this load and couldn't have chosen a more precise moment to do it. The whole set was just covered including the reflector. Pandemonium reigned and we couldn't believe what was happening. We all got a good laugh out of it though and set to work to clean up the mess. It required a complete wardrobe change before we could redo the shot. The crow flew up to join his friends who caw-cawed away as if praising his efforts. But it seemed to us like a wild scene from the movie 'The birds'!”

EARLE KEATLEY

Earle Keatley MPA of Oshawa, Ont., had an assignment in December to shoot equipment beside a harbour location. “Rather than use a helicopter I chose to shoot from the top of a gigantic oil tank that gave an ideal vantage point. The tops of those tanks are humped up at the center, so I eased over to the edge for a clear view. It was really cool up there during the shoot but with much hand waving I was able to direct the machines into the right location and get the photographs. With that completed the people below disappeared into the warmth of the office while I was left to get down on my own. I started to climb back up over the hump in the roof to reach the ladder but found I kept sliding back towards the edge. A coating of ice and frost had frozen over the whole surface. With all my gear I just could not get a sure footing on that incline. Well, to get back up I literally had to melt my way up. I put my hand on the metal surface, melted a spot, eased myself up a foot and then pulled my gear up behind me. Then, I had to switch to the warm hand to melt the next spot. It took me over fifteen minutes to finally make it to the top and clamber onto the safety platform. I could have been trapped for hours or slipped right off the roof without anyone being the wiser. That was something I had not calculated on!”

PRAVIN THAKRAR

Pravin Thakrar of Mississauga, Ont. recounts a problem he experienced while delivering a customer's order. “I was carrying an armload of framed photos to my client who had a door where you press a button to make them swing open. Since both hands were full I decided to use my head to press the button. But just as I bent forward I got a couple of big sneezes and banged my head on the button... and then, again on the door, as it opened. It was quite a surprise and most painful, causing me to drop the pictures while I rubbed the pain in my head. Luckily, the photographs were OK.”

STEPHEN BISS

Steve Biss of Toronto, Ont., remembers the first assignment he was sent out on his own. "My boss sent me to photograph children crossing a road for a safety league brochure. I had a 4x5 Graflex at that time, equipped with a magazine that held 12 films. I photographed the whole darn eleven pictures on the first sheet of film. No one had explained to me that I must pull the exposed film through to the back of the magazine before taking my next shot.

Steve continues, "At Brigdens, as was my habit when I loaded film, I would enter the darkroom with my hands full of empty holders then reach back with my foot and kick the door closed behind me. Well, on this particular day I reached the point where I must have done it once too often. I entered the room, kicked the door, closed my eyes as I turned out the lights and loaded a dozen 8 x 10 film holders. When I finished I turned around and saw, much to my horror, the door WIDE OPEN and light flooding in. A box had fallen to the floor and got in the way of the door, so it had opened again and I didn't know it! That 8x10 colour film, the whole box of it, was expensive to throw away."

"I nearly fell off the top of a building trying to get a photo with my 4x5 Graflex. You looked down onto a mirror-image much like the Hasselblad. The image was reversed in direction and made it difficult to maintain balance while looking into the viewing hood. There was a man fixing telephone poles up in the air and I was required to get a picture. I compensated in the wrong direction and almost fell off the darn edge of the roof. The same thing came up again while photographing on a rolling boat. I compensated the wrong way and I fell into the water. That Graflex was completely wrecked!"

Steve Biss was in the Armed Services during WW Two and was stationed in Ottawa. "They sent stuff into our section for printing that required 16x20 display prints for an exhibition. This time it was prints of flying bombers and when finished I turned them over to my spotter for retouching. She was very meticulous at her job and I instructed her to spot them carefully which on this job she did most thoroughly. Later, I got an irate phone call from a Squadron Leader chiding me, "You took out all the *** flak!"

"We just thought it had been a lousy negative with big dirt spots all over it."

STANLEY J. WINDRIM

Stan Windrim, of Mississauga, Ont., must be one of the favourite photographers that I have interviewed. He has supplied me with so many interesting vignettes and still he continues to state that: "Nothing ever happened in my life, worth recording." Possibly we can recognize ourselves in this quiet Canadian. Stan's ability to see the funny side of life has produced seventeen anecdotes for me.

Stan recalls when he was sent on a photo assignment to Eastern Canada. A family had won a skiddoo in a national contest and it was up to Stan to record the happy winners with their prize. On the way there he imagined he would get a picture out in the snow. But when he arrived he found the family had assembled their prize skiddoo in the living room and being the best piece of furniture were using it to sit on while watching television. Since they were most reluctant to take it apart again, he had to take the pictures just where it was!

Stan did a lot of public relations photography for a tire company and was assigned to produce pictures publicizing the animals at the local Riverdale Zoo with some tire products. On his first venture he put an enormous tire beside an elephant at which the elephant promptly stood on it and Stan got his picture. He couldn't predict what to expect but that picture was widely used throughout the country. The client was well pleased, so the ideas started to percolate on what to do next. Stan was sent back to see what would happen with an orangutan. To get the closest view he was allowed inside the safety fence and when the tire was rolled towards the ape it spat gobs of spittle back at Stan making it darn hard to get any pictures. The tire was repeatedly retrieved and rolled towards the uncooperative subject until finally the ape grabbed the tire and twisted it all out of shape. So there were no pictures that time. For another attempt on a cold winter morning, Stan was back to the Zoo accompanied by an assistant. They arrived loaded with tires and camera gear and were greeted by the curator who indicated that he was busy for a while. But since Stan knew what to do, they were given directions to the right building. They struggled through a tiny entrance into a room, lit by only one small window at the far end of the building. As they entered the monkey inhabitants were screeching so loudly that it was hard to concentrate and to add to the problem, Stan's cold glasses instantly fogged up with the humidity. Stumbling in the darkness Stan stood on something and kicked it aside just as his assistant found a light switch. When the lights came on Stan found himself standing amongst the biggest alligators he had ever seen. The two made a panic dash for the door and did a Laurel and Hardy act trying to get out. One camera took a bad beating as they burst out to the open... and safety.

"I had a small wedding where the photography was to cover only the church and the reception. Things didn't start off well as the young lady was an hour late for the ceremony. As it turned out she had been in an automobile accident and was taken to the hospital where they calmed her down with a shot of valium. When she arrived she didn't seem to be with it. The wedding went through quite well until we reached the time for the signing of the register. I set up the bridal group with the priest and was reaching to get some flowers to add a touch of colour to the table when I realized the bride was gone. Nobody could figure where she was, but we finally located her sauntering down the aisle by herself. By the time we arrived at the reception everything was an hour and a half late, the maitre de was pulling his hair out and I still had to get the group photographs. In these final pictures the bride looked like she had been shot through a screen door. Although the pictures were quite passable, I got the blame for the weird look on her face."

"In 1986, hockey star Red Kelly ran for election in Mississauga and he brought Prime Minister Lester Pearson for a major rally. I arrived to take pictures for the local newspaper but couldn't get anywhere near the front to get closeups of the VIP's. So the caretaker of the school suggested I go down to the basement and find my way through to a set of stairs which would lead up to a trap door. It was pitch dark down there and it took some fumbling to finally find the stairs. As I popped up through the trap door I was dazed by the light, but soon woke to the fact that I was in the middle of the stage and thousands of people were staring at me. I was like a Jack-in-the Box coming up through the floor. Rather than retreat to the darkness and get lost again, I clambered up on stage with all my equipment and I was in a perfect location to get some good pictures of Pearson chatting with Red Kelly at the podium. Everyone seemed to take it for granted and I wasn't challenged at all. Today, they would have thought I had a bomb and the security would have pounced all over me."

" I had a job to photograph the Goodyear blimp as it flew over the Toronto skyline along the edge of the waterfront. I and the account man took the ferry heading for the Toronto Islands where communications had been set up. On the way over the blimp suddenly arrived early and started running through its passes. In a panic I started shooting from the rear deck of the ferry and I was still shooting the middle of a run when the ferry landed at the island. I finished the last few pictures, but before we could get off, the ferry pulled away and we found ourselves stranded and heading back to Toronto. They couldn't stop the ferry, so I knew I would miss out on all the arranged photos and we couldn't reschedule another fly-by. I figured I was in deep trouble with the client - everything was down the drain. But Lady Luck must have been looking after me as we realized we were on the ferry's 'milk-run' that visited each of the islands. As a result, I was given the perfect shooting platform out in the middle of Toronto harbour. It couldn't have been better since I was much closer to the blimp with the city lights balanced to the afterglow of the setting sun. It was a matter of being in the right place at the right moment for this one time in my life."

"I had an elaborate slide show to shoot which took three weeks to pull together; it wore me out completely. There were three copies produced: one for Western Canada and then a French copy and an English copy to travel to Quebec, Halifax and Truro. On the flight back from the Maritimes the cargo door of the DC3 flew open and the whole shipment fell out, scattering projectors and a thousand slides across the country side. I suddenly got a panic call from the client that yanked me out of my state of recu-

peration. The show was lost but it had to be put on in Toronto, two days hence, when 500 people, including the top brass, were to gather for an annual meeting. The question was: could I produce it again in two days? I delved into my cull slides and within an hour felt we might make the deadline. I didn't get much sleep, ate in the car during the runs to the lab, duped about 200 pieces and just had to think about it every moment of my life. It was the most cram packed assignment I ever lived through which I certainly couldn't do today. But we made it in those two days!"

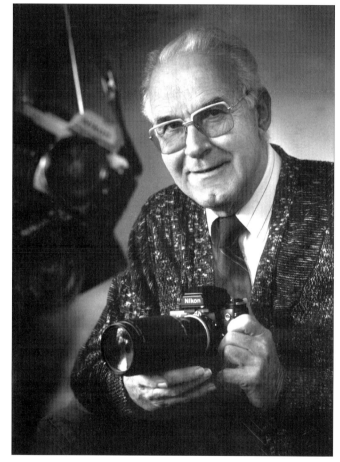

"I was shooting a boxing match when George Chuvalo knocked his opponent out with a smashing right to the head. This chap fell through the ropes and landed in front of me with a splat, spraying a shower of sweat all over me and my cameras. I thought he was out, stone cold, but the next thing I knew he was up and grabbed me, then started using me as a punching bag. By the size of his muscles I don't think I could have lasted very long. Luckily, I was pulled to safety – but such are the pains you take in this business."

"I was hired by this chap to take pictures of his birthday party that was held at Spadina House which is a pretty spiffy place. He wanted everything shot candid style so I was wandering around trying to get pictures. The guests were all high-brow celebrities and I felt I was out of my class. It was a bit tedious so when the host invited me to make use of the bar and food table, I fully participated. There was a musical combo out in the yard but it was a bit too cool there to attract listeners. They, too, were bored and asked if I could supply them with double-rums from the bar. As the evening wore on, I kept them supplied which, I swear, made them play better. About 11 PM when everyone moved inside, I noticed that the combo had stopped playing. On checking them out, I found the violin player slumped over and had lost his bow while the piccolo player was off trying to find some food. I realized I had destroyed the musical aspect of the party. They were so bombed out they had to leave their car and take a taxi home! Still, they were happy."

Some photographers have a streak of luck that protects them from harm in the most dangerous of situations. When Goodyear closed down their New Toronto plant they gradually demolished all the buildings until they finally came to the last standing object which was a towering smoke stack, a landmark for the area. As Stan relates, "It was an historic event so a big crowd gathered despite the bitterly cold day. I checked with the Chief Engineer to see what direction the chimney would fall, in order to get the best angle of view and be out of harms way. He said it would fall in an easterly direction towards the city, so I chose a southern viewpoint and waited for the extravaganza to happen. I was ready with a motor driven Nikon and a full load of film. When the charge went off I started the camera and through the viewfinder watched curiously as it performed its ballet dive DIFFERENT to what I expected. The stack was falling towards the south, in my general direction, and I was frozen to the spot determined not to take my finger off the button until the 36 shots had clacked through the camera. I've been asked why I didn't run and I can't give a good answer. I just had to see that film through to the end! When the stack hit the ground there were bricks and stones flying in all directions. I thought I was in the Battle of Britain with the amount of debris that landed around me... but I wasn't hit! And then there followed this tremendous cloud of dust and soot that shot up from the ground and spread in all directions. It was like a movie set where someone arrives in heaven and is greeted through the fog. It hung so heavily, it tied up all the traffic on the Lakeshore highway so

that it took two hours just to get out of the parking lot. And yes, the film did turn out OK!"

"I had another close call while photographing a bolt-making machine in an industrial plant. The machine crunched short lengths of steel rod under tremendous pressure to produce the head on the bolt. Next, grooved metal dies, the size of 4x5 film boxes, ran back and forth to create the threads. The finished bolt was then ready for the heating oven. I was proudly setting up a new 4x5 Linhof and positioning the lights around this gnashing monster to get the details of the operation. I was merrily working away when suddenly there was this tremendous BANG and everything came to a halt. The dies had exploded and steel shrapnel flew in all directions... luckily neither I nor my camera were hit. I was the center of attention as no one could believe I wasn't mutilated. Looking at the remnants of the two blocks I had to wonder as well. But that is one of the little joys of taking photographs in an industrial location."

Mr. Windrim set out on a cold morning to photograph a high class home in Burlington for a real estate company. Stan says "I arrived to find a huge Winnebago in the driveway and since it blocked the view of the house, it had to be moved. A lady came to the door wearing only slippers and a negligee so I assumed I had got her out of bed. I explained who I was and asked for the keys to the Winnebago. While we were talking she stepped out from the doorway and a gust of wind slammed the door shut. I thought, this is a bad way to start a morning especially after she said the house keys were locked inside! Here she was out in the cold in her negligee, me with my camera, and a dog barking like mad on the inside. She suggested we might get in through the bedroom window but I didn't realize WE meant ME! I stood on an old rain barrel and eased myself up. As I was ready to go through the window she cautioned that the dog was a little vicious... NOW she tells me! The lady got a hold of my rear and gave an almighty heave, shooting me into the room and hitting a potted plant that exploded dirt all over the rug. The dog was now in an uproar and yapping at my heels, so I made a dash for the door. I got the lady in fast but it took yet another 20 minutes to find the Winnebago keys. That was when I asked HER to move it out of the driveway as in no way was I going to touch it. I finally took my picture and left quickly. If I remember correctly, it was only a thirty dollar job!"

TERRY ROBERTSON

We've come to respect Terry Robertson MPA, of the Bochsler Photographics + Imaging in Burlington, Ont., for his talent and knowledge, always cool and in full command. But that isn't the way Terry tells the story when he reveals some of his experiences.

"I finished an assignment in Vancouver," recalls Terry, "and had extra time to wander around town just like a tourist. I noticed a window washer some ten to fifteen floors up on the side of a building. Since I had washed windows in my high school days I took interest in scrutinizing his techniques. Its not as easy as one might think. Sitting in a bosun's chair at the end of a free-swinging rope, the problem is to maintain your location as you sweep the windows with your squeegee. Your actions constantly push you away from the window and it had always frustrated me. But this guy had the solution! He had a suction cup to anchor himself to each window and thus was able to maintain both his stability and his wiping pressure. I was transfixed by this revelation that had evaded me those many years ago. I kept walking down the street still gawking back to this marvel. I must have been about a block away when suddenly my feet gave way underneath me. I looked down to discover that I was up to my ankles in wet cement right in the middle of a newly poured sidewalk. Four burly construction workers came out of nowhere, screaming and yelling at me for my stupidity. I exited the quagmire as gingerly as possible, made a profuse apology and beat a quick retreat to the hotel before the concrete dried into my shoes and socks. So that's my most embarrassing memory of Vancouver."

But here is Terry's all time horror story where everything went wrong on an assignment. "I was to fly with a client to Montreal to cover a two-day shoot of 24 different pictures involving a truck company. I stressed we take an early flight to scout locations the first morning which would leave a day and a half for shooting. We really needed an assistant but there was no budget for it. Besides, my client insisted he knew the people at the plant and

everything would go smoothly. To start off we missed our 9.30 AM flight as the client thought he had booked for 10.30. That loused up the whole morning. Touring the plant we found everyone spoke only French and the day was totally wasted without a translator to get things moving... no pictures at all! We headed for our rented car only to discover the head lights had been left on and the battery was dead. Another hour wasted getting a tow truck in to start the car. At the hotel I phoned André Amyot MPA to help line up a bilingual assistant. He gave me six names to call while he tried another six. But no success, it looked like our second day was going to be a wipe-out too. By luck, an electrician was located in the plant who could speak English, as well as French, and he assisted us to arrange the workers in good industrial illustrations. We really hustled and squeezed in the 24 shots in eight hours. Elated to complete the assignment, we rewarded ourselves with a rest and dinner. But that almost cost us our flight back to Toronto as we arrived at the airport with only ten minutes to get through security and onto the plane. I carry my cameras on board as hand luggage with the exposed film in a separate plastic bag. I put my camera bag through the screening system but handed the bag of film to a young lady, requesting 'hand inspection'. She was arguing with another passenger who wanted to get oversized luggage through, so she wasn't attentive to what I was saying. To save time we went through separate check-ins, picked up my camera case on the other side and just managed to make the flight. We could now relax as we figured the job was in the bag. But not so! Arriving at Toronto we were waiting for the bus when I had this awful feeling. I opened the camera bag... and THERE WAS NO PACKAGE OF FILM! I had left it behind at Montreal. I felt the blood drain out of me totally. 'This just does not happen – its unbelievable.' I explained to my client and he laughed... while I cried. 'Terry,' he said, 'some how, this all has to work out.' I immediately phoned Dorval to reach the Lost & Found department but everything was closed down for the night. At home I fretted away the hours as I could not sleep. Finally I put the call through and, yes, they did have the bag of film still in the Security area but they would not ship it out. I had to come and get it from them. Well, once again I turned to friend André Amyot for some much needed assistance. He razzed me for the problems I had been put through in covering the assignment and couldn't believe that, on top of it all, I had lost the film at Dorval. It shows how sincere are the friendships developed within our association because, on hearing of my plight, André volunteered to drive to the airport, extricate my precious film and ship it direct to Hamilton by Bus Express. Without his help, I would have had to make a return flight to Montreal. The film was processed, everything was fine and the client got his prints."

Terry and Rick Bell MPA were to fly to a Maritime photographers convention, Terry to be a guest speaker while Rick was to run a seminar. The plane was waiting by the terminal, loaded and ready to depart. "Through our window at the back of the plane," says Terry, "we could see the ground crew was still loading gasoline. They have big hoses that attach underneath the wings. Anyway, the loading of the fuel ended but then we saw this big stream of gas pouring out of the wing. We wondered whether to raise an alarm as it continued to pour out making a sizable pool. We're getting worried but no one, outside, seemed to take any notice. Catching the stewardess' attention we asked if it was nor-

mal. Her eyes widened in horror and she ran for the cockpit. Now we really knew that something was wrong, but the pilot, in the calmest voice, came on the intercom to request passengers please return to the waiting room by the door at the front of the plane. Since we were in the last two seats, we were the last passengers to get off... all the while knowing the full danger of the situation. Some one had forgotten to close one of the lines, resulting in a ten inch cascade of fuel spewing onto the ground. We could have exploded into a monster ball of fire at any moment!"

"I had what could be called a happy accident. On one of my first assignments with Tom Bochsler, I accompanied him to a steel mill to photograph a white hot ingot just after it came out of the furnace. Tom worked on one side of the glowing block while I shot a different angle on the other side. Being a new apprentice I was given the Hasselblad ELM to use for less chance of errors. But I wasn't aware that on a long exposures - 1/8 second and longer - as soon as you take your finger off the shutter button the motor advances the film, even before the exposure is completed. When we processed the film every frame that I had taken was streaked into the next. It looked like an utter disaster - a complete failure as far as I was concerned. But Tom saw the potential and suggested to the client that it would make a good cover shot. They went for the idea and it turned a bad situation into a very happy accident."

CLAUDE GAGNON

Claude Gagnon MPA of Timmins, Ont., was flying into Kenora to do some mining photography. "We were in this eight-seater aircraft," recalls Claude, "with pairs of passengers facing each other. There was an elderly lady sitting opposite me who was having ear-pressure trouble during the take off. Some chewing gum was offered which she most graciously accepted. She broke the gum stick into two pieces, rolled them up... and stuffed them into each ear! It seemed to make her more comfortable."

NORBERT R. HOFERICHTER

Bert Hoferichter MPA of Mississauga, Ont., has lived through a variety of experiences as a commercial and portrait photographer before becoming a teacher and the Director of Creative Photography at Humber College in Etobicoke.

"In one of those unnerving episodes of my life I arrived at a bride's home with my assistant to start the portraits at 3 PM. The place was totally deserted and despite repeated knocking on both front and back doors, we were unable to raise any response. I decided to wait 'til at least 4 PM. In the interim I phoned back to the studio to have the details checked in my appointment book. At 4.15 I saw a lady walking up the street with two shopping bags; with relief I recognized her as the mother of the bride. When she saw me she calmly asked, 'Hi Bert what are you doing?' I replied, 'I'm here to do your daughter's wedding.' Well, at that she broke into gales of laughter and I was perplexed by her actions. 'I'll tell you what, Bert,' she said. 'You have the right date... you have the right day... you have the right month... but you've got the WRONG YEAR! You are a whole year too early.' Well, I must say that I'll never do that again as it was an experience never to forget!"

"I was involved with a movie shoot for Ontario Place to produce a film called BIG NORTH. We were working outside of Thunder Bay in a provincial park to photograph some bears. There was a film crew of six people with myself shooting the stills. We had no luck in spotting any bears all day long, so I decided to scout around for some scenic shots taking a lane way through tall bushes down to a lake. I humped all my equipment along with me. Low and behold, what should show up but a mother bear with her two cubs. A mother bear always spells danger, so the film crew scampered back to their vans while I was isolated and stranded - the bears being between me and safety in the van. To compound the problem, the mother was on one side of the road, that I had followed, while the cubs were on the other side. My retreat was cut off completely. The cubs were taking their time feeding while the mother was ripping apart an old log to get at an ant colony. Periodically, the she-bear would stretch herself up to check her cubs and survey the area for intruders. For the next hour, I patiently waited for them to finish and move off, but they just kept on feeding. I, at least, made use of the time by photographing them with my longest telephoto, but I knew at some time I had to make

a move to get back to the crew. My patience was wearing thin, so I decided to make a mad dash the moment she put her head down to feed. I crept forward as far as possible, positioning my equipment for unimpeded running. I intended to be like a football player making a 50 yard dash to a goal line. With my head down, sweat on my brow and heart pumping madly, I chose the moment and took off. I got up speed and tore along the pathway to safety. I didn't know it, but at that same instant the she-bear had decided to join her cubs on the other side of the road. Fate couldn't have planned it more precisely, because just as I reached the danger zone, this furry blob came loping out of the bushes onto the road right in front of me. We collided with a BANG! I was a complete wipeout, sprawling onto the gravel and clutter. I instantly looked up to see her reared in the air and eying me warily. Bears look awful vicious when you are that close and your life is in jeopardy. It seemed an eternity as we eyed each other... I was terrorized to make any move... then she slowly lowered to all fours and retreated to her little ones. We never saw each other again...... thankfully!"

"I was covering a political campaign in Mississauga involving Joe Clark who, at the time, was running for Prime Minister. I was assigned to record him with local MP Don Blenkarn. The setting was at the Port Credit Yacht Club with the VIP's on one of the sailboats. I was alternating shots on several Nikons that hung around my neck. I had worked with Mr. Clark before so I guess he knew my name. 'Bert,' he said, 'have you ever dropped one of them [cameras] in the lake?'... 'NEVER!' I replied and kept clicking away. To get one of the Nikons out of my way I swung it around to my back. That was the moment the safety clasp decided to come apart and the strap parted sending the camera flying overboard into the water. I can still remember how elegantly I swung that camera around my neck and then thinking.... 'Where is it?' Then realizing it was in the lake.... camera body, zoom lens and motor drive. Would you believe the ill luck and poor timing? I gave a kid twenty dollars to dive and recover it for me."

"After the PPOC National Convention in PEI, I was passing through the Airport Security checkpoint, heading for home. With all the sunshine during our PEI visit I had allocated time to shoot colour scenics with my 4x5 equipment. The exposed film was unloaded into a box and put into my carry-on baggage. Not wanting it to be X-rayed I asked for hand inspection. After clearing personal inspection I returned to the desk to pick up my belongings and found an inspector opening up my 4x5 film boxes. He already had one lid open, so I slapped it down fast with my hand just as he was ready to open the final lid. There goes my work for the last four days, I figured. The inspectors would not take no for an answer, in regards to opening up the box, since they were determined to see the contents. Finally I had to take the film back to the Air Canada check-in counter where I got into another discussion as to why I would not allow the contents to be inspected. The check-in clerk asked, 'Why are you so stubborn? I can take my film out of my camera anytime in daylight.' She was obviously talking about a 35mm cassette camera while mine was unprotected sheet Ektachrome in a box. She could not see the difference. We finally worked out a compromise by taping my little box inside a huge cardboard box which was then put on board with the rest of the luggage."

"I had a commercial assignment up north in the fall and again I was part of a video crew taking the still photographs. I had to produce a sequence of slides that would tie in with the AV presentation of leaves falling from the trees. It was a very calm day and too early in the season for falling leaves, so we sent one of the crew up into the tree to shake the branches while we took the shots from below. The guy was shaking the leaves while I was shooting with a motor drive. In the whine and clatter of the camera, I heard a scream but I kept shooting to get lots of shots. Suddenly into my finder, I saw this body passing downward through the leaves. All I recognized was a pair of shoes passing in front of my camera. The chap unfortunately broke his arm in the fall, but we did capture his descent in slides and in motion picture... and of course the falling leaves!"

EVERETT ROSEBOROUGH

"Advertisers actively pursue 'tie-ins'! An airline is the 'official transportation' of a basketball team or a film-maker displays ads for the Olympic Games, and so it goes; the great event attracts the attention while their product shares the limelight. A great liner, The Queen Mary, was launched in Britain in 1934 so the maiden voyage was to be an event thoroughly covered by the media. How logical it was to have a 'tie-in' using imports that would be transported on the first trip to America. The two main department stores in Toronto must have thought of the same idea, simultaneously. An undeclared race was hatched to see which could first display the token imports of china, linens and furniture from Britain."

"There were some elaborate plans made, all kept highly secret; each store would fly their goods in chartered aircraft from the New York harbour, a few hours after the docking. Willie Morehen and I were instructed to be at the Hamilton airfield by mid-afternoon. Customs clearance had been arranged with a company executive on hand to sign declaration forms while delivery trucks lined up to whisk the precious cargo to the stores."

"I saw complications if darkness should intervene, so packed accordingly. Have you ever photographed in an open field at night... especially with slow '30s film and flashpowder? Willie brought his 8x10 while I packed a 4x5 camera... and four half-pound bottles of Victor flashpowder. Considering the location, the size of the aircraft and the type of cargo, I reasoned that an eight ounce charge would not seriously overexpose. Nobody in his right mind would hand-hold a flashlamp containing such a quantity, so it was reasoned to build a small bonfire into which the powder, wrapped in newspaper, could be thrown from some distance. An anticipated difficulty was the rocking of the aircraft by the blast."

"After viewing the scene, the party left for the Royal Connaught Hotel, there to wait the phone call announcing the departure from New York. The executive participants had decided to pack their own equipment, too. A great row of bottles appeared on the mantlepiece of the suite: Rye, Scotch, ginger ale and soda.

As the day waned, it became obvious that a night landing could occur, except that the Hamilton landing field had no provision for lights. Orders were hastily issued to have trucks and cars from the Hamilton store ring the landing area and be ready to turn on headlights with the first sound. In our 'command post' suite the phone jangled incessantly. With each ring the entire group would leap up, breathlessly awaiting progress, only to settle back with yet another drink in hand. This went on for hours."

"One of the party chose to recite 'The Lady of the Lake' in its entirety, a bit thickly, in an Irish accent much modified by Scotch. At 4 am the phone announced that the merchandise had finally been located deep in the hold, but with a little money could be aboard their aircraft by 5. It turned out to be a lot closer to 6, by which time the entire decoration of the mantlepiece had been consumed. Everyone took off for the airfield, into fresh air and a new sunrise. Thankfully it was daylight."

"At long last a biplane bumped down the field and the unloading commenced. The reciter of 'The Lady of the Lake' proceeded gingerly across the turf, one foot after the other to make sure there was ground underneath then draped himself across a wing, holding on for dear life. Time was everything, our photography had to be quickly completed but the tipsy bunch were having too much difficulty standing. It was then or never. With film exposed, the cortege left for Toronto at high speed."

"We immediately set to processing our pictures and rushed through a half dozen seven-foot bromide enlargements. By the time we arrived with the background prints, the windows were filled with merchandise and cards proclaiming the 'firsts'. But across the way, our competitor blazed his own triumph. They had chosen to use a seaplane whereby they could land at the foot of Yonge Street, much closer to home. It is rumored that by some strange means their freight was conveniently stacked close to a cargo door."

"About noon, our company President took a stroll to admire the results for himself. This was followed by a terse command: "GET THOSE PHOTOS OUT OF THE WINDOWS!' "

CHARLES van den OUDEN

Charles Van Den Ouden MPA of Owen Sound, Ont., raises the question as to why photographers are often accused of working too slowly. "At a recent commercial shoot for a water bottling company, I was photographing bottles of water in a setting in the middle of a stream. We built a small dam out of clean stones and dressed the bottles to make sure they looked cool and fresh. I set up the tripod deep into the water so that the camera was just at the creek's surface. I had spent a lot of time framing and focussing the camera (after all I am paid by the hour) when I happened to look down under the surface of the water. I must have been standing in one spot for quite a while because a small school of trout had chosen my shadow as a nice place to hang out and retreat from the sun."

"Here is a little technique which is certainly not my invention and which I never believed would work until I had the proper occasion to use it. I had photographed a lady and used every technique I knew to soften the deep smile lines in her face. Knowing how fussy my client was, I was particularly pleased with the proofs... but my client hated them! No matter how hard I tried, I couldn't convince her that negative retouching and print finishing would create a pleasing final photograph. So I agreed to do a reshoot and the lady returned in the very same outfit as the first session. The proofs looked just the same as the first. It was at this moment I recalled a technique I had heard, along the way, and that was to have the proofs printed backwards. The client loved her new set of images and she described them as 'looking exactly like me'. She was, of course, looking at her image as she was accustomed to seeing it every day... in the mirror!"

BRUCE A. DUNSTALL

In l956 Bruce Dunstall returned from the United States where he had been working for the Miami Herald. A buddy suggested he apply for a job with the Ontario Department of Highways just for the winter. Well, Bruce got the job which lasted some 29 years. As Bruce explained on retirement, "That was the longest winter I ever spent in Canada!"

Bruce recalls some of his experiences. "We were helping the TTC make a movie to encourage passengers to stagger their working hours. What we needed was a scene of a jam-packed subway to prove the benefit of off-hour travel, but the subway system worked too well and we lacked that crowd scene. We explained our predicament to the Supervisor who immediately knew what we meant and closed down some of the turnstiles. This created a crowd in no time and it backed right up the stairs. Suddenly, into the midst of this, came a big guy with a huge bass violin trying to push his way through. Bingo! I couldn't have asked for a better shot and that was the scene we used in the film."

"I was invited to Guelph to shoot an annual bowling tournament so I packed my two Leicas and travelled up there. They were short of bowlers so I put on my bowling shoes and joined them. I asked my wife to bring in one camera with the 35mm lens from the car. That would be sufficient to cover the event: -a few action pictures and about six presentations at the banquet. Everything would fit nicely on a 36 exposure roll of Tri-X. In my camera bag there was one camera loaded and one empty; you guessed it, my wife brought in the unloaded camera. I didn't check it, although I usually check them: so there were no pictures that year. The following year they invited me back to do the same thing. They had a surprise presentation at the banquet for me, the photographer. I unwrapped a box about 8x10 in size and it was filled with a whole bunch of little film boxes. An enclosed card read: 'In future, load the camera before you load yourself!' It was a bum rap but the sentiment was appreciated."

"After photographing snowplows for 25 years," says Bruce, "I think anyone would get blase about shooting them. If you've seen one, you've seen them all. But when the D.O.T. trucks were re-equipped with a new type of blade the PR department ordered up new photographs for editorial and publicity requirements. I was chasing through the Huntsville / Bracebridge area looking for plows in action with good background scenery, but without luck, I was coming back down Highway 11. I had seen a few plows but they really weren't suitable. Besides, shooting conditions were bad as a new fall of snow sifted down.

Finally, away off in the distance I saw this one heading north towards me. Son-of-a-gun, it was just what I was looking for and I was determined not to lose it. I quickly pulled my car off the road and in the rush put myself into a snow-filled ditch. I couldn't worry about that for the moment as the plow was almost upon me. I grabbed my Hasselblad from the car seat and lunged out the door only to be snapped back as I was still held in by the seat belt. That lost precious time and I almost missed the shot. Luckily the window was down so I thrust myself through the window with just enough time to crank off two shots on the camera. Bang!..Bang! Just as I got off the second shot a transport truck passed on my side of the road and sprayed up a mountain of salty slush all over me. With me hanging out the window he couldn't have aimed better and I was completely soaked with the interior of the car looking like a dirt pool. With the car stuck in the ditch, the camera caked in slush and not being sure I even had a picture, I figured I had too many strikes against me. In addition, I had set the exposure for fast black and white film but found I had loaded colour. But thankfully somebody must have been looking after me, as the colour came out just perfect. And to top it off, the truck that had splashed me formed a perfect frame to the oncoming snow-plough. I had got the shot away just in the nick of time before the big soaking. The photo got tremendous play on the covers of four important magazines."

DOUGLAS W. BOULT

Doug Boult MPA HLM of Wellington, Ont., began his photographic career in England in 1951 then worked in Canada as an industrial and advertising photographer. In 1968 he established the Photography Department at Sheridan College, accumulating awards and honours throughout the world. He is now retired as Professor Emeritus but continues as a force in NAPA.

Doug recalls, "In 1959, I was assigned to photograph a group of the Simpson's stores executive which included the Chairman of the Board, a very elderly gentleman. We took along an 8x10 camera and lighting equipment that used the #22 flash bulbs which were the size of 100 watt light bulbs. We thoroughly pre-tested everything as we intended to use the "open flash" exposure system. I arranged the group with the old gentleman seated at the centre; he seemed ready to nod off at any moment. For the first shot I removed the slide from the holder, opened the shutter, and fired off the flash. There was an incredibly loud explosion as the bulb in my assistant's extension blew apart. I was so surprised I forgot to close the shutter, thus ruining the picture. Then I was petrified to see the old gentleman fall out of the chair to the floor. 'My God!', I thought, 'I've given him a heart attack.' Thankfully it was not so and, after much reassuring, we settled him down for a second shot. I steadied the group.... raised the flash gun.... and at that the old gentleman cringed in his chair, covering his face with his hands. It took some time before we could uncoil him and convince him that the new bulbs would not repeat the explosion. So we DID get the picture finally with success."

"I was shooting at a furniture show working at the top of a twelve foot step ladder. I was under the focussing cloth adjusting the 8x10 camera while my assistant made the arrangements to the room setting. I felt the ladder shaking and was about to complain of the distraction when I felt someone tug at my trouser leg. I peeked from under the cloth and was startled to see an elderly lady standing on the ladder just below me. Before I could say anything she blurted, 'Is that a ONE MILLIMETER lens?' With tongue in cheek I agreed, 'Yes Ma'am, it most definitely is.' She looked down at her female companion and said, 'There I told you so!' She thanked me most kindly, climbed back down to the floor and toddled off into the show."

"When I was just starting as a photographer in England, I undertook to shoot a local wedding. I had only an old Thornton-Pickard quarter-plate camera, given to me by a retired photographer. It was a single lens reflex, equipped with a focal plane shutter. I was warned never to carry it by the handle on the side because the loose wooden body would widen and create havoc with the shutter assembly. I was doing quite well at the wedding until the point when the bride and groom came down the aisle after their marriage vows. As the couple started their long walk, I grabbed for my camera... BY THE HANDLE... and there was an immediate clatter as the entire shutter system collapsed into the bottom of the camera body. I quickly called to the couple to stall for a few moments while I feverishly knelt on the floor and took the camera apart. It felt like hours were flying by while I refitted the blinds and rollers into place. All the while, the guests in the church and the wedding party were wondering what the heck I was doing on my knees. Like all miracles, I had some elastic bands with which I pulled everything back together. Unbelievably, I was able to complete the wedding, but from that day on I never went on a job without a back-up camera."

"During a visit of the Queen Mother, I was photographing for a Toronto regiment of which she was the Honorary Colonel-in-Chief. As official photographer, I was assigned a special room to take the group shots, being allowed only six minutes to complete the task. Besides all the dignitaries, the room was quite overrun with security types... Toronto police, RCMP and Scotland Yard... and I was the only photographer. As with all Royal events, I was wearing a very visible I.D. pass which gave official clearance. After I had completed the photograph, they set up a receiving line for formal presentation of each of the guests to Her Majesty. I packed away my gear then went through the reception line, receiving a personal compliment from Her Highness. I then brought out a 2 1/4 SLR for candid B&W shots and circulated amongst the guests. Her Majesty and the Lt. Governor were sitting beside a small table, animated in conversation and occasionally sipping cocktails. I know well enough NOT to photograph Royal personages while they are smoking or drinking, so I waited until both had put down their glasses and then took a shot from some distance away. As they continued to talk so pleasantly, I moved ever closer and eventually found a good spot where I knelt for the best vantage point. While peering into my viewfinder, I suddenly noticed a HUGE figure blocking my view. I was swept up by this person and bundled forcefully out the nearest door. He was from the Special Forces of Scotland Yard and berated me severely, despite my visible identification. Although I offered to put my camera away, he would not allow me back into the room. So I packed up and went off to have the colour film of the group shot processed and get something to eat. Four hours later, I arrived home to find my street crowded like a movie set. There were police cruisers, RCMP cars, dark black limousines and groups of uniformed officers scattered about MY HOUSE. As I got out of my car, all eyes focused on me and someone yelled, 'There he is!' My heart skipped a beat and I immediately thought that something terrible had happened to my wife and children. The crowd followed me into the house, raising all sorts of anxiety with my family. After being pointed out by the accosting officer from earlier in the evening, a senior Scotland Yard official announced I was to pack a small case as I was about to be taken to Scotland Yard for interrogation... IN LONDON, ENGLAND! I argued for my Canadian rights while they threatened special laws covering British Royalty. It all came down to the demand that they wanted the film I had shot at the reception. To prove I had not photographed the Queen Mother drinking, nor even with a glass in her hand, I offered to process the film and show them the results. So a group followed me to the basement with only one officer able to squeeze into my tiny processing space. I carried on a rather strange commentary through the wall to describe each step of what I was doing. The fixed film was eagerly inspected by one of the RCMP who was pushed forward as an 'expert' and it was agreed, frame by frame, that the Good Lady was not seen drinking. BUT!.... off to the side of some frames there was a small glass sitting on a table. It was agreed that I should cut off that side of the roll of film for presentation to the Scotland Yard officials, for which the RCMP would dissuade them from taking me to England. Well, the whole thing finally quieted down. I got to keep the remains of my decimated film while they went off with the long thin strip showing a dainty glass on a table. It could still be sitting somewhere in England in a vault where they keep such things!"

"I visited the old Riverdale Zoo in Toronto so often and got to know Dr. Scollard, the curator, that they gave me special privileges to shoot inside the cages of some of the animals. A photographer was visiting from the West and was similarly interested, so I took him along getting clearance to shoot inside the cage of a large female chimpanzee. The handler assured us that she was quite docile but cautioned us not to make rapid movements nor startle her. I hadn't noticed that my colleague had attached a flash to his camera and he rashly went right up to the unsuspecting animal and fired the flash right into its face. The poor thing gave out a distressing screech and let fly with a stream of liquid excrement straight at the photographer hitting him squarely in the chest. The chimp and I scattered to the furthest points of the cage leaving the novice reeking with a strong odor in retribution for his insensitivity."

DON FOLEY

Ever have a bad day? Compare your woes to those of a photographers who had his own special gremlins on assignments.

Don Foley CPA of St. Catharines, Ont., was commissioned to do aerial photographs for the regional government. On one of the

flights, the pilot (an instructor) asked Don if he had ever flown a plane and whether he'd care to try his hands at the controls. "I was agreeable," recalls Don, "so he proceeded to give me some basic instructions. After we did one of the photo passes along Lake Ontario he told me to take over the controls while he would guide me through the procedures. Adjusting myself to the controls I moved my foot backwards and hit a fire extinguisher on the floor. It immediately let loose a mist of white CO_2 that completely filled the cabin. I thought it was smoke and fully expected the engine to conk out at any moment. We were coughing and gasping for air so the pilot opened up the windows. Even then we couldn't see a thing as the whole interior, including control panels and the forward screens, were covered with white powder. We just kept going round in a wide circle at 95 miles an hour. The pilot finally realized that I had hit the fire extinguisher and luckily was able to get us down safely. I suggested he inform the tower that we had cut the flight due to foggy flying conditions!"

"Periodically, I lecture at local high schools and one day I arrived to teach B&W photography, accentuating available window light, to a class of grade eleven students. I demonstrate with 35mm cameras as that is all the students have to work with. I had just re-equipped myself with a new automatic camera that had all the fancy electronic gadgetry; it was a bit perplexing since I was used to an old Cannon with straight manual controls. I loaded the film into the camera and I heard a bunch of beeps and noises. I figured the camera had loaded itself, so I set it on the tripod and went through my demo on the quality of light, composition and posing etc. As we were shooting, the camera didn't sound right, -I was sure I couldn't hear the shutter releasing. I looked at the little window on the top and it read 'EE'. Could that mean - empty? Did the film go through the camera when it loaded or did I finish it off already? So I said to the teacher that I needed to open up the back of the camera to check if the film was going through OK. I needed to use his darkroom. Since the time for the lecture was limited we hustled down the hall into a darkened room with no lights. The teacher said to follow him, so in the darkness I followed his footsteps around a corner, through another door where it was pitch black. 'Fred,' I questioned, 'are you there?' He said follow me and I heard another door open. In this final room he turned on a safelight, showed me the work table with an enlarger on it then turned out the light. I cleared the film in seconds and told Fred he could switch the light on, again. 'Fred! Fred!' There's no answer and I realize I'm standing there in total darkness all by myself without any orientation as to where I was. I didn't know where the light switch was and couldn't even figure where the door was to get out.

Normally, I'm quite at home in a darkroom so I started feeling along the walls and banging into every thing, darkrooms with black painted walls can be eerily black. So I thought, just relax... concentrate, there must be something I can do. I realized that I've got a modern electronic camera in my hands (now empty) which has a little light that illuminates the camera settings on the viewing screen when you are in a darkened location. Its just a tiny diode and gives off a very faint amount of light. So I held the camera close to the wall, pressed the shutter and, sure enough, I see a puff of light. As faint as it was, my eyes were becoming quite sensitive to any light. So I'm creeping along the wall, firing my camera and looking for any light switch. Nothing... nothing... I found a corner, then there was more wall. Although I still had no idea where I was, I'm beginning to find my way through the maze.

Finally... a doorway! But that only led me into another room... its full of sinks and taps... its the processing room. There had to be a light switch somewhere, so I spent another five minutes and finally found it. I flicked it on... only to hear the noise of the film dryer start up. Now, I'm really starting to sweat, it's soaking through my hair, it's running down my face. I retraced my steps, stumbling into a broom closet along the way until I was back at the enlarger table. There had to be a switch for the safelight so I worked along the wall, flipping this, flipping that and finally found the safelight switch.

With this one little light as an anchor point I now walked backwards, feeling along the walls. I found another short hallway that led to a different door. I was sure it had to be the right way. I was beyond the glow of the safelight, so I was back to my old situation using the light in the camera. I opened the door and it was still total darkness, but at least I figured it must be a connecting walkway. I'm feeling along the wall and sure enough I find another door... open it up... and its THE HALLWAY! You can't imagine how sweet and fresh hallway air is after you've been trapped for 15 minutes.

Back in the classroom Fred commented about my lengthy delay, but I let him know that unloading the film took only 3 seconds (I had accidentally tripped the rewind button), but finding my way back in the dark, took the rest of the delay. So with so little time left, my lecture changed into a demonstration on how to work under pressure to get a portrait completed in 5 minutes, which normally would have taken 20."

"While I was sweating my way through that maze in the darkroom I thought, 'By God, I've got to remember to tell THIS ONE to Marg!'"   [Maybe it inspired the title of the book – author.]

PAUL COUVRETTE

This is a story of what not to do with your favourite photographic equipment.

Paul Couvrette MPA of Ottawa, Ont., was touring the American South West on a photo shoot with Andy Hobelaid MPA of Windsor. "This event took place in Death Valley," recalls Paul, "where we climbed to the top of a high bluff which was almost vertically straight up and shaped like a cone. At the top there was space to stand of maybe five square feet. Andy and I were squeezed onto this platform and as I swung my equipment from my shoulder, my Hasselblad film back which I hadn't attached properly, went flying off, bounced once... and dropped over the edge of the cliff. In a split second I'm over the edge after it. With the laws of gravity I'm thinking: 'If I'm falling at a particular speed and the film back is falling at a particular speed, all I need to do is add some momentum to me and I'll catch it.' That crazy thought flitted through my head as I was racing to catch this thing. The trouble is, -and I'll have to reexamine the laws of gravity, it really doesn't work. The Hasselblad back must have bounced 20 times while cart wheeling down the slope and I was constantly four feet behind it, running and sliding at top speed. Suzanne was at the bottom of the cliff, watching all this, and figured I was going to end up in a hospital, for sure! But I wasn't thinking of the consequences, I just wanted to save my equipment. I finally caught up to it a few feet from the bottom. The leather was torn off and it had dings and bumps all over, but I had it and I felt good about it. So I climbed all the way back to the top of the bluff and finally got there, parched and looking like hell. Hobelaid is waiting with a big sarcastic grin on his face. I attached the battered film back to my camera, I wheel around and do a shot of the scene. It must be said that I'm known as the guy with the lucky horse shoe up my ass, so I chuckled, 'Well, Hobelaid, it's just perfect!' He couldn't believe it. When I got back to Canada the film came out OK. The Hasselblad back, although it looks like hell, has never been sent in for servicing and it works perfectly. I don't know if that's a commendation for Hasselblad, for the speed of my running, or for my lucky horse shoe. It all worked that eventful day."

MICHAEL ODESSE

Michael Odesse MPA of Penetang, Ont., was shooting for a local boat manufacturer. "They wanted perspective views from the air with their boats racing through the water. That required a helicopter to be brought in which was a small two-man job with no doors. It was really tiny and cramped with just enough room for the pilot and myself. I had never been in a helicopter before so looked forward to the experience. The helicopter lifted off quite fast and headed across the water skimming the surface then sweeping up over the islands like a roller coaster. The pilot gleefully said it was just like Hawaii-Five-O. I warned him that if he kept doing it, I would surely throw up. But it all worked out well until near the end of the day when I turned white and then green and he landed in less than 10 seconds; he didn't like the idea of having to clean off everything. That ended the shoot as I was so-o-o sick."

"During that eventful day, we had a shot that looked directly down on a boat that was tied up to a dock. We found a national park location that wouldn't have bothersome telephone poles and hydro wires. It was still spring and the season wasn't open so there wouldn't be any people around. We scouted ahead, the boats arrived and were just tieing everything down and positioning the models when a Ministry of Natural Resources boat showed up with the Park Superintendent. He wasn't pleased at all, but only because he had not been asked. So he gave us a full minute to do the shot and get out of there. When we pulled in to hover over the boat, we were actually quite close to the trees. I was just about to shoot when all of a sudden the helicopter pulled away. The pilot said the air was not coming back under the helicopter and we were at the point of crashing down onto the boat. He warned we could only go over one more time. When we made the run we actually dropped about 25 feet, and he jerked us away awfully fast. We got the shots but no wonder I was so sick."

"We don't do weddings any more but I can remember some really crazy incidents. At one wedding, I knew that the groom liked to party and was quite the drinker. He would sop up booze no matter what kind it was. The bride and groom had just completed their vows when the priest came down to offer the chalice to the couple. First the bride took a little sip of the wine followed by the groom who took a small drink also. Then without hesitation, he tipped the whole thing back and downed the lot. The priest, quite stunned by this gauche gesture, gave the congregation a look and had to go back to the altar to consecrate more wine so that he could finish the service."

"We have a two acre property where our home and studio is located. With the waterfalls and landscaping I put in, it was the ideal setting for weddings. My assistant had a wedding to shoot at 2.30 PM while I had another at 3 PM. We had enough space to handle both if they overlapped but when my party arrived early, I didn't reckon with the problem of parking. The earlier wedding had to leave and, in order to extricate their cars, drove all over my manicured lawns leaving deep ruts and gashes. They totally ruined our front yard –so that was the end of shooting weddings."

CHARLES DOLLACK

Charles Dollack MPA HLM of Toronto, Ont., worked through a wealth of interesting experiences before retiring from commercial photography to Florida.

"During ration restrictions imposed in World War Two, about 1944-45, photographers found it hard to complete many of their food assignments. At the Rapid Grip studios we were commissioned to have a cake made and photographed for a newspaper advertisement. The cake was to be twice the normal size with white frosting and coconut trimming. Time was too limited to have it created by a commercial baker, so Kay, our studio coordinator, volunteered to make it at home. Ingredients such as shortening, lard and cooking oils were hard to obtain so she had to use substitutes to make the recipe work. It turned out a beautiful three-tiered creation, ready for the Friday morning shoot. Approval of the finished photograph was given in the afternoon so all the food was removed to the galley where the studio employees could partake of the goodies. The cake soon disappeared down their hungry throats with every succulent bite being savored to the utmost. Kay dropped by on Monday to ask about the shoot and to reclaim the cake. I explained that after any shoot the food is given over to the employees. She gasped a mighty, 'OH, My God!... I couldn't get any shortening so I had to use three bottles of CASTOR OIL. I hope everyone had a nice week-end!' "

Clients seemed to delight in giving out assignments on Friday afternoon which had to be ready for Monday morning. Charlie recalls when a pharmaceutical company rep sent in a number of contraceptive items to be photographed in colour on such a tight time schedule. It looked like the week-end was shot to hell again. "Checking over the items," says Charlie, "I discovered that one of the pessary packets had a large stock number printed across the front, so it was unsuitable for photography. I phoned the client who agreed it was an error, but since his stock room was already closed for the week-end asked if I could get a substitute from a drugstore. He suggested that I explain to the pharmacist who it was for and why it was needed. By chance, my good wife was in the office doing the books and she volunteered to go to the store while I carried on with the rest of the photography. She had no problem explaining the purpose of the request to the druggist. But when he said it would cost a given amount she explained that she only wanted to borrow the pessary and would bring it back in twenty minutes. As fate would have it, two old ladies were standing near the cash register and heard only my wife's last remark of 'using it for twenty minutes and bringing it right back'. The women, with a gasp, gave my wife a hard and disdainful look and marched out of the store. Both the pharmacist and my wife had a side-splitting laugh when they realized the mix-up of information."

"In the middle of the 1950's when stereo photography was gaining momentum in movies as "Bwana Devil" and "The Wax Museum" wedding photographers hitched a StereoRealist to their 4x5 cameras to provide 3-D slides of the wedding. In another application, children used red and blue eye glasses to view their stereo comic books. I was commissioned to use this same two-colour system to produce 3-D photos of a model for a soap advertisement. This went well as the negatives only had to be in black and white. Prints were sent off to the printer for half tone reproductions. About ten days later my client brought a stack of printers proofs about twelve inches thick and explained that, unbelievably, the print shop owner turned out to have only one eye while his pressman was totally colour blind. So how in heck could they ever expect to print a two colour anaglyph if neither could see anything in 3-D. The job eventually went to another printer where the employees did have two good eyes."

JOHN NARVALI

Not all stories by photographers are funny; some can be described as stranger-than-fiction. Here is one as told by John Narvali of Toronto, Ontario.

"My assignment started off as a quick executive portrait of a junior Vice President in a large company. I was called in by the President's secretary so had the finished prints delivered to her, rushing to meet a closing deadline. During that particular week I had a photo student assisting me on a work-week arrangement. On the envelope containing the portrait the student wrote the name of the President rather than that of the junior V.P., due to the fact that the last names were identical. It seems that this envelope, without ever having been checked, was rushed on to the printer who was finalizing the company's annual report. The rest of the story is agonizing history for me. There was no time to get proofs OK'd by the client and as a result the photograph of this junior Vice President was used prominently on the inside front cover in place of the President's portrait. When the printer found out the error he almost went insane as this report was a 30 thousand dollar project with a 14 thousand copy run. So fire and brimstone flew in all directions, to say the very least. I had visions of a lengthy lawsuit but I was determined to remain cucumber-cool to the end. But my day of reckoning finally arrived when I was called to the phone... the President, himself, was on the other end of the line and I knew this must be my Doomsday. I was prepared to receive the worst. 'Mr Narvali,' said the President, 'I'm arranging a retirement party for myself and was wondering if you would be so kind as to take the photographs. I had planned to retire at the end of this year, but it seems that your mix up on the portraits has turned out to be an inspiration. My wife and I are leaving directly after the party for a two months holiday.' I learned that the junior V.P. was, in fact, the son of the President and had been pegged to assume the top office upon his father's retirement. So everything turned out well. But to this day I have no desire to go anywhere near that printer again!"

ANDRE AMYOT

Have you ever been down a mine? Well, read on and hear about the experiences of several photographers.

André Amyot MPA HLM of Longueuil, Quebec, recalls an assignment to photograph a gold mine in Northern Quebec. "We went down to the 1500 foot level and then travelled to the end of the gallery. There we found a big pile of mineral cuttings ready to be hauled out for processing. The floor was covered with a foot of murky water. All the machinery operates by air, so pipes and thick hoses run everywhere with pressures of 100 lbs. per square inch. To commence the shoot we decided to first scout the area for the best placement of our lights. I took the lead, followed by an engineer, some workers and then my assistant, André Couture. All of a sudden I heard this tremendous SWISH-SH-SH-SH. In the confines of a mine tunnel, every sound seems a hundred times louder than normal. One of the hose connections broke beneath the water and blasted a wall of water in all directions. I got totally soaked and immediately took refuge in a big scoop-bucket on the front of a nearby machine. My assistant wasn't quite so lucky. The hose was flailing in every direction and he got hit in the middle of his chest. Luckily he was wearing a little 35mm camera and like the sheriff who stops a bullet right on his badge, my assistant was struck by the hose right on the camera. That is what saved him as he was bowled over and had his safety hat knocked off. The hat provided the only source of light so he was in total darkness as he ran to get away from the thrashing, snaking hose. He ran back into the gallery and luckily did not smash into a wall in the pitch blackness. Finally, someone managed to reach a valve and turn off the pressure. It was a tense few moments as the hose might have hit someone in the face or chopped off a head. It was a deadly situation."

"On another assignment we had to descend a long steep incline that led underground. With extra assistants it was easy to get all the equipment down the slope, but when we came to leave it became an arduous task to pull all that weight up the forty-five degree ramp. We were all feeling the effects and I was really short of breath. Ahead, I saw three workers, silhouetted in the mine opening, with their reflection mirrored in a puddle of water. Just the dynamic picture I was looking for..! So I dropped to my knees to visualize the scene from a low angle. In this rolled up position everyone thought I had collapsed with a heart attack. They were really alarmed asking if I was sick or something. 'No no no!' I yelled. 'I'm OK. I'm just looking at this terrific shot. So we dropped all the equipment, turned the three guys around and got a dynamic reflection photo that made the front covers of a number of mining magazines and even won several awards in competition."

GEORGE HUNTER

George Hunter of Mississauga, Ont., in the mid 1950's was shooting photographs at a uranium mine in Northern Saskatchewan. After working underground most of the day, George returned to the surface and began taking pictures of a 'cobbing' operation inside the mill. As George explains it, "This is where the high grade uranium is carried on a conveyor and passes beneath a Geiger counter. When a piece of high grade ore comes along, a light flashes and a bell rings. There was little activity so I approached the belt with a Hasselblad around my neck and WHAMMO.... the lights came on and the bell rang continuously. Two mill hands, thinking they must have hit the jackpot, jumped into action and frantically began hauling all the ore off the belt into the high grade chute. I retreated so as not to interfere... and just as quickly as it had started the commotion stopped and it became quiet again. It wasn't until the third time I approached the belt with the same hectic consequences that we realized I was the one tripping the Geiger counter with a contaminated Hasselblad. Somehow the camera had picked up radioactive dust while I was making underground photographs."

WILLIAM R. SILVER

Bill Silver CPA and Mike Dupont MPA of North Bay, Ont., were shooting an underground assignment at the 5600 foot level of the Falconbridge mine in Sudbury. "It was Mike's assignment and I was along to give assistance. We were about a kilometer down the drift from the cage and were finishing the last shots. My headlamp had burned out early, but that was no problem as I worked under the lights from Mike's hat and that of our Supervisor. Well, Mike's lamp quit and we finished packing with only the single beam. Wouldn't you know it, just as we were ready to leave, the Supervisor's lamp also went dead. We were suddenly in total darkness... deep inky-blackness that makes you feel so alone and cut-off. In a tiny shaft with a mile of rock over your head you suddenly feel trapped in your own grave. You experience that only in a mine when your light goes out because there is absolutely no other illumination and you can't see a darn thing. Luckily we were in an area where there were trolley tracks, so in total darkness we had to feel our way along the tracks for the whole kilometer to reach safety. Needless to say I now carry at least one flashlight in my kit on every assignment... just in case."

WILMOT BLACKHALL

Wilmot Blackhall SPA of Lindsay, Ont., accompanied Herb Knott of Toronto to photograph a spectacular dynamite blast that would cut out a horseshoe shaped wall of an open pit mine. "We were standing beside a truck for protection with a big man standing beside each of us. I got six frames off during the blast before all the debris and dust made it impossible to get anything more. When everything was over they told us that a week before, with much less explosives the stones had sailed a mile beyond where we had been standing! Our guardians were actually there to drag us under the truck for safety if the debris headed the wrong way."

ANTHONY E. FISHER

Tony Fisher MPA of Toronto, Ont., has covered a wide variety of assignments in commercial, advertising and industrial photography.

"One time I was doing progress photos of the construction of the University of Waterloo residences. They wanted some overall

views that required climbing to the top of the crane and then crawling out on the boom for the best views. They were pouring concrete at the time, and when they pour concrete they don't stop for anything... it is a constant pour. So the Superintendant said, 'Alright, when the crane stops to load the concrete into the bucket, you climb up and go out to the end of the gantry. Once you're in place we'll start pouring again. When you're done, give us a wave and the next time we come down to load the bucket, we will allow time for you to get down.' So I climb up this crane and its darn cold up there since its the middle of winter. But I had come prepared with heavy clothing and a snowmobile suit. Its all grease up there and in no time I was covered, head-to-toe, in this black grease. I work my way out onto the gantry and tie myself down with a safety harness. I am used to heights and this crane is no problem as it is only 20 feet above the top of the building. But then they swung the boom out and it is suddenly 200 feet above the ground. I get some shots and they swing back in. Back out again a couple more times, and I had all the shots I needed. I waved down to indicate I was finished, but nothing happened. They kept doing this for another full hour, swinging out - swinging back. A joy ride, to be sure, but I was freezing even with my snowmobile suit and I was getting scared. I kept waving and waving. Well, they finally let me down and they were in hysterics with laughter. They thought it was the biggest joke to leave the photographer stranded on the boom. But if I had been borderline or feared heights I could have really freaked out on them."

"We were flying back from a shoot in Arizona and as we approached Chicago, the pilot announced they had a problem with the landing gear. But not to worry, they sent the first officer to our area to check out the problem. My assistant stood aside while the officer lifted up the carpet under his seat and checked through a porthole located there. The landing gear was down and OK. So he went away, but five minutes later he came rushing back and checked the porthole on the other side of the plane. He had looked through the wrong side and could have caused a serious accident if the wheel HAD NOT been down. This really upset one of our models who was afraid of flying and she almost flipped out... especially when we landed and there were fire trucks lined up along the runway!"

"I had an aerial job to do at Niagara-on-the-Lake, a short hop across the lake from Toronto; so we rented a helicopter. I went down to the Island airport and, just before we took off, the pilot asked if I wanted to fly with the door off, or land in St. Catharines and take it off there. Since it was a fairly warm day I agreed the door be removed right there. We took off and started following the lake shore rather than flying directly to Niagara. As it turned out, single engine aircraft and helicopters are not allowed to cross the lake; so we had to follow the shoreline and with the door off I froze... it was so darn cold. We got to the site, shot the job and then spent another 40 minutes flying back to Toronto. The pilot was OK because he had his coat and his gloves on. When he asked if I wanted to shoot extra stuff around the city I told him, 'No way!... Land the damn 'copter! I'm freezing... I'm finished!'"

BRODIE WHITELAW

Brodie Whitelaw of Scarborough, Ont., understands how Murphy's Law can spoil any well planned assignment.

"I was working for Brigden's in Toronto and had a routine shot to illustrate a client's internationally-known fabric as used in ski fashions. The art director suggested a situation where a female skier would be receiving pointers from a famous ski instructor. A male model, presumably a boy friend, would stand in the background. Models were selected with the clothes custom made to fit exactly; that was some three weeks before the actual shoot in January. Came the day, we headed for Collingwood Ski Lodge where the instructor was based. Leaving Toronto we had bright sunny weather, but at our destination the sky was overcast and it was starting to snow. We expected to see the photography completed by the next afternoon. The client had brought along his wife to enjoy the short overnight stay."

"The next day was blowing snow; so, not to waste our efforts, we decided to run through a garment check for fit and any final corrections. The stylist reported difficulties with the ski pants as they were tight around the waist and had to be let out. It turned out our model was 'slightly pregnant' and now was beginning to show. This created a problem by cutting down the useable positions she could be in. In fact, the only pose we could use was leaning-over ready to take off downhill. The increased girth was adequately concealed. So the shoot was set for Wednesday... but the weather was no better. The same with Thursday. Back in Toronto the weather was beautiful and they were phoning to find out what was keeping us. Luckily, the client was along, otherwise they would have thought we were having a wild time on the slopes at their expense. Finally on Friday, the weather cleared beautifully but with one problem -the temperature had dropped to 32 degrees below zero. That was Fahrenheit in those days and it was damn cold. At that temperature both models and photographer would freeze like boards before reaching the selected shoot site."

"The only way to get our photography done was to shoot just outside the back door of the kitchen. Luckily, we had a clean background, new snow and a sloping hill with a blue sky and puffy clouds. The trusty Deardoff was set up just outside the door. The models and ski gear were quickly positioned to check focus and composition then quickly brought in to avoid frostbite. The clothing for the models was rather lightweight, considering the frigid situation, especially with no hats and light shirts for the men. When sufficiently warm again, everybody ran to their positions allowing just enough time to grab two exposures on 8X10 Ektachrome, then it was a dash back to the kitchen again. Even the lens was brought in to avoid the shutter freezing up. We were only able to make six colour exposures plus one black & white before the weather closed us down again. Only one person suffered frostbite to the ears. With that, we packed up and headed back to Toronto under white-out conditions. The client and his wife departed on their own and unfortunately were stranded when their car slid off the road. Our processed shots

were a great success and widely used; so everybody was off the hook. It could have turned into a total wipe out. Ironically, the ski instructor mentioned to me that a week previous he had spent three days at the Summit resort, immediately north of Toronto. We could have whipped off the shot in half a day as the weather had been excellent!"

MARCEL RAY

Marcel Ray of Toronto, Ont., was both a professional musician and an accomplished portrait photographer catering to the musical and theatrical trade. "Years ago," recalls Marcel, "I was engaged to play in 'The Prom' at Varsity arena. It was a very popular summer symphony held outdoors in, what was then Toronto's biggest football field. They built special bleacher-seats that banked up around the orchestra and seemed to go up forever; we used the location for rehearsals. Someone had decided to have a photograph taken and since the union was most strict about overtime, the photographer understood he had only ten minutes to shoot his picture and no more. He had big banks of flashlamps strung out to light this monster picture and had his camera away up at the top of the bleachers at the back wall. Everything was in readiness, the camera focussed, the lights tested and synchronized. Because of the elaborate setup of flash bulbs he could take only one picture; so at his count of three, everyone was to strike their normal pose and hold it until the picture was taken. The photographer ran up the 200 steps and climbed a ladder to reach his camera position by which time he was really out of breath. At the start of the count, the concert master and all the violinists brought their instruments up to position with chins so tightly tucked down so that it looked like everyone had his head tucked into his armpit; you couldn't see a face.

Our frustrated cameraman realized the uselessness of the pose and came running down all those stairs again. He pleaded could we do something different... even half way. The concert master was an avid amateur photographer and knew exactly what he was doing as he struck the farcical pose. It was marvellous to see how the rest of the orchestra picked up on the ruse and instantly struck the same pose. It was really a rotten trick with precious minutes whisking away. The photographer had to run all the way back up again and we finally let him get his picture. It was a near catastrophe for a while and I felt sorry for the photographer."

"We had a conductor, Sir Adrian Boult, leading a summer rehearsal. He was a very aristocratic Englishman, most polite. While we were rehearsing we heard these noisy heels clacking across the wooden floor. It was a young press photographer, a beat up scruffy looking guy trying to play a hard line imitation of Sam Spade the detective. He jauntily put his foot up on the podium and stared at Sir Adrian as he continued to conduct. At a rest point in the music it was found that the photographer was there to photograph the maestro. 'Go ahead, any time,' said Sir Adrian and he continued on with the rehearsal. The photog didn't move and since this was bothering all of us Sir Adrian finally stopped and asked if he wanted something special. If he wanted a pose, Sir Adrian didn't mind and would agree to it. The photog put his Speed Graphic to his eye ready for the picture. Sir Adrian raised his arms in a gesture at which the photog lowered his camera in disgust. He didn't like the pose. Sir Adrian must have held the pose for a minute before he finally looked around to see what was happening. 'Show me what you want done,' was his retort. So the guy jumped up on the podium and struck a pose at which Sir Adrian exclaimed haughtily, 'No no! You're thinking of that other chap, Tchaikovsky. I can't do that pose, its not my style. If you don't like this pose then take the picture while I'm conducting.' The photographer wasn't happy with anything so turned and left the building!

ERIC TRUSSLER

"This story from Eric Trussler MPA, now of Calgary, Alberta, tells of an experience, when in his younger days, he was extremely shy. He worked for a Toronto commercial firm where he felt safe in the intimacy of the darkroom and the studio. One day a customer phoned in an assignment and Eric was told to go to the Royal York Hotel and take a picture of a speaker on stage in the ballroom. "If you stand in the wings," suggested his boss, "he will see you with your camera and come over to have his picture taken. You can get out of there quickly, – its just a simple assignment." No problem, thought Eric, despite the fact he had no experience as a press-type photographer and preferred to shoot only in the studio. Arriving at the ballroom, the biggest in the hotel, he took a position in the wings with his Speed Graphic to await his subject. Several times the celebrity glanced in Eric's direction; each time Eric beckoned him to come closer, pointing to the camera. But it was of no avail. Repeatedly he beckoned and repeatedly nothing happened. Finally the speaker did walk towards a now-smiling Eric but, to his horror, the gentleman took him by the hand and pulled him right out into the middle of the stage. There before Eric was a sea of inquisitive faces which, individually counted, amounted to 4000 staring eyeballs! Whispering in his ear the orator asked Eric for his name, then turned to the audience and announced: "This is Eric Trussler who has come to take my picture. Would you excuse us for a moment?" The crowd roared its approval. So a trembling Eric, by this time a reluctant star on stage, cautiously proceeded to focus and snap the photo. Had he set everything right? – had he cocked the shutter? – would the flashbulb fire? – had he pulled the slide? To his relief and the cheers of his new found fans the bulb flared into action and the shutter clicked...! The photo was on the film; with great relief, it was finished. With weakened knees Eric headed for the wings.... and safety!

"During the construction of the Toronto subway I used to walk its full length , once a week, to photograph anything that looked new and interesting. When they reached St. Clair Avenue I would enter the dark catacombs through an opening just big enough to squeeze through with my Speed Graphic and a bag of flash bulbs. The first time I entered at that location, I opened a little gate and started down a ladder that was nailed to the wall. On unfamiliar territory and in darkness I suddenly found myself hanging on for dear life as the ladder came to an abrupt end and my feet were dangling in mid air. As my eyes adjusted to the darkness I found a ledge I could stand on and finally work my way down to the bottom. That scare made me more cautious. On another visit I was to enter through a door where a platform should have been located. It was a very sunny day so I waited for my eyes to get used to the darkness and after several minutes I could make out two boards. 'Oh great,' I said, 'they've built the platform' and I stepped through the doorway.... to nothingness and plunged four feet to the track level below. I heard one of the workers say, 'Oh God! some guy's fell in the hole!' I pulled myself together but I hurt all over. I finally ended up at the doctors for X-rays and they found three ribs and the breast bone broken. They taped me up and I headed back to finish the job. That was the only time I've ever been off sick!"

"I flew to Montreal for an assignment and packed flash bulbs to shoot the job with. I was working in a 'clean room' wearing special clothing, gloves and shoes when one of the bulbs blew up. It went off like a cannon and burnt holes in my shirt, burnt holes in the paper. Everyone in that clean room came to a complete halt with their eyes fixed on me as if I had dropped a bomb. As a result, the job finished early and since there was lots of time left until my flight to Toronto, I called up a lady who had given me a number of assignments and invited her out for a social drink. We headed for a bar and I ordered a martini but didn't know they only served 'doubles'. We yakked away for some time swapping business stories and suddenly I had to go to the washroom. The receptionist said, 'First door on the left down there.' It was only when I was through the door and it had slammed behind me that I noticed I hadn't entered the washroom. It was a mechanical room for the air conditioning. There was nobody around and the door locked behind me; so I climbed the stairs up to the next floor. Still nothing, so I went up to the next floor. I'm wandering around, completely lost, when I see a door with a window in it. I spotted two people in a garden outside and banged on the glass until a man opened the door from his side. I found my way back into the building, worked my way back to the receptionist and said, 'NOW let's try that again.' I finally got back to my friend in the lounge and she said, 'Oh! I thought you had left for Toronto'. By this time I realized it was time to head for the airport so I made my goodbyes. Seeing the bus still outside I ran out to the driver and said I had to be on that bus, hold it please while I get my equipment from the check room. When I got back I was just in time to see the bus pull away without me. All this time the double-martinis had been working on me and I was really looped. I hired a cab to take me to the airport and flew from Montreal to Ottawa then to Toronto. As the passengers were coming off the plane they were all discussing the terrible storm we had come through, –thunder, –lightning, and the plane bouncing all over the sky. Me, I didn't remember a thing. In fact, I don't even remember stopping over at Ottawa!"

Eric recalls an aerial assignment in the early 50's when he was to photograph a bank building at the corner of ,King and Bay Streets in Toronto. "As usual," says Eric, "I had the door off the plane and used a Speed Graphic camera with a twelve exposure film magazine. As we circled I would make a shot in B&W and then repeat the picture on Ektachrome film. You yanked on a lever to draw the film into a leather pouch and then transferred it to the back of the pack. On one of the circuits I pulled the lever and the WHOLE magazine came sailing off the camera and was flying out the door. 'Dear God!' I thought, 'Down below are dozens of people crossing the street.' My hand shot out and, wonder of wonders, the magazine landed in my hand! In that split second it passed through my mind that this could be the end of my career.... for when they pulled this leather and metal box out of someone's head, there, in bold print would be the name ERIC TRUSSLER - Photographer!"

RUTH EASTON

Ruth Easton of Toronto, Ont., recalls a vacation trip to Morocco, shooting pictures in all directions as she went. "When I travel," she says, "I shoot film as if it is water! On this particular evening I had been at a night club to see some belly dancing. I was using flash on my camera and had a few shots left over when I left. As I came into the narrow streets there was a Moroccan lady, in local dress and veils, talking to a soldier. I thought it was great so grabbed a shot, but the soldier immediately took offense and threatened to smash my camera. He said that I must not shoot ANYTHING military. My guide protected me and after much verbal abuse I got away with the picture. It was later explained to me that the woman was a 'Lady of the Night' and the soldier didn't appreciate being pictured with her!"

MARY ELLEN NEALIS

Mary Ellen Nealis and husband, Bill, of Fredericton, New Brunswick were doing a summer shoot for Tourism-New Brunswick at a country hotel. "Some of the settings I had to photograph were the special suites called theme rooms. We were to photograph the 'Victorian Room' which had an elaborately decorated jacuzzi, so they gave me the keys and we headed up with all the equipment to start the shoot. We had the strobes and all the umbrellas set up and were ten minutes into the session when there was some one at the door. There was a fumbling of a key in the lock then two people stepped into the room. A shocked look came over the couple's faces and I suspect we had caught them on a get-a-way weekend. It must have appeared that we were there to record their dream visit. Although we tried to explain why we were there, they quickly left with faces a bit red. The front desk had made the error by issuing the same room before we had completed the photography."

BARTON STRONG

Barton Strong of Hamilton, Ont., is a medical photographer. "I guess you could say I got into photography through the back door, like so many people did in the 1960's. Since there were so few photography courses in those days, I graduated in electronics technology and my first job was as an audio-visual technician for Mohawk College. I also had a small business doing a variety of freelance photography - weddings and portraits, industrial etc., but that was more like a hobby of mine. As the AV department grew they asked me to do more photography and eventually I became their full time photographer. The same rise through the ranks happened when I changed jobs and became Chief of AV services for a hospital in Ontario which included shooting medical photography. I liked it so much I was able to evolve to full time photography with the hospital, basically because of my experience with freelance commercial assignments. Here are a few anecdotes pertaining to my experiences in the medical field."

"This particular event took place in the late 70's when I had a freelance assignment to photograph the birth of a child of a prominent Canadian. I was in the delivery room with the operating team and the mother. The father was there too, and seemed preoccupied as he kept looking at his watch. Basically, he was there to help his wife with her breathing exercises, giving her support only sporadically. As it got closer to the actual birth he seemed agitated and more preoccupied with his watch. I was photographing the procedure as well as the interaction of parents, doctors and the nurses. Two minutes before the baby was born, I finally found out what was bothering him... why he was constantly looking at his watch. He suddenly announced that in 3 or 4 minutes he was going to be on television and he didn't want to miss it. He asked if there was a television set in the hospital that could be wheeled in, so he could see himself during this interview. Being the prominent citizen that he was, the staff managed to find a portable TV. They brought it into the delivery room and as his son was being born, he was sitting immediately beside his wife watching television. He

would help his wife breathe then turn to the television to make some comment. Even his wife was mesmerized by the TV, offering her own criticisms: 'Gee, you look good in that shot, you should remember to make sure the left side of your face is always to the camera.' The birth was almost anti-climactic... everything was secondary to what was happening on the television. It amazes me to see how people regard themselves sometimes. I wonder if I would behave in the same manner if I were as important as this fellow was. Thank goodness I was there to record all those pictures; some day they will appreciate seeing what really happened."

"I took a series of photos during the construction of one of the first tennis-bubble installations. It was a fairly new innovation, designed by a California company. It faced severe tests as it was being built in the middle of winter. The contractor sent their own engineer from

California to oversee the installation and he was there several months but seemed eager to get away. Towards the end it got bitterly cold and there was a big storm looming. The engineer said there would be no problem as the bubble could withstand anything so they went ahead and inflated the bubble. I'll never forget watching it slowly rise then fill into its final majestic form. The storm came that very night and by the next morning we had three feet of snow piled up everywhere. When I drove past the site of the bubble the whole thing had collapsed. It had ripped open by the fury of the storm and the weight of the snow... the roof material was in shreds, the supports were broken, the hardware was spread all over the ground. I immediately went for my camera to record the remnants of this beautiful structure. When I got out to the site, I spotted the California engineer standing on top of the remains of the bubble on a big air pocket. He was motionless, shoulders hunched forward, crying his eyes out. I snapped quite a few dramatic pictures and later told him that I had pictures of that dark moment in his life. He was quite embarrassed but explained: 'The real reason for my crying was not because the bubble had collapsed, but because the night before I talked with my wife in California. I was told of the birth of a new son and I promised I would fly home on the very next plane. Now I can't! I'll have to spend another month or two getting things sorted out here.' I never did use those photographs; I just put them away in my file as a memory. Periodically, I look them over and feel sorry, all over again, for that poor fellow who missed out on the joys of his son's birth."

"I once photographed a series of case-studies involving different forms of child birth. I followed a number of couples through their preparation classes and then photographed the actual birth. There was a young Jewish couple who were together during the birth of their child . It was very late at night and the father was watching the birth. At the moment the baby was born, the father suddenly yelled: 'Nobody touch him, –I have to be the first!' He reached down and with bare arms, picked the baby up. Over the objections of the doctors, he held the baby high in the air and said a prayer to his God, dedicating his child to the work of the Lord. It was a most touching moment. There were tears in his eyes and in the eyes of his wife. The doctors and nurses were all quiet... they never said a word, just stared in amazement. But I had the privilege to photograph the whole thing and produce some very dramatic photographs. Those are fond memories which I will remember for years to come."

"In this game you quickly learn by your errors and I recall what might be described as a young photographer's nightmare. It happened during the first year of my professional career. I had a rush call from another college to take pictures of some dignitaries for a local newspaper. The newspaper photographer hadn't shown up so I was requested to fill the gap while everyone waited my arrival. I quickly loaded my camera with B&W film, threw my gear in the back seat of the car and took off down the highway. As I went around a sharp bend I hit a pot hole in the road and my camera flipped off the seat and got tangled amongst equipment on the floor. The motor drive button got jammed by a piece of equipment and it happily started taking pictures of the roof of my car. I heard the thing clacking away and tried to grab it, but it was out of reach. By the time I pulled over to the side, the whole roll of film had gone through the camera. Since I hadn't brought extra film with me, there was nothing I could do but turn round and go back to the office. My boss received several calls wondering where I was and they finally cancelled the shoot when no photographer showed up. I learned a lot from that particular incident."

"While still with Mohawk College, I was assigned to photograph Prime Minister Trudeau on one of his whirlwind tours of Hamilton. I was elbow to elbow with twenty press photographers, jostling the body guards while trying to get the perfect picture of Trudeau. For a while, it seemed like everyone was jumping on each others shoulders. All of a sudden, one photographer handed his camera to his assistant, jumped through the line of RCMP body guards and embraced Trudeau, so his assistant could snap a picture of the two of them together. After the initial shock, Pierre managed to smile for the photo but the bodyguards were certainly not amused. They hustled the photographer away for questioning so I wonder if it was all worth it.. although it must have been a great picture to keep for his grandchildren."

"I was asked to hook up a brand new video camera to an operating room microscope in order to record the progress of some micro surgery. I followed the instructions to the best of my ability and managed to get it working. I recorded the operation and immediately afterwards, a group of the surgeons wanted to review the video to analyze the results of the surgery. Since it was an unusual case, I was requested to take the tape to a conference room and run it on the television set, there. Since I had another assignment, I hurried away leaving the surgeons to run the tape through themselves. About half an hour later I came back to check on their progress and was astonished with a most unusual sight. As I opened the door there were fifteen rear ends stuck up in the air. The surgeons were bent over, like ostriches with their heads near the floor. They were viewing the operation which I had, unfortunately, shot upside down. It seemed totally incongruous with images of blood running upwards and the surgeons giving comments from their upside-down position. It was one of the most unusual sights I've ever seen. Believe me, I quickly learned how to properly hook up a TV image-recorder to the operating microscope."

JAMES H. PEACOCK

Jim Peacock MPA, of Calgary, Alberta recalls when he first started in medical photography in Toronto. "I wanted to experience shooting surgical operations and to prove to myself that I COULD withstand the sight of blood. The operating theatre had a glass-walled gallery from which I could safely observe and shoot. Being rather new I decided to shoot with the 4x5 Linhof and began setting up as they wheeled in the patient. I fiddled around, got the lens on, decided to change for another, then selected where I should locate for a well composed view. With these fine necessities attended to, I got under the focussing cloth for the final framing of this epic medical shot. As I started to focus on the surgeon he suddenly walked out of the picture. To my surprise he had completed the operation, a simple appendectomy, while I was fiddling away my opportunity. As Chief Surgeon, he left his juniors to close up and finish. It really impressed me the speed needed to photograph in the operating room."

FRANK D. LITTLE

Frank Little, a Toronto medical photographer, found humour mixed well with the seriousness of his profession.

A young lady, twenty-one years of age but who had grown only to the size of an eight year old, arrived from South America for treatment of her affliction. "I was required to photograph her at intervals during her three months stay. She duly arrived at the studio for the sitting which required she be recorded only in her underwear. This proved to be a problem since the young lady had a strict puritanical upbringing in her home country. I knew only a few Spanish words, but with them I attempted to put her at ease. Whether it was my age, my beauty or my linguistic abilities, the young lady relented and cooperated fully with me. But the attending physician, a highly trained specialist and esteemed throughout the hospital community, was banished to stand in a corner with his face to the wall until the proceedings were completed."

For a display on how nurses care for the geriatric patient, Frank was photographing a nurse combing the hair of one of the dear old ladies in the hospital. "To make conversation and hopefully to put the lady at ease, I asked her if she liked to dance. She replied in the affirmative and asked why I wanted to know. I told her that there was a dance on Saturday night and wondered if she would like to go. Her face instantly changed to a glare which burned a hole between my eyes. 'Young man,' she growled, 'before my husband died seven years ago, I promised I would never go out with another man. And I don't have any intention to start now.' The nurses won't let me forget that perfect put-down."

"When photographing under the chin of an elderly widow I knelt on the floor to shoot the angle I wanted. While in this position I asked how long it had been since a man had been on his knees to her. Without a blink she chirped, 'Too damn long sonny - too damn long.'"

"I was on the ward as an elderly gentleman was being prepared for admission. The Orderly was doing his best to get the old gent to cooperate but without much success. Finally he said, 'Come on Mr. Smith, we'll get undressed and have a nice hot bath then hop into bed, OK?' The old man looked at him curiously and asked, 'Here mate, you ain't one of those blokes that likes boys are you?' "

"One of our staff photographers was having trouble with his bowels and was full of gas, with little control over it. One time he erupted with a long loud burst of gas, much to the amusement of the rest of us. Some body yelled, 'That sure tore your old ass hole, didn't it Willy!' He turned at the sound of strange laughter to find himself surrounded by a class of young nurses and chaplains. He was so embarrassed he couldn't pass wind for a week."

"Years ago we had an Ektamatic processor with sets of rollers that pulled the film through the machine for developing. One of the lab technicians, who was keen on very wide bright ties, was in the darkroom running some film through the processor when we heard loud curses and roars. Not knowing what might be wrong we quickly dismantled the door from its hinges to find our friend with his glorious tie caught in the rollers and fast disappearing. Not only that, his beard was but a scant few millimeters from following the same course. Being compassionate people we left him exactly as we found him, undaunted by his curses and threats of painful death, until we could get all the photos we wanted."

"When training new lab technicians to use Nikor processing reels, we let them practice with dummy rolls of film with the lights on. But they close their eyes to get used to the idea of feeling, rather than seeing. A month after breaking in a new recruit, he was in the darkroom loading ten reels, happily humming to himself as he worked. Suddenly he realized it was not normal to see the film go on the reels. Absent minded, he had only closed his eyes and forgotten to turn off the lights It sure blew that training method all to hell."

"When I had my commercial studio I was photographing three young boys for a Father's Day gift. When I ducked under the focussing cloth on my old studio camera, the youngest lad asked what I was doing. I jokingly replied that I was eating a hamburger in there. While checking the focus I didn't notice that this lad had disappeared and as I lifted the cloth we were nose to nose. Without a blink he quipped: 'You is a dod dam liar... there's no hamburger in there!' "

CINDY MOLESKI

Cindy Moleski of Saskatoon, Saskatchewan trained as a medical photographer but is now in the field of portraiture. "Nothing funny ever happened to me while I was a medical photographer," remembers Cindy, "but I never will forget my most agonizing moments. A seventeen year old boy, normal except for his height of 3'4" had to be photographed in the nude. It must be said that I, too, was pretty young at the time and looked even younger. Being the only photographer on duty I had to do the assignment. The young man was visibly upset while my face must have shown my surprise when I was confronted by an adult, rather than a little child, as was usually the case. When the shooting session was finally over, I turned away and advised him to dress. On his way to the dressing room he tripped over the edge of the backdrop in his excitement. Horrified, I turned to see him sprawled on the floor, frozen in embarrassment. My heart really went out to him as I helped him up. Later, a gentleman was wheeled in to have pictures taken of stitches in a delicately sensitive area. I soon realized this was not my vocation and switched to portraiture, since I was not prepared to handle some of the assignments in medical photography."

EVA DZILUMS

There is many a slip to challenge the calmest of nerves as proven by this story from Eva Dzilums MPA HLM of Toronto. She was covering a convention for the Ontario Hospital Association with thousands in attendance. It was a major event with Coretta King heading up the list of celebrity speakers. Says Eva, "I had the assignment to photograph our keynote speaker so I took extra precautions to see that everything went right. I brought along a full complement of camera equipment and made sure to get a good variety of pictures from all angles to ensure complete coverage. When Mrs. King finished I carefully tucked away that special film in the pocket of my camera bag. The location for the presentation was the theatre of the Metro Toronto Convention Centre which has a long flight of stairs to exit the auditorium. When the King party left at the breakup of the session I stumbled while going up these stairs, spewing the contents of my camera bag down the full flight of stairs. It was particularly embarrassing since all the OHA executives were present and watched me scramble about retrieving the bits and pieces. I wanted to escape as fast as possible. Some 5 to 10 minutes later, I finally took time to repack my equipment and to my horror the precious roll of film was missing! All sorts of things flashed through my mind - where could it be? - how could I explain its loss? - was I going to be fired? In a panic I headed back to the scene of the spill. It seemed like a lifetime to get there and painfully to make the search... step after step down the whole flight of stairs. I was in a turmoil. But there at the very bottom was my little cassette of film. Despite the hundreds, who had walked over that area to leave the theatre, my film was still intact; it so easily could have been crushed."

As a corporate photographer Eva shoots in a variety of situations, recording hospital activities for public relations, annual reports as well as medical reports. During surgery assignments she has found that highly trained doctors, oblivious to the world around them, often turn "Hollywood" when a woman photographer comes to take their photograph. She has found that doctors are quite thrilled by this female attention. "You see very interesting things," says Eva, "that don't show up in everyday life. On one

occasion I was to photograph the action during a bone transplant. A group of technicians was off in a corner while one doctor who had completed his part of the operation, was continuing his investigations. He appeared to be cleaning quite a large bone. I was fascinated and stood staring long enough for him to look up and catch my mesmerized gaze. He asked, 'I'll bet your wondering what I'm doing?' I replied with a questioning... 'Uhhaaa...?' He stopped me in my tracks with: 'Well, we are making CHICKEN SOUP!'.... 'Yuk!' "

JAMES ATKINSON

James Atkinson, President, Medical Media Production Group, has travelled the world while working as a medical photographer. "In Winnipeg, I was photographing a little boy flown down from the North for treatment of frost-bitten feet. He was Cree and the only words I could converse with him in his native language were: 'Hello, my little one.' Each morning I made a routine of going up the extra flight of stairs to visit him in his ward and salute him in Cree, then go back down to work. The prosthetist made the boy a special pair of shoes with little wooden blocks at the front to give him balance. As a surprise one morning the nurses had him dressed and waiting in the middle of the hall. As I came to the top of the stairs he made his first few steps toward me with his arms outstretched. That was a tremendous thrill and a very special day for both of us."

"In Africa there was an occasion when I was to photograph an Afrikaaner who had been in the bush for years and had never seen a strobe flash. I am usually careful to set the flash off a couple of times before I start shooting, so the patient can get used to it. This fellow looked like he had been around, so I thought there would be no problem. I set up to take a full frontal face shot and snapped the exposure. He reacted to the 600 watt/second flash as if he had been in an explosion. He flew right off the chair and ended up on the floor... much to my pain and consternation."

James continues, "At a Toronto hospital we had a procedure to inject a patient with a substance which could be photographed as it passed through the eye. Blue light was used to fluoresce the dye substance while a yellow filter on the camera would enable us to see and photograph it. Occasionally a patient would feel ill from the effects of the injected chemical. We had a rather large woman come in for the procedure; she put her chin in the head rest while I made ready with the camera. A rather small doctor was working with me, about half the size of the lady. He administered the injection and stood behind her. Sure enough she said she didn't feel too well. I took as many photographs as she could endure and then went for help. The lady attempted to stand with the doctor's assistance but toppled over backwards, on top of him. When I came back he was scrunched underneath her. All I could see were two flailing arms as he tried to get out before she crushed him completely. Such are the occupational hazards of a medical vocation!"

"Stopping off in London, England," recalls James, "I had to get a third booster shot for yellow fever before leaving for Africa. I was staying near Westminster Hospital, so I went to their Emergency Department and asked where I could get the injection done. Before I could explain it was for yellow fever they said: 'Follow that line to the basement and they will give you your shots there.' I went all the way down two floors and finally got to the place where I had been directed, but it was a VD clinic, so I told them THAT was not what I was after and they referred me to The North London Immunization Centre on the other side of the city. Some two years later I found myself working at the same Westminster Hospital and my first job was to go down to the same VD clinic to take a photograph. Pam Bentley, who was working with me said: 'You'll never find it. I'll have to take you over and show you how to get down there.' I protested that: 'No! I know exactly where the VD clinic is, as I have been there before.' She burst into laughter and gave me a funny look. She could only assume that I had been a patient at the VD clinic. So, before going off to take the photographs, I felt it important to our working relationship to explain the whole story of how I was looking for a yellow fever shot!"

ROY V. COOKE

Roy V. Cooke, for years Director of the Audio Visual Department of a Hamilton hospital, tells this story. "A major surgical procedure was scheduled for the operating theatre. Due to the complexity of this operation, a variety of skilled staff were involved: an anesthetist, an orthopedic surgeon, an ear, nose and throat specialist, a general surgeon, surgical nurses and supportive technical personnel. This operation was scheduled to last for seven hours, so the preparations were fine tuned to work as smoothly as possible. My role was to produce a 16mm motion picture, detailing each aspect of the operation. I spent considerable time, the day before, preparing the equipment and then an hour of sterilization of the final set up. We rigged the cine cameras on a mobile ladder with a platform that reached above the operating table. This whole platform was draped with sterile sheets to isolate it completely from the operation. While I was busy setting this up the staff were laying out the appropriate equipment, scrubbing up and prepping the patient. After this lengthy procedure the operation was ready to begin. The first request by the surgical team was to see the pre-operative X-rays to visualize the anatomy. After a stunned silence and then a few choice words, it was realized no one had ordered the X-rays. This HAD to be done before the operation could proceed. The only choice remaining was to bring in a portable X-ray machine while my carefully draped installation had to be dismantled and removed. It only took a few minutes for the X-rays, then I had to completely reinstall my equipment, starting from scratch. So much for an early start and plenty of careful planning!"

"On my very first day as a medical photographer, my first assignment was to document pathological findings during an autopsy, using colour photography. This entailed more than an hour of handling and photographing numerous wet and bloody organs and tissues. To say the least, this caused considerable queasiness in my stomach. When I arrived home from my first day

at the hospital my wife announced that to celebrate the occasion she had painstakingly prepared a sumptuous dinner of sirloin steak with all the trimmings. When I heard this I turned green all over again and declared that my appetite had disappeared completely. As a matter of fact, I lost total interest in meat for quite some time.

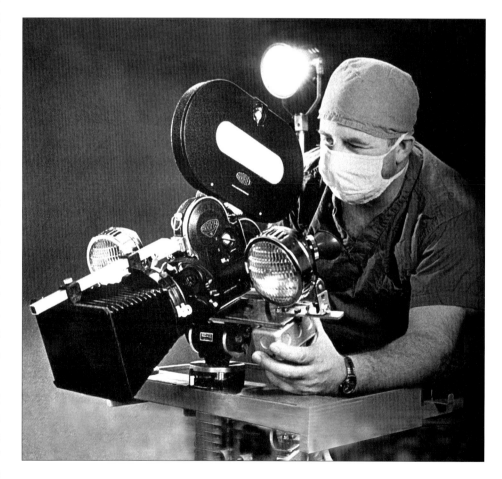

STANLEY J. WHITE

Before immigrating to Canada, Stan White of St. George, Ont., was a commercial photographer in England. Stan taught photography for 21 years at Oakville's Sheridan College and is now Professor Emeritus. He is Canada's authority on 3-D photography, designing and constructing his own stereo cameras. Author of "Beyond the Third Dimension" Stan is sought after to lecture throughout Canada and the United States. He relives for us some memorable experiences.

"While still in England, I was called upon to photograph a number of monster drying ovens and air ducting installations for Carrier Engineering. This particular day, I was at the Austin Motor Works to shoot paint drying tunnels which must have been 50 yards long. To record them we used a technique called 'the wagging hand lamp' which required us to set our camera on time exposure while we waved a tungsten lamp at arms length, literally painting the scene with light. With everything pitch black (clothing too) I could walk right into the picture and light the whole length of the tunnel. I would start at the far end and walk backwards keeping the light facing away from the camera. The light put out quite a punch, giving brilliance to the metal interior. It was the only way to handle the problem and it did a most beautiful job. Anyway, I was in the tunnel wagging this lamp wildly around when, all of a sudden,the cord shorted out and I found myself zapped with 220 volts of electricity grounding through my arm and feet to the metal floor. I was frozen in my tracks but made some frantic swings to dislodge the lamp from my locked hand. It seemed an eternity before I got free and the lamp hit the floor in a bloody great shower of sparks. I considered myself really lucky to be alive after that experience and with distraught nerves staggered out of the tunnel. At that very moment the agent who had been pressuring me along on the job for the past two days arrived back from scouting other locations and grabbed me by the arm. 'OK!' he said. 'We're late for the next shot. So what kept you so long?' He hadn't seen a thing and I couldn't expect to get ANY sympathy at all!"

"In my days as a photography teacher I gave a lecture on shooting full-length figures with studio flash. It seemed a good idea to have the students practice what they had learned in the lecture, so I arranged with the Life Drawing studio to supply three live models, all dressed in character, for the following session."

"When I arrived at 9:00 AM there they were - three wonderful characters. A very authentic looking sailor who might have been steamed off one of the old Player's cigarette packets; a most attractive young lady dressed as a belly dancer who had just the right excess to accentuate her every movement; and the third model, a fellow dressed as a Catholic Priest."

"I divided the class into three groups, each working with a separate model. As might be expected, the students were so preoccupied with the technical necessities that they gave little direction to their models. In fact, they simply stood them up like cows. With the idea that I might relax the models and perhaps help the students to be creative, I took the belly dancer across to where the priest was standing. There I sat him down on a chair and placed her on his lap."

"It is a rare occasion when an instructor finds an opportunity to demonstrate the multiplicity of his talents, rather than the usual dissemination of mundane f stops and shutter speeds. On this day I was not to be denied. Giving the operation of the camera to one of the students, I set about directing the models."

"The poses that I contrived could not in any sense be considered indecent, by the standards of the day, nevertheless they were decidedly bawdy. I kept up a continuous line of patter, embellishing here and there with double entendre. At one point, I ruffled the priest's hair, undid his collar and had the dancer leave a well formed lipstick kiss on his cheek. My purpose was to encourage the students to be spontaneous, showing them how the present may be emphasized by evidence of the past. From time to time I would allude to this or that internationally renowned photographer as though I was on a first name basis."

"Things were going rather well, I thought, except for an unexpected presence. A curious figure had joined the periphery of the students and I couldn't help noticing him since he was dressed as a clown. He seemed to be trying to catch my eye, but he was no match for me as, in my youth, I had had experience as a waiter and I had no intention of allowing him to interrupt my continuity. I was on a roll and little did I suspect that the proceedings were destined to come to an abrupt halt."

"Out of the corner of my eye I noticed a student coming from the film loading rooms with a batch of holders. I recognized him as a student from one of the other classes. Pushing his way to the front of the group he exclaimed in utter disbelief, 'My God! What are you doing with Father Flanagan?' My sensory perceptions may not have proved adequate to the reality of the moment but for the first time that morning I correctly perceived the significance of the clown... HE was the third model. The point did not escape the notice of the students and the place was in an uproar."

"I can only liken the experience to a time, back in public school, when I was first confronted with a vulgar fraction: it was the only other time in my life when I had cause to ponder whether I had been born with sufficient intelligence. Now, the significance of the clown... the real model... that Father Flanagan was a real priest... the realization that I had reached the zenith of idiocy. There was a strange consolation that whatever I did next, there was no way I could make a bigger fool of myself. Dreamlike, I moved forward and extricated Father Flanagan from beneath the abundant charms of the belly dancer. Mumbling some incoherent apology, I offered him my lowly comb and with my handkerchief, fumbled to wipe away the lipstick on his face... it only smeared to a bigger mess."

"By degrees the morning lapsed into a kind of subdued normalcy, not unlike the aftermath of a bereavement. Needless to say, I gave all the students a good passing mark, even those who stood their models up like cows! As to Father Flanagan, he turned out to be a rather decent fellow and did not seem all that perturbed by what had happened. I gave him the benefit of the doubt and put it down to him being in the business of professional forgiveness. The student, a parishioner of the good priest had brought him to the studio for a portrait and was most pleasantly surprised as Father Flanagan had a reputation for being rather dour. But the student said he got some very pleasant expressions. I believe he used the word 'beatific'."

"There were other humorous moments at the college where some students came to the program knowing little about photography. Under the stress of a deluge of information in the first few days, it is not surprising that one or two will not quite get their instructions straight. One day I was called into the darkroom to look at some sheets of 4X5 film which had curious marks all over them. It was obvious they were unevenly developed but these films had me stumped until I noticed, sitting in the developer tray, were two 4X5 film holders. Both film AND holders had been developed together!"

"A teaching colleague was given, at very short notice, the unenviable task of putting together an end-of-semester business seminar for our students. Frantically, he phoned the library sources for any appropriate audio visual material. There was little to choose from and when he got the films there was no time for a preview. However, from the titles, one looked promising and he decided to start the seminar with it. Within half a minute the lecture theatre was in pandemonium as the screen filled with dancing girls to the delight of the students. It turned out the movie was a 1940's Hollywood musical- 'How To Make A Million'. The library had confused it with an inspirational film 'How I Made My First Million'."

"A teacher's reward comes through the evident success of his students. But the student who has given me the most whimsical pleasure was the fellow whom I taught photographic lighting for two whole years. He went on to be, of all things, a lighthouse keeper!"

DOUGLAS W. BOULT

Doug Boult MPA HLM of Wellington, Ont., Professor Emeritus of Sheridan College in Oakville, assembled this list of excuses offered by his photographic students during his teaching years. They were given as reasons for late or missing assignments or, in some cases where the completed work did not rise to the acceptable standard.

–The prints are not too good because, by the time I got to the location, it was dark.

–My mother had promised to take me to lunch, but she didn't.

–The emulsion was on the wrong side of the film.

–No-one wanted to have their picture taken.

–I couldn't take the house because the owner came out with a double barrel shot gun.

–I have been sleeping with my horse and my parents don't know about it.

–A train ran over my exposure meter.

–Do you remember how you warned us that someone might pee in our developer... well someone did!...and it was all brown.

–Our cat died and it belonged to my sister.

–It was sharp when I shot it.

–My father keeps goats, so one of them probably ate it.

–I 'f'ed it all the way up and all the way down, but none of them were any good.

–I shot it in colour but it came out in black and white.

–This person couldn't smile; they don't have any teeth.

–I did what you told me and it came out to f 10, but I don't have an f 10 on my camera.

–I thought the '8' on the shutter meant 8 seconds.

–I asked for Indoor film but they only had Tungsten, so I shot it on Daylight- it was on sale anyway.

–I couldn't help it; when I print at home I don't have any proper safelight.

–I tried to shoot the Soccer game that evening but I couldn't find anywhere to plug in my extension cord.

–I couldn't help it, nobody told me about M and X.

–The sun didn't come out that day, so I used the moon.

–I thought Polycontrast was for transparencies.

–You can see the flash didn't work at all, even though I used a thousandth of a second for every one of them.

–I didn't have enough developer, so I shook the tank a lot.

–They are over exposed because my Nikon doesn't have f 45.

–I tried to do Rembrandt lighting but I only have one light.

–I put my print in the dryer but it never came out and nobody knows where it is.

–The film I used only gave negatives which is why I don't have the slides.

–I wasn't sure of the ASA which is why I shot colour.

–It blurred because I used a Wide Angle lens.

–For that Depth of Field thing, can I stand the three people next to each other?

–She wouldn't let me use flash because she said her mother told her it would go right through her clothes and show her bra.

–All the 90 mm lenses were signed out, so I used the 240 mm.

–The reason I shot this person in the nude was because they wanted me to. Her mother was there too.

–f. stops and shutter speeds still confuse me. Can I shoot it on Polaroid instead?

–I did it in the style of that photographer. Joseph Crush [Yousuf Karsh].

–A prominent photographer that I know is George Kodak, but he died a long time ago.

–I know you said not to shoot our relatives but I included my father in the group because he is bilingual.

–How come you gave him a higher grade than me? I used the same girl and she doesn't even go to this College.

–It would have been alright, but YOU told me to do it that way.

–The cable release didn't work and I only had the 'B' setting to work with.

–The film was blank and its not my fault.

–The slides look good with a bright light on them.

–Is it necessary to read about a photographer who is dead?

–I looked in the viewfinder and it was all in colour.

–I was going to bring it in today but my mother sent it to England.

–My father says its very good. How come you only gave me a 'C' for it?

–I showed my Grandmother that last assignment you didn't like. SHE likes it!

–Can I do that Window-Light portrait from outside the building as long as the window is included in the picture?

–The reason I am behind so much is because I haven't been able to get into my locker for over a month now.

–The next assignment will probably be late because I have to go to court with my girlfriend. (The pair were later charged with murder).

–How much out-of-focus is really acceptable.

–When you say 'one-to-one solution' do you mean TWO?

–I'm so far behind now that I think I would rather do all the assignments at the end.

–I never have felt like doing much in February!

–I have to go on a short vacation. Can I shoot some assignments there?

–Can I do a Vertical shot of a Round building?

–The model was too tall for the lens I had.

–I did try to spot the print but I only had a ball point pen.

RAYMOND BAKER

From Thunder Bay, Ont., Ray Baker MPA informs us that, as a teacher of photography at Confederation College, he occasionally has a student who wants to rewrite all the theory that was ever written in a text book. "One such student, I'll call Henry, would relish any novelty, news item or tidbit that he found in a photo magazine or product release sheet. He constantly tinkered to develop new and revolutionary chemistries, camera gadgets, etc. The problem was that this testing interfered with his course work and he was on the verge of failing the program. One day, Henry informed me he was heading down to Duluth, Minnesota and asked if he could pick up anything for me. I suggested he stay and get some work done for his projects instead. I later found him in one of the darkrooms spinning a helicopter propeller on a sheet of photographic paper which he said was a paper sensitometer. That did it! I told Henry there was indeed an item he could look for in town

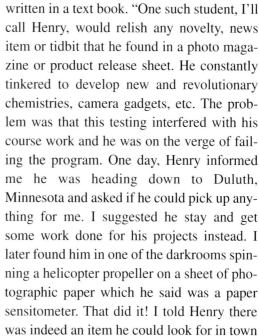

because I hadn't seen it for years. His eyes lit up and his interest was immediate; I told him that I needed a chemical called 'Focuseen' which I had used during my own student days to sharpen out-of-focus negatives. Henry toured the whole city and reported that the retailers thought he was crazy. He could not find it in Duluth so he persisted and went to Minneapolis looking for the mystery chemical. He never did get it and it seems that some people never learn!"

ROBERT S. BRAY

Bob Bray MPA of Edmonton, Alberta is reminded of the occasion when a lady came into his studio to order her family portraits. She had done all the early consultation by herself but on this final session she was accompanied by her husband. "I was projecting the proofs to 30"X 40" on the wall and the husband asked how much it would be for a print that size. I said it was 'fifteen-ninety'

and he replied, 'Well that's not too bad, we'll take three of that grouping and one of the others.' I looked in astonishment at him and asked, 'Three?' It turned out I was talking about $1590.00 while he was thinking $15.90."

"When studying photography at the Northern Alberta Institute of Technology I could be pretty temperamental like all young artists. I had been in the darkroom all day making B&W prints, when the lab tech yelled in to say he was going to turn on the lights as it was the end of the day. I screamed that my print was just going into the developer but he said he would give only one more minute. While my print was still processing the light came on and ruined it. I had worked so long to get the perfect print with a lot of burning and dodging... and he flipped the light on. The 16x20 paper, I was working with, belonged to the Institute and the tech told me to turn the paper in. So, I turned it in with the lid off just the way it was when the light was turned on. I was kicked out of school for a day for that little trick!"

"While taking that photography course I used my brother for an environmental portrait. I had him standing in the water at the edge of a shallow creek while I was composing the photograph in my camera viewfinder. I was telling him to back up a little bit and then a little bit more. It was only ankle deep at the edge but then there was a sudden dip down. He took one extra step backward and disappeared completely out of my viewfinder. Luckily he could swim, but it was a poor way to treat a sitter, even if it was my own brother!"

CAROL and RAYMOND HEBERT

Running a photo studio in Windsor, Ont., hasn't been a bed of roses for Carol and Ray Hebert MPA. Like many of to-day's young photographers, they had to struggle in their early years to get established. Carol recalls the first convention they ever attended and relates the following story. "The convention was in Washington, D.C. in 1976. We had absolutely no money but desperately wanted to attend this particular event as it listed so many top speakers that we yearned to learn from. We scraped together just enough money to take care of the registration and travel expenses, but in doing so, we could only budget for a single big meal a day. We couldn't afford a breakfast but would eat lunch about 2 o'clock in the afternoon when we could still get a big meal at luncheon prices. Then we'd have to pass up dinner making do with just pop and chips in our room."

"On our first day we headed down for our lunch and ended up as table partners with some American delegates. They literally took us under their wings when they heard it was our first convention and we were from Canada; they, in fact, picked up the tab for the meal. This friendliness by the Americans was a most welcome plus to the convention while the unexpected easement to our financial straits gave hopes of eking out the whole convention. We realized that we could combine our $5 lunch money with our 'chips' money and go out for supper. Luck must have been really shining down on us as someone picked up the tab for that meal too, and throughout the rest of the convention either a member of the trade or a friend paid for our lunches or dinners every day we were there. That convention had such an effect on our lives that we decided if we could ever be of assistance to other photographers then we would do so." For years the Hebert's served their association, lecturing whenever beckoned and serving as executive officers.

The 1986 PPOC National Convention in Quebec City carries a particularly vivid memory for Carol. "That is the year," she recalls, "that both Ray and I received our Master's Awards. It was the highlight of our careers. After the Awards Banquet we were invited to a celebration and were in the suite of Joseph and Louise Simone of Montreal. The room was gloriously festive with everyone dressed in their best finery, partying and having a good time.

Then suddenly, the fire alarms went off and I saw a look of shock come over Louise Simone's face. I told her not to worry because, at that time of night, the drunks got out of the bars and pulled the fire alarms just to be funny. But the alarms persisted and my own belief changed to concern. I had brought my children to this convention to share the excitement and splendor of our awards presentation. I had tucked the children into bed in their room before coming down to the party. I now realized that I was on the 6th floor while my children were in possible danger on the 14th floor. The alarm kept ringing and ringing and my concern rose to a frenzy. I called the front desk and they said it WAS a definite fire alarm. They urged us to get out of the building immediately!"

"No matter what I am in life: a photographer or a business woman, I am a mother FIRST... my children come before anything else! Ray and I headed for the elevators but, as everyone knows, they don't work during a fire. We resorted to the stairwells which were now filled with hundreds of guests descending down against us. From that point onwards my mind was a total blank, dedicated only to saving my children. I felt the whole world must be coming down against me as I struggled up through the maze, floor after floor, the 6th up to the 14th. When I finally reached the top, the staircase had emptied and, as I stepped into the hallway, I realized I was lost. The hotel was laid out with wings going off in different directions. I knew where my rooms were in relation to the elevators, but now, entering from the fire escape, I was disoriented.

The alarm bells were blaring away madly. I was panicking and ran down the hallway only to discover it was the wrong wing. I was frantic, I went back to the central corridor, followed another wing but that was the wrong one, too. By this time I was screaming my head off but no-one could possibly have heard me over the clamor of the bells. I finally saw a corridor with a baby bed in the corner and knew this was the right one, as I had seen it in there earlier. I hiked up the long skirt of my evening dress and was running as fast as I could when someone rushed past me almost knocking me down. I was thinking: 'Who the H*** is that!' I thought I was the only one left on the top floor. When I got to the door of my rooms, I found out who had brushed past me... It was Joseph and Louise Simone. Foregoing their own safety, they had forced their way up through the fleeing crowd to provide protection for MY children and had reached the rooms before me. They are the most sensitive and caring people and my gratitude will never end. The top floor had already been evacuated but Ray and I will never forget the Simone's for their act of concern and courage."

STEPHEN RUDD

From all appearances, photographic conventions run smoothly but behind the facade there are crises to test the resilience of those running the show. But with every crisis there is humour. Stephen Rudd MPA was in charge of running the portrait programs at a PPOC convention in Toronto and had arranged with a model agency to supply a young lady for boudoir photography by speaker Steve Palen. The model was experienced with photographers, on a one-to-one basis, and would be wearing a bikini and a negligee. But on previewing the ballroom where she was to pose, she was confounded by the size of the audience and the display of sample photographs which included many nudes. Butterflies turned to stage fright when Mr. Palen presented her with a silk negligee.The young lady fled in terror from the hotel, taking the gown with her. Without the model, Steve Rudd checked with the agency and found she had reported: "they expect me to take my clothes off in front of 200 perverts... all with cameras." Well, now there was panic. Where to get another model at such short notice. The speaker reworked his program to stall for time while Steve ran to the hotel beauty salon and asked one of the pretty operators to help out. Apprehensive, she said she had never posed before. Steve pointed out that normal sitters, going into a photographers studio, are not models. It would be up to the photographer to guide her into proper poses. She finally agreed, went through with the session and said she quite enjoyed the experience.

DOUGLAS W. BOULT

Doug Boult MPA HLM of Wellington, Ont., in charge of the commercial speakers at the above convention, was to pick up James Tampin arriving from England at the Toronto International airport at 5 PM. Due to a monster traffic snarl, Doug found by 4.30 he couldn't get near the terminal, so he parked his car in a nearby lot and walked in. The arrival lounge was jam packed with thousands of people as many flights arrived all at the same time. Mr. Tampin's flight number indicated he would be coming out 'Gate C' so Doug patiently waited there for over an hour-and-a-half... but no sign of the visitor. Then he discovered that they were letting the arrivals out 'Gate B'... but still no success. "An elderly lady," recalls Doug, "was brought out in one of the airlines wheelchairs. She just stood up and walked away with her son, leaving the wheelchair in the middle of the crowd. Everyone was tripping over it and I tried to get it taken away, but to no avail. Finally, in desperation and fatigue I sat down in it myself. Within five minutes I was knocked over with the chair landing on top of me. Nobody stopped to help and it looked like they were going to just walk all over me. So I righted myself and got back in the chair then started pushing myself around. I was almost upset a second time when a man pushed past with his luggage. I finally went to the counter to have my name announced and, in backing up, I ran over a man's foot. On looking up to apologize, I realized it was MY speaker, James Tampin; I had only seen him in a photo. 'You're Jim Tampin!' I screamed with joy and rose from the chair. Jim looked at me in stunned amazement thinking a miracle had just cured my lameness. Well, it was 8 PM when we finally left, pushing a buggy of luggage three quarters of a mile to my distant parking space... but my mission had been accomplished!"

NICKI ALBRECHT

Nicki Albrecht of Toronto, in charge of Props and Equipment, suddenly realized during the National Banquet that the rear-projected slide program had stopped. Checking backstage, she was horrified to find the operator slumped over on the floor. But it turned out he had eaten a dinner with a wine sauce to which he was allergic; sleep was the natural reaction and he did so on the floor. He was roused and the show went completed.

JOE K.R. STONE

Joe K.R. Stone CPA, of Fredericton, New Brunswick was in Toronto for a PPOC Convention. With Mike Saunders and their wives they were hosting the President's reception in the Maritime suite, prior to the Awards Banquet. "Everyone came to visit," recalls Joe, "VIP's from all the provinces as well as visiting speakers and our own delegates. All were dressed to the 'nines' in exquisite gowns or trim black tuxedos. It was quite an elegant affair, something we are not prone to push in our own home territory. With that many visitors we were fast running out of wine glasses, so my wife gathered up some of the used glasses and prepared to clean them in the little washroom off the suite. Now, my friend Mike Saunders is a bit of a character and is usually unflappable to any situation. When my wife started to clean the glasses I had Mike's wife bring him over to the washroom where I kept the door closed so nobody could see us performing our menial task. I

took one glass and got down on my knees before the toilet to make it appear as if I had been washing them all in the toilet bowl. When Mike peeked in, he did a double take, then jumped in and slammed the door behind him. 'Oh my God!' he screamed, 'Don't let anybody see you doing that.' He calmed down enough to add: 'I don't care where you wash them but DON'T let those people from UPPER CANADA see you wash them in the toilet!"

PEGGY WRIGHT

Down in the Maritimes they have fun conventions, particularly when practical jokers like Peggy Wright HLM, Joe K.R.Stone CPA and Ev Waterfield get their heads together. A number of years ago, as part of a convention, some large plastic capsules were used to enclose names in a scholarship draw. The capsules reminded the culprits of containers used for urine samples, so a plot was

hatched. They set to work collecting a supply of hotel stationery on which they drafted an official sounding letter from the management. It was indicated that there was a suspected case of dysentery in the hotel and the Department of Health required all guests to leave a urine sample at the front desk. Strict compliance was required. They then taped the letters and capsules to the doors of fellow conventioneers. Most people recognized it as a prank and chose to blame it on innocent Cliff Wright MPA who was noted for such pranks. The next day he was publicly presented with all sorts of samples, ranging in colour from 'coke-red' to 'mouthwash-green'. But at least one person was taken in. Terry Waterfield was getting a newspaper at the front desk when a 'very prominent trades-person' approached and discreetly deposited an envelope with an amber coloured vial. Some months later that trade rep was asked by Joe K.R.Stone about the state of his kidneys and it was only then, he realized he had been taken in by the prank. No-one ever did hear what the hotel thought about it.

TERRY ROBERTSON

Every convention has its problems but with the dexterity of its committee workers the programming continues without any appearances of failure. Terry Robertson MPA of Burlington, Ont., tells of a near disaster during an Ottawa convention. Speaker Linda Campagna, M. Photog Cr. was most explicit in her list of instructions regarding the equipment and layout she required for her slide-lecture. "We had everything arranged for her when she arrived, two tiers of tables, three projectors on the top level, three on the bottom, a four-track cassette player for sound with everything pulse coded and synced. While she was checking it out with her slides and tapes she leaned on a table and the leg collapsed –everything came down in a horrible CRASH! The projectors slid off in a pile, the recorder, the sync system, everything was thrown to the floor. About fifteen glass super slides were broken while Linda received bruises to her leg. We reassembled everything but found to our chagrin, that the recorder would not work. We were in a panic to find a replacement as the equipment supplier said they didn't have another one. We put out half a dozen desperate phone calls but didn't come up with anything. Things were looking bad so the committee workers put their heads together. It was Paul Pedersen of North Bay who said he once knew a chap who was a musician and that was the kind of equipment he used. It was a long shot, but he knew he now lived somewhere in Ottawa. We looked through the phone book and finally came up with his number. I phoned but he said: 'I don't have one but I do know who might have one.' He gave us a phone number and I called this next chap. You can't imagine how difficult it is to explain over the phone to a stranger who you are, what you want and why you need it so desperately. During the whole phone conversation with this fellow there was a terrible clamor in the background; he was having a party and couldn't hear half of what I said. 'Tell me again!' he would scream and so I would yell the whole story into the phone again. Finally, it dawned on him and he said, 'You know, I think I have what you want.' That was 9 PM Sunday night and Linda's program was scheduled for 8 AM the next morning. Without that machine she couldn't run her program. We struck a deal of a bottle of Vodka which Tony Fisher MPA conveniently happened to have in his room and which conveniently I relieved him of... for the sake of the convention. So the commercial program by Linda Campagna was saved by a bottle of Vodka."

PETER J. BENINGER

Peter Beninger CPA of Chelsea, Quebec was given the task to photograph fellow photographer Lyle Webb MPA SPA as they rode the ski lift to the top of Whistler Mountain in British Columbia. As delegates to the PPOC National Convention, they were heading for a barbeque supper at the remote location and it seemed the ideal time to get a breath-taking snap for the folks back home. Peter was to precede Lyle in one of the chair lifts then turn around and take the picture with a beautiful scenic background. Peter tells the story this way: "Lyle Webb handed me his newly-bought camera, one of those fancy things that has automatic focus -a real "Buck Rogers" kind of camera that takes care of all the details. I got on the lift with Nicki Albrecht and Leo Sciarrino while Lyle and his wife followed in the next chair. When I turned around to take the picture, for some reason the camera wouldn't work –but it was guaranteed to be an automatic idiot-proof camera. I handed it over to Nicki but she couldn't get it to work either, then it was Leo's turn. Nobody could get it to work. We wasted the whole trip up and were finally dropped off at the top of the mountain; of course Lyle was quite disappointed. To think that with all our efforts and so much beautiful scenery, no one had succeeded in shooting even one picture. Now with such a gathering of professional photographers, you would think we could find someone who could show us how to operate this automatic machine. We kept asking ...but to no avail. FINALLY, the mystery was resolved much to the consternation of all concerned; it was discovered that Lyle had lost the batteries out the bottom of his camera! Without batteries –no pictures... no matter how automatic and how idiot-proof it was!"

TED SMERCHANSKY

This story comes from Ted Smerchansky Hon. SPA, a twenty-five year veteran traveller for Winnipeg Photo Ltd. He's lived through many unusual experiences while on his road trips. Ted recalls flying to Philadelphia to speak at a photographers' seminar, arriving at his hotel late in the evening after a long rerouted trip from Winnipeg.

"I was lying in my bed, trying to fall asleep, when a crowd of people arrived in the room next door to start a boisterous party. I checked with the front desk but found there were no other room to move to and so finally had to phone my loud neighbours to tell them I was having a hard time falling asleep. A man answered the phone and suggested I join the party, rather than complain. But it didn't interest me, particularly when I had to be up by 7.30 AM to teach 100 photographers who had registered for the seminar. A second plea for quiet, an hour later, did not work nor did a call at 2 AM; but I must have fallen asleep out of exhaustion after that."

"When I woke up the next morning I decided to phone the room next door to find out if they really had a good time. The guy who answered was really annoyed that anyone would wake him so early in the morning."

To continue the punishment Ted felt that since the gentleman was now awake then he might be hungry. "So I ordered them an unwanted and unwelcome breakfast from the room service!" As Ted was leaving for the seminar he asked the maid to make up his room -giving the room of his neighbour to be cleaned. "I could hear the scream from the room before I even got on the elevator!"

"Well, that surely wasn't enough so I phoned the maintenance department asking to get the TV fixed and as I passed the front desk asked to have the bell hop pick up the luggage.... all in my neighbour's room.

"I had to drop back to my room later that morning and was on hand to see the noisy couple departing from their room. Not having ever seen or met, I bid them: 'Good morning!... How are you today?' Their answer was thoroughly satisfying as they unloaded their complaints: 'This is a terrible hotel. Couldn't sleep in because of all the disturbances!' I asked what possibly could have happened. So the lady went down through the list of grievances: phone calls, maid service, unwanted breakfast, bellhops, TV repairmen. 'You are the only nice person we have met at this hotel, today.' she said. With that I wished them a BETTER day and silently suggested to myself... Lest we forget!"

JOHN ABBASS

John Abbass of Sydney, Nova Scotia has a special memory of an early Maritime Convention. Kodak Canada had distributed to studio owners yellow vinyl cutouts in the shape of a footprint which they could use to attract customers into their business premises. John talked the Sydney Hotel to allow him to stick the foot prints to the tile floors leading from the front entrance, through the lobby to the convention registration desk. John assured the hotel management that he would remove them immediately after their photo event. But the glue proved to be so tactile that they never would come off, no matter what was tried. Allen Benjamin was in the hotel many years later and, although they were a bit fainter, the footprints were still there! Much to the chagrin of the hotel and to John Abbass, those prints never disappeared until they were completely worn off by the passing traffic.

GLEN GILLHAM

Glen Gillham was for years the technical representative for Ansco Canada and later under its title as GAF. He was a consistent worker behind the scenes for the photo associations, being a favorite master of ceremonies and frequent auctioneer. He had the

gift of the gab and knew how to put the spark of life into any occasion. At an OSP convention in Toronto's Royal York Hotel, Glen did his best to start the event in a lighter mood. The hotel was over crowded, with rooms at a premium, so he moved some of his furniture into one of the main elevators, creating a little sitting room. With table, chair, foot stool, rug and reading lamp, all the comforts of home, Glen completed the tableau by relaxing in the chair to read his newspaper. Each time the elevator opened at the main floor, guests were taken aback as they seemingly blundered into a private room. "It was amazing, the reactions it produced," recalls Glen. "I kept my back to the door so I wouldn't have to make eye-contact and be drawn into a conversation. They would gasp, 'OH, pardon me!' then backed away dumfounded. With a simple 'Quite alright', I'd let the doors slowly close and await the next rendezvous!"

RICHARD D. BELL

After the barbecue festivities for the 1981 PPOC National Convention at Toronto's historic Fort York, Richard Bell MPA and his entertainment committee had the task of returning equipment to his studio. A monster log for a sawing competition was loaded into Rick's car, projecting some five feet beyond his rear bumper and causing the rear end to drag precariously. His car lights decided, at that moment, to black out, so all agreed to travel in convoy to the destination. The Fort York event was a costume affair so Rick was dressed as Laura Secord. The convoy was moving along Queen Street when a motorcycle policeman pulled along side to check the darkened swayback car. Peering into the drivers window he was met with a vision of loveliness. There sat Rick in an ample bosomed print dress complete with a flowered bonnet and a wide black mustache. Rick flashed the officer a smile and remarked: "Your not going to believe this!" The policeman studied the car... the log... and then the mustached maiden. Surely no excuse could match the visual impression. The policeman roared off with a smile and a shake of his head.

MARTIN FLEWWELLING

When you are chosen to speak at a national convention you rework your program, rehearse repeatedly and check all your props to make sure that everything will run flawlessly. Martin Flewwelling MPA of Saint John, New Brunswick was to give a portraiture demonstration at the PPOC Convention in Quebec City which required live models. "We were organized to the nth degree," says Martin, "slides, props, backgrounds and lighting equipment. The models showed up an hour early for the rehearsal so that they would fully understand their parts in the demonstration. The theme of my lecture was based on how the photographer must establish rapport between himself and the sitter in order to bring forth recordable emotions. As the photographer, you must become intimate with your subject in order to create those feelings. Yet, with all our planning, with all our preparations, with all the rehearsals, we failed to anticipate one possible flaw. The two models turned out to be totally French speaking while I, in all my 'Englishness', was unable to establish any communication with them. When props or lighting fail, you override the problem. But in this case, despite gestures, leading and pushing, it was impossible to achieve my theme."

DAVID C. BROWN

Talk about bad weather tossing a curve into expectations for a trip, David Brown CPA SPA HLM of Saskatoon, Saskatchewan remembers a trip to a March convention at Kelowna, British Columbia. "I was assured that there would be no snow at that time of the year; so, I was to leave the frigid prairies behind and come prepared for some balmy BC weather. 'Don't bother to bring any skis' was the edict. It was arranged that Ed Keeling MPA SPA HLM of Calgary and I would drive through the mountains to our destination. Our 'nice drive' turned out to be a horror as a blizzard swept through the West and there was snow all over the place; Kelowna was turned into a winter wonder land. Still, the seminar brought a heavy turnout of photographers and it was impossible to squeeze into the packed hall when Doug Boult MPA HLM gave a lighting demonstration using a nude model. Several of the executive and Kodak Reps chose to participate in outdoor recreation using the golf clubs brought along by "no-snow")"Don MacGregor MPA SPA HLM and orange golf balls supplied by Kodak; the challenge was to hit a ski bell outside the hotel. In our stray shots we discovered a snowman

at the bottom of the ski run and inspiration suggested it was the perfect venue with which to pull a prank on Adrian Price SPA, the only member of the executive who had gone into the program. We decided that the snow man must go into his room. I had no trouble getting a key from the front desk then we set about carrying sections on a piece of plywood up the fire escape. We were tempted to set it up in the middle of his room but it was a brand new ski lodge so opted for the bathtub. The three tiered snow man was a monster when finally assembled and it overpowered the whole bathroom. I'm not sure if Adrian knows, to this day, who were involved and this is probably the first time he's heard the story about the creation of the Kelowna Monster. It was still melting when the convention finished and I wonder what the house staff must have thought when they came to clean the room."

RENE RUYG

Rene Ruyg MPA of Belleville, Ont., after attending a photographic class in Winona, went out to dinner for the evening with four fellow photographers, Terry, John, Frank and Susan. "After an excellent meal we sat and talked and during this period, I began to have itchy eyes, and my lower eye lids began to swell. In addition, upon closeup inspection in the restaurant's washroom I noticed large hives on my abdomen and chest. Returning to my friends I indicated I was having a mild allergic reaction to something I had eaten. We decided to go to the drug store for something for the hives."

"With Susan at the wheel, John and Terry noticed my throat and face now covered with hives. My tongue had started to swell, and I was having trouble breathing. At the drug store the pharmacist took one look at me, and told my friends to get me to the hospital without delay. Frank had her draw us a map and we were on our way to the hospital."

"During the ride I became progressively weaker, nearly passing out, but for the none too gentle prodding of Terry and John. At the hospital I was taken into the trauma room. Amid lots of drama and commotion the ER team did their thing. I regained consciousness in a few minutes, and was completely stabilized within half an hour. It took three hours before I was ready for release. The attending physician emphasized I couldn't have been any closer to death when I was brought in. And had it not been for my four friends... I would have died that night. Although I had only eaten one and a half shrimp in a shell I took an acute reaction to the iodine, commonly found in shellfish."

"So to 'the Winona Shrimp Gang', whose close attention saved my life, I dedicate this story: Terry Jarka, John McClain, Susan Wynne and Frank Robbins."

ALBERT E. TROTTER

During the Second World War, Al Trotter MPA of Chatham, Ont., was flying over Germany in a Halifax bomber, tagging along as an Observer. "We were pretty safe at 22,000 feet where the ack-ack couldn't reach us. I was busily taking pictures out of a side door that opened up and I was wearing a safety harness but not a parachute itself, because there seemed no apparent need for it. All of a sudden, the plane dropped 5000 feet in what must have been 5 seconds and I was sucked out of the aircraft... actually sucked out with  my feet dangling in the air stream. I felt like one of the Three Stooges in a crazy slapstick movie! Luckily, I had my arms wrapped around a post in the middle of the doorway and was holding on for dear life; that post seemed all that kept me from heading for terra firma. The guys, inside, dragged me back into the plane but during that terrible episode I was mesmerized by the view of Germany passing below my feet."

W. D. WALLY WEST

In his younger days, Wally West SPA HLM of Prince George, British Columbia, photographed quite a few banquet groups. "I travelled over to Nanaimo and photographed a ceremonial feast, then as usual to get a rush proof, I dropped into a friend's home to do the processing. She had some visitors and I guess all they heard when I dashed through was: 'Can I use your bathroom? I'll clean up the mess afterwards!' They all had a good laugh but, at the time, I couldn't figure out what they were laughing about. I always carried enamel trays with me to do the processing in. I developed the film and when I put it over to the hypo, the tray was empty. There was a chip out of the corner and all the chemical had drained away. So my film was ruined. I had travelled all the way from Victoria to Nanaimo for nothing. Without a picture I couldn't make any sales. But that's only one of the many things that could happen to a photographer in those rough makeshift days."

"In 1939, I photographed the Royal visit of King George and Queen Elizabeth. Associated Screen News hired me to photograph the official banquet at the Empress Hotel. I had always used flash powder to cover such banquets but this was different and the officials wouldn't allow me to use powder. So Screen News sent a whole case of big #4 flash bulbs which I had never used before. I had to design and make my own flash gun that would hold four bulbs at one time in order to get a big boost of light. Along with the bulbs came a sheet of cellophane with which I was ordered to cover the bulbs, just in case they exploded when fired, as was often the case. My partner, Art, and I set up the camera for the official head table shot and got the flash all ready with all the elastic bands holding the cellophane. Off to my right in an alcove was a radio announcer giving a live broadcast. He was describing the Royal couple and all the details of the surroundings. You could hear a pin drop in the banquet hall as no one talked and all eyes were glued to the head table. So I took the photograph and ALL the bulbs flashed... and, would you believe it, every darn one blew up! It was like a cannon shot. I had the protective cellophane in place but no-

one seems to have checked that. The Queen, who was sitting beside the Lieutenant Governor, was heard to say, 'Well, that starts things off with a bang!' Of course the announcer immediately broadcast details of the explosion to the world. President Roosevelt who was being kept informed of the tour, phoned all concerned from the States when it was reported that the King had been injured. The Eastern newspapers ran off with a wild story: 'Photographer dares to approach within five feet of the King - flashed his bulb and ruined the crab cocktail!' It just escalated out of all proportion and everybody was talking about it. I was allowed to process my film but then it was whisked away for a security check, then distributed to the pool of news media. After that I was put over to using a movie camera and not allowed to use a hand camera. I was assigned to Government House where the Queen was reviewing her Regiment. The Queen personally came to me and asked if I would please take a group photograph of her with the Regiment. In utter embarrassment I had to explain that I couldn't achieve her wish because they wouldn't allow me to have a still camera any more."

JANE SLOAN

Jane Sloan, HLM of Sidney, British Columbia recalls for us events in 1949 when she was working as a stringer for many world renowned magazines and newspapers. At the time great attention was being given to the protest actions of the Doukhobor Sons of Freedom with their burnings and bombings in the Kootenay area of British Columbia.

"The Freedomites chose to strip off their clothes as they watched the results of their arson, so there were countless opportunities for bare-buff 'news' photos. There was this one time when I was pre-sented with a great opportunity for a true 'art shot'. I noticed a long-bearded old man sitting naked on a ploughshare, looking rather sad. The soft overcast light was coming from just the right direction with the back-ground sweeping in for a beautiful art-study. Knowing he wouldn't keep that pose for long if he spotted my bulky 4x5 Speed Graphic, I hid the camera behind my back and saun-tered ever so casually into a good vantage position. As I brought my camera from its hiding place he caught me from the corner of his eye and immediately stood up and faced me. Damn! No newspaper at that time would use a 'full frontal' nude shot. So I simply lowered my camera and took off for more saleable shots. Those Doukobors, who saw all this, thought I had given up out of embarrassment, so they laughed and teased me for quite some time afterwards."

"The local B.C. Provincial Police used to give me a rough time just because I was a girl. On one of my assignments four of them picked up my little Austin with me in it and turned it cross-ways on the narrow bridge to the Doukhobor settlement. It took a lot of maneuvering to extricate the car and be on my way. Of course this gave them the big joke for the day.

On a similar assignment I had driven a reporter from Life magazine and two others, from Toronto, up to the village. While interviewing and recording the activity at one location we noticed a fire in progress about a mile away. The four of us raced back to the car and piled in for a fast getaway, necks craned and ready for the swoosh. I put the car into gear and floored it..... the motor roared but the car didn't move! That was when we spotted the cops laughing their heads off and I knew they had been up to another prank. They had propped the back end up to keep the wheels off the ground. Can't you just picture it?

DON FOLEY

Don Foley CPA, of St. Catharines, Ont., was on his way to a Kodak seminar in the Chateau Laurier in Ottawa. He was dressed in a white high-necked 'intern' shirt, white pants, white shoes and, to top it all off, Don's gray-white hair. "My wife, Marilyn, and I got on the hotel elevator and were joined by a family. A little girl, about 5 years old, looked up at me and her eyes went bright and wide. She tugged excitedly on her mother's hand and exclaimed: 'Mommy, Mommy, THERE'S JESUS!' Needless to say my wife does NOT see me quite in those terms!"

DAVID A. and MARY ELLIS

David Ellis MPA HLM of Scarborough, Ont., and wife, Mary, say that you know you are getting old when the flower girls and ring bear-ers from twenty years ago, return for their own wedding coverage and make it explicit when they call you "Sir" or "Ma'am".

M. JACKSON-SAMUELS

M. Jackson-Samuels csc, Cinematographer and Director of Photography of Toronto, Ont., is known in the industry as "Sammy". After World War 2 he apprenticed with The J. Arthur Rank Organization then immigrated to Canada in 1950. His filming has covered the danger and dust of a coal mine to the splendor of Buckingham Palace.

"I filmed 49 episodes of "The Littlest Hobo" back in '68-69 in which they used twelve look-a-like dogs to act the part of the main dog character "London". The dogs lined up for make-up each morning, as the blaze on their front chest was made to match exactly. All dogs were trained to respond only to commands in German so as not to be confused by the English speaking actors. I arrived one morning to find London sitting on my seat at the camera and peering intently through the view finder with a paw on the wheel for the pan and tilt. I was surprised by this mimicry until a voice yelled: 'Sam, I guess you're fired. He does it for dog biscuits!' "

"About 1960 I filmed a TV series at the Kleinburg Studios, near Toronto featuring an English Mountie when the RCMP were still held in awe. The actor was not very 'Mountie-ish' as after each day's shooting he would get roaring drunk. His only elegance was a flashy sports car which he drove to the studio each day. After one drunken binge he woke up lying at the side of Highway 27, semi-nude, his hands tied and his car gone. He had been mugged! He sheepishly said he had fallen asleep by the highway. A day later his car turned up at a police station., – completely polished and the missing suit neatly folded on the seat. Why would that happen? Well, can you imagine the faces of the muggers when they opened the car trunk and found a Mountie officer's uniform? They panicked and not wanting to get involved with the RCMP who ALWAYS got their man, they cleaned off their finger prints and returned everything safely.... to an English actor."

Sammy's most memorable assignment was to shoot a TV commercial at Buckingham Palace whereby Prince Philip would solicit funds for the Royal World Wild Life Fund. It was quite something for any of the Royal Family to appeal for funds on television. "I got this call on a Friday afternoon requesting me to be in London, with all my camera equipment, –fully cleared through customs and ready to shoot Monday morning. To a news-reeler, short notice is not strange, but for a working cameraman and director of photography to undertake a TV commercial at such short notice, is unthinkable. There are all sorts of bits and bobs to line up. I did accept the assignment and immediately started a phone search for a reliable crew who could dress well and not be stressed out by the importance of the location. Then I called a film service in Britain for the lights as they work, over there, with 240 volts at 50 cycles. That meant my camera had to be battery operated. I took two cameras and two of everything – God forbid something should go wrong. With everything assembled it was sent out to the airport, we only had time for a quick confab. Then Sunday evening we were off on our flight to London, arriving

Monday morning and were met with a giant Daimler car. Working for His Royal Highness did wonders as we, and all the equipment, were wisked through customs without challenge and were at the gates of Buckingham Palace in half an hour."

"First to meet us was the Prince's equerry who enquired which of the 300 rooms we would like to shoot in. Too time consuming to inspect them, I had a flash of inspiration and opted for the Queen's study where she gives her Christmas message. I figured that if they shoot there for British television, they must have lots of electricity. Ha Ha, was I wrong! Every Christmas a 30 man crew from the BBC bring in their own generator and miles of cable – that's BBC style. Our little crew of 3 were led to a beautiful15 x 15 room with a fireplace at one end and the Queen's desk, with a background of paintings, on the other side. I opted for the desk as it was by a large window that flooded the area with soft daylight. We needed only to fill in from the other side. Simple lighting that needed only 30 minutes to set up and we would be ready."

"Well, that wasn't to be, because the Prince arrived and dismissed our location as 'too starchy'. He suggested doing it by the fireplace in an arm chair. The director wasn't about to argue with him, so we moved everything over to the fireplace. Unfortunately we lost our window light and now needed an artificial key light. That meant adding a big light to supplement the small soft lights that we had set up. Not wanting to blow a Royal fuse, I asked the head electrician how many amps I could draw from an outlet and was floored with: 'I'm very sorry sir, here at the Palace we only work in volts!... With that I knew I had to find another outlet so picked up a 50 foot cable and went out to the corridor figuring that 10 or 12 feet down the way, another room must hopefully be on a different fuse. I pushed a door open and to my horror, there at breakfast was Her Majesty the Queen. A maid stood by with eyes bulging as I burst through the door. I was at a complete loss for words, offering only the limp wire in my hands as an excuse and implying we were making a movie. With that I slammed the door shut and finally found an outlet to successfully finish the shoot. But I'll always remember that job for the image of the Queen sitting at her breakfast with a large box of Kellogg cornflakes on the side. It shows that the Queen is really human, and eats the same food as everybody else!"

HILDA (ONIONS) GEE

Hilda (Onions) Gee MPA of Calgary, Alberta, has a charming tale of a bride she photographed last summer. The young lady had grown up on a ranch and wanted to be photographed with her favourite horse in her bridal attire. The photo session took place

after the couple returned from their honeymoon. "I wanted the mountains in the background," says Hilda, "so the location was chosen up in the hills near the ranch. A sister-in-law rode up with the horses, while I chauffeured the bridal couple with the clothes and my equipment in a four wheel drive.

It was only when they started dressing for the shoot that the bride realized she had forgotten her strapless bra; so I produced a large roll of packing tape and a pair of scissors. There, under God's blue sky, the bride held up her ample breasts, while her sister-in-law and I taped them into place. You can imagine the fun and laughter. After the photo session as the bride slipped out of her dress, the groom was more than willing to playfully assist in removing the tape. While the bride was at the tail gate of the car, I got one of my best shots. It showed the bride dressed only in white heels, panties, her bridal veil and a brilliant smile. It was a fun shot, and everyone enjoyed the session."

NICHOLAS DELIGEORGY

Nicholas Deligeorgy MPA of Toronto is a master of ideas which he has taught to fellow photographers. He carries corsage-pins with which to secure the bride's dress when shooting in a park on a windy day. He also carries after-shave lotion to apply to his hands before adjusting the brides veil. Thus, the bride is surrounded by a pleasant fragrance while he works closely with her. Nick carries a veritable tool kit in his car which includes brush, comb, hair spray and extra nylons for the women as well as all sorts of gadgets, spray cans and cords for his flash equipment. When shooting a wedding on a hot day this conscientious photographer brings along a cooler containing fruit drinks and sandwiches for the benefit of the wedding party whose energies may be flagging during the long shooting session. For total preparedness, Nick travels with a change of clothing, deodorant and wash-packs.

Nick recalls the story of a photographer who was shooting a wedding in one of Toronto's favourite parks that has a tiny bridge stretching over a lily pond. The photographer's Hasselblad camera was knocked into the pond and he immediately jumped in to retrieve it. The camera was covered in mud and water was draining out of every crevice. The photographer rushed to a nearby house and asked the people to wrap his camera in a plastic bag and put it in their freezer. Then he dashed back to his wedding and completed the photography with a backup camera. On Monday he returned to the house, picked up his frozen camera and headed off to the repair center. With the water frozen, nothing had a chance to rust, expand or deteriorate. The camera was thawed, dried and given minor touchups and it was as good as new.

PATTI LIVINGSTON

When it comes to energy, ambition and adventure, Patti Livingston MPA of Saint John, New Brunswick takes a back seat to no one. With the variety of assignments she covers each year – press coverage, environmental portraits, weddings, Royal tours, football games and VIP personalities, she is on her toes all the time.

Being a female photographer has disadvantages, but it makes Patti into a dynamo when thrown into the "press scrum" to capture a photo of some visiting VIP or politician. Recalls Patti, "When photographing Royalty it is like war. You have to battle the British press whenever they show up as they have no courtesy at all. On one tour I was thrown onto the cobblestone street, denting a lens and cutting my elbow which needed several stitches. But when you are hyped to get that perfect shot and have to rush back to the office, 100 miles away, to meet a deadline then what's a little blood? I won the PPOC Press Category with my shot of Queen Elizabeth grabbing for her wind-tugged hat. She had a fabulous expression on her face."

When Pope John toured the Maritimes, Patti was caught up in the crowd for his visit to the Moncton Cathedral. "I came with five cameras and with a variety of lenses, including a 500-1000 zoom in case I might be kept too far back to get close-ups. As it turned out, I couldn't have been closer and my editor said that, on TV, it looked like I was going to climb on the Pope's back. I actually reached out and touched him, which was a beautiful spiritual experience."

Patti will always remember that assignment for another reason. "I had brought a portable darkroom with me to make prints on the spot, but since I was on a high I decided to return to the studio. So I grabbed up the processor machine and carried it down a flight of stairs to my car. It is a great way to come down to reality when you find that the activator solutions are running down the front of your pants... and me with nothing to change into... and with a distance to drive. But that assignment was a 100 percent success."

Patti also has fond memories from many of her wedding assignments. "I was shooting a wedding with a very cooperative couple. The setting was almost too elaborate with a covered bridge spanning a river and in the distance a decorated yacht and a lighthouse. The couple had their yacht anchored away from shore to protect it from the rocks. They enacted their departure for me by hopping into a dinghy and rowing out to the boat while I shot from the shore. Following their progress through the camera viewfinder I noticed that the "JUST MARRIED" sign on the back of their boat was gradually sinking... lower and lower into the water. The groom had thrown out a white rag that was in the bottom of the boat, but unknown to him it was used to plug a leak. They realized their dilemma and started bailing frantically. With the situation getting worse they headed back to shore. Thank goodness I always carry a hair dryer in my truck; so we made good use of it making the bride and groom as good as new! After that we chose to go up on a cliff overlooking the yacht and there took their special photo. The little red row boat was forgotten."

"One of my wedding couples hired a limo for the big day but things seemed to get off on a wrong footing. The limo never appeared at the home so she was late arriving at the church. She was in a panic –her face was as red as her bouquet of roses. After the ceremony the driver was waiting outside the church and was most apologetic. I picked out a beautiful location by the waters edge and had the car maneuvered into the setting. The bride and groom were in a romantic pose with their reflection in the water. With the light fading I quickly snapped this memory and we made ready to depart. Suddenly rocks, mud and water started flying in all directions... it was our buddy, the limo driver, as he got the car stuck deeper and deeper into the sand and mud. The sparkling white limo gradually changed to dingy brown. Needless to say, the bride quite lost her love for big impressive cars!"

"On another occasion we had reached the end of what was a fairytale wedding. The bride had created an eye-dazzling setting with a myriad of candles around her wedding cake. She beckoned to the groom to join her in cutting the cake, but then suddenly I saw her vigorously beating her arm with her hand. In horror I saw that her sleeve was going up in flames; being the closest, I jumped to her assistance and smothered the fire. Luckily the giant puffed sleeves saved the bride from being badly burned. I then pinned the remains of the sleeve so that the damage could not show. Fighting back tears she continued to pose for our final shots. Outside there suddenly appeared a gorgeous double rainbow which restored the sparkle needed to complete the wedding. So things turned out well after all."

"After a working-holiday overseas, I staged an exhibition of photographs called "STEP INTO IRELAND". It went so well with 500 people showing up for the opening day, I knew I had to create either a book out of the pictures or a calendar. There were wonderful memories from my bus tour so I opted to relate those tales in a book, called 'ABSOLUTELY IRISH!'. To reach one of Ireland's highest waterfalls, our bus had to follow a narrow country lane and was forced into a ditch when trying to pass a car coming the other way. Not to be deprived of our quest, we trekked the long four miles to the falls despite rain and heavy mist. It was well worth the effort. While away, the bus was extricated by a farmer with his tractor. When I spotted two donkeys in a field, the bus obligingly stopped on my request. I set off after them, but every time I got near they moved away. My frustration was at a pitch with the tour director honking the horn to get me back. In despair I gave up and started running back. But I heard a strange noise behind me, it was the donkeys chasing me! I stopped... they stopped... I got the picture... they're in the book!"

On the evening of August 27, 1991, Patti was on the stage of the Ottawa Congress Centre to receive her PPOC Master's Award and Gold Bar, despite the fact that the previous night she had been confined to hospital with a severe attack of asthma. Patti was determined not to miss the highlight of her career which was to have her mother see her presented with the award. "My mother has been the biggest fan and greatest supporter in advancing my career. She has always been a positive thinker. So in no way was I going to miss that event."

With a zest for life, Patti Livingston is a person who pursues her career at full speed. Whether taking press and wedding photos in New Brunswick or travel photos in Ireland or Europe, she has a talent and flair for the work she pursues.

LISA JONES

Lisa Jones of Aurora, Ont., remembers when she was assisting at a Jewish wedding reception. The wedding party was dancing the Hora, with the bride and groom raised high on two chairs. With the bouncing and jostling, the chairs separated at the middle and the bride suddenly slipped down between them. The only problem, the dress was so stiff it stayed up with the chairs –while the bride slipped down and was left dangling in her underwear.

STEPHEN RUDD

Stephen Rudd MPA of Toronto, Ont., must lead all photographers in collecting awards for his photography. He's been honoured three times as Ontario's Professional Photographer of the Year while adding other awards such as The Kodak Gallery Award, International Day Photographer and International Wedding Photographer of the Year. He's in demand on the international speaking circuit as one of Canada's leading photographers.

Stephen's experiences over the past decade provide many interesting stories. "We arrived at one wedding reception," he recalls, "and I noticed that the cake was leaning to one side just a tiny bit. The bride wanted the receiving line taken care of first but I jokingly asked, 'Would you cut the cake, first, before it falls over!' She complied with my request and no sooner had we finished than this beautiful four-tier-creation toppled right onto the floor... PLOP! It had a cream filling and became one big gooey blob. They had to move the table away to clean up the mess then replace the cake with a cardboard replica. I took a picture of the 'blob' to prove to the caterers that it hadn't been eaten."

"One of my bridegrooms was determined to have the best of everything. He must have spent $80 thousand on the wedding with over 500 guests. He ordered a black antique limo for the bride and himself, a limo for the parents, one for the guys and another for all the girls. He went so far as to have a special bouquet just for the time I was photographing the bride at her home. The bouquet for the church was protected in a cooler to offset the hot summer weather so that it would be in perfect shape by the time we got to the park pictures. He chose St. Michael's Cathedral for its prestigious history and setting. The aisle looks like its a quarter of a mile long. They have a buzzer system between the front and back of the church to keep everyone in touch. I went around to the back to do some photography of the groom then positioned myself to record the girls as they came down the aisle. Everyone was in place and the music commenced as the first bridesmaid made her appearance. Half way down this long aisle, the procession came to a sudden halt and didn't move for some five minutes. Seconds can seem like hours at a time like that – the groom even looked round, but there was no sign of his bride.

The music continued to ring out 'Here comes the Bride' but no-one was moving. So, I skipped out to see what was wrong. There, in the back of the Rolls Royce, was the bride... out stone cold! Each time she struggled to regain her feet she swooned again. It looked like we would have to carry her down the aisle. She had been excited about getting married and hadn't eaten for two days. Then, just before leaving for the church, she had a couple glasses of champagne to celebrate with the girls, – it hit her like a ton of bricks. The more agitated she got, the worse she felt. We had to convince her, 'The wedding won't proceed without you, so lay back and relax. When you feel better that's when the wedding will start. Right?' To give her food at that point would have made her sick. About half an hour later, she finally got it all together and down the aisle she went. And you can believe the groom had the most delighted look on his face. He was sure she had taken off! The wedding ran beautifully after that."

"A Rosedale client insisted that his daughter's wedding was going to be the best and the most elegant. No hotel could handle the number of people invited, so a large marquee tent was set up on his estate. The reception was catered by the best chefs, with the finest china, with wines and champagnes... the best of everything! The wedding ceremony was held beside the swimming pool where everything was elegance and decorum. Following the ceremonies and the dinner there was a garden party. By that time, the groom had changed to a morning suit with top hat. It became apparent that he was not of the same class structure and had a different set of values. One of his buddies bet that he could get the groom to jump in the pool for $200. Everyone, particularly the bride and her father were protesting, 'No way! Not on his wedding day and in a full tuxedo.' But his buddy was sure the groom would do it, if dared. Well sure enough... POW! He takes a beautiful dive into the pool with his full wedding regalia. His brother, the Best Man, said, 'If you can do it, then I can do it too!... KABOOM! He's in too! Then, they went after the bride's father. He's so straight laced you wouldn't believe it. And KAPLASH... he's in the pool! They had everyone in stitches and they really didn't want to get out. An hour later the wedding couple were ready to leave and, to be unique, a rickshaw was on hand to carry them away. There was the groom in his soaking wet hat, sitting with his wife in the back of this rickshaw. For a final toast to the couple, they started popping Dom Perierre champagne, and that's where the bride's father turned the tables. Figuring the groom didn't need anything to drink, he invited everyone to pour the champagne on the groom... which they did. It was a real social event! Can you imagine the consternation when Freeman's got those tuxedos back and they were shrunk three sizes too small?"

"I was photographing this tall elegant bride, six feet tall at least, and was confounded to find the groom was only five foot seven. All day, I had to work around the problem to minimize the height difference, having her sit while he stood in many of the photos. Jokes flew all day about who would wear the pants in the family. At the end of the reception, I normally finish with a photo of the groom whisking the bride up in his arms to carry her off. So I said to him, 'Come on, lift the bride up in your arms.'... 'Are you crazy?' he replied. At that the bride picked the groom up and it looked like she was holding a Charlie McCarthy doll. The bride said, 'Relax! I can hold you for hours!' Then she whisked HIM over the threshold and away to the car."

Stephen is a certified underwater diver, using his photographic skills on trips to the Gulf of Mexico. "Felix, my instructor, took me out for some night time diving to hunt for lobster. They use Hawaiian slings with which to spear the fish and wear heavy gloves to pick them up. It was spooky for me, jumping overboard in the dark, but I had my own light and pretty soon I wandered off on my own. Low and behold, I saw this monster lobster that was bigger than anything the others were catching. So I tried to grab it but it was scooting all over the place. You are supposed to grab the lobster from the backside so that its tail can't work and thus has no propulsion. I didn't have a spear or glove but I wasn't going to let this one get away. I grabbed him and... BOOM... he's jerking me

all over the place... up this way... then down again. Luckily a lobster can only do this for 30 seconds so I held on and finally got it over to the boat. Everyone was astounded at its fantastic size. But then the PAIN set in. In that watery struggle the lobster had dragged me through a bed of black sea urchins which are a mass of prickles, like porcupine quills. I had them sticking out of my

knees, feet, arms and hands. The poison was agonizing and I spent the next day soaking in hot water and painfully extracting the barbs. Left in, they would have caused much damage. The lobster was great, but I don't think it was worth the pain."

DOUGLAS A. PAISLEY

Douglas Paisley MPA of Sarnia, Ont., has a long list of honours for years of service devoted to the Canadian and American photographic associations.

This first story is from Doug's early career. "I was sent out to shoot progress photographs of a large industrial plant that was under construction," recalls Doug. "In those days we used an 8X10 camera with a wide angle lens. Each month I had to tote a heavy case with camera and holders, plus a tripod up to the top of a steel tank to get the overall views. The ladder

was surrounded by big safety hoops so it was like climbing up through a tunnel with all that gear. But once on top of the tank, there was no safety device of any kind. The roof curved in a slope to the edge then dropped straight down to the ground. On this particular day, it was exceptionally cold and the top of the tank was coated with a film of ice. It was quite a struggle to haul the equipment up and get everything ready for pictures. With fingers numbed, I took off the lens cap and accidentally dropped it. With anguish I watched it slowly slide down the icy surface to rest about four feet from the edge of the roof. In those early days, the lens cap was used as the shutter and here I was just starting the assignment. If I lost that cap there was no way of replacing it, and I would sure-

ly lose my job if I didn't complete the assignment. It called for some hard thinking and plenty of desperation. I sat down on the cold tank, then with my hands and the seat of my pants, eased down towards the edge of the tank. The cap was caught on a strip of ice. I was taking my life in my hands, as the nearer I got, the greater was the slope of the roof; the chances of slipping increased with every move forward. Fear gripped me but with determined care and stealth I eventually gained the precious cap. At that spot the roof seemed to round off steeply with a 45 foot drop to the ground. Now, I had the problem of climbing back up. When I made my first move up, my hands slipped and I got nowhere. I couldn't get any traction, and at that location, any wrong move might send me hurtling over the edge. I now feared to make any move at all! After sitting for some minutes trying to work out a solution, I must have melted the ice where I was sitting –just enough to let me move up a few inches. That was the answer to my dilemma! So it became an agonizing sequence of 'melt and move'... 'melt and move'... until I had gained the safety at the top. I survived to tell the story, but I often think how photographers jeopardize their lives to obstinately complete their assignments."

"One day, my insurance agent dropped into our portrait studio to sell a new type of policy. Since, as he described, portrait photographers had a safer way of life, I was to be offered a better policy with lower premiums. I looked at the policy and thought: 'Can this be true?' That very morning I had climbed forty feet up a ship's mast to get a photograph looking down over the deck. With sixty pounds of equipment, I had to struggle up the mast steps which are little rings that you stick your feet into. Then, in the afternoon, I had an assignment down a manhole in the road, where I walked some 400 feet through a tunnel away from the river. We were inside a large sewer which was roughly five feet in diameter. In the darkness we trudged along until we came to a wall of bricks that had been slapped up to seal off the tunnel. Braced against this wall was a heavy timber which was secured in place by a few wooden stakes. I asked the engineer what was behind the wall as I noticed a lot of wetness on the floor. He said there was a solid wall of water behind it. He explained that when their work was complete, they would tie a rope around the timber and from the safety of the manhole, would jerk out the brace. The wall would collapse and send everything dashing towards the river. Realizing that this flimsy stick of wood was the only thing holding up that wall, I visualized myself being swept through the sewers by an avalanche of water. The 400 feet back to the manhole seemed too far away... we couldn't even see the light that far. So I was awfully glad when I finished the assignment and climbed back into the open air again. Now, with the insurance agent, I was thinking if he had been with me for this one day, he would surely have doubled my insurance, instead of offering a reduced premium!"

"Back in 1947 I worked for a studio where we had to shoot, sometimes, fourteen wedding groups on a Saturday. In those days we would arrange a dozen people or more into one photo and shoot with an old 8 x10 Century view camera. On this particular warm summer day I was busy under the focusing cloth, checking the image on the ground glass, when I saw the bride suddenly fall backwards. I immediately came out and found the bride out cold on the floor. The rest of the bridal party was intently watching me, and were unaware that the bride had fainted; nobody had seen anything. To the surprise of the groom, I gathered the young lady up in my arms and carried her out of the studio for some fresh air. Everyone stood around in shock!"

"Once a week we travelled to small towns in our area to photograph babies in their own homes. We took along a small table to set the baby on, and always cautioned the mother to sit close by, keeping her hands off the table but to be ready to grab the child if anything happened. Again, I had my head under the focussing cloth and saw the baby tip right off the back of the table. I jumped out to find the mother sitting there, intently watching me. Then she heard the squalls, as the baby let us know he wasn't happy. Luckily my soft drapery had cushioned his fall. There are days when falling backwards is strictly between the photographer and his subject, as no one else seems to notice."

"I was photographing a wedding, starting with the usual family groupings at the home. When these were completed, the father left for the church taking the mother and the bridesmaids, while I completed some single portraits of the bride. I asked how she was getting to the church and she suddenly realized that her father had left without her. That was when I became a chauffeur and arrived with the bride to find the father waiting at the curbside, anxiously checking his watch. He still didn't realize that HE was supposed to drive the bride to the church. I reverted to my task as photographer and carried on with the wedding."

"What started as a child portrait took a sudden twist to my surprise. I met two ladies with a child in the lounge of the studio and after chatting for a while moved to the camera room. I put the child on the platform then turned to the younger woman and suggested that the mother sit on one side while the grandmother should sit on the other side. To my horror, the older woman whom I had called grandmother angrily told me that SHE was the mother while the younger woman was just a family friend. Thank goodness the child was friendly!"

JOHN AND GAYLE KINDURYS

John and Gayle Kindurys have a studio in Simcoe, Ont., but make use of the parks in the area for environmental portraits of their wedding parties. While waiting for the arrival of a wedding group, John decided to light up a cigarette. But no sooner had he done so, than the bride arrived with all the others. John looked around for a place to dispose of his cigarette. Stubbing it out, he tossed the butt in a niche of a tree behind him, then turned his attention to the wedding party. Halfway through the shoot, the bride gave a startled yelp, "The tree is on fire!" Sure enough, smoke and flames were belching out of the tree hole. The shooting session quickly ended as wedding members scampered in all directions for water from the nearby houses. Apparently the still-live cigarette had fallen into dry leaves inside the tree, then smoldered into a blaze. That was a hot shooting session to say the least!

DIANE and BRIAN HALLIDAY

This is the favourite story that Diane Halliday tells about her husband, Brian. They run a family business in Mississauga, Ont., and when photographing weddings, both attend in order to make posing and shooting easier. They were covering a wedding and were midway through the reception, when Brian got an urgent call from nature. So he dropped his equipment in a corner and sped off for the nearest washroom. Of course, it was just at that moment the bride needed some special photographs taken and Diane searched high and low for half an hour, but could offer no solution for the disappearance of her husband.

Meanwhile, Brian had taken to the tranquil privacy of one of the cubicles and was safely seated when, to his horror, he heard the voices of two women entering the washroom. In his haste, he had mistakenly chosen the ladies washroom. What to do? Make a quick exit or wait it out? Well, fate has a way of playing games at the most inopportune time and for Brian that was his worst moment. The dance-band took a break just then, and as usual, all the women in the hall headed for the washroom. Brian's life suddenly turned into a siege of terror as the flood of women filled the washroom and grabbed every available cubicle. To avoid detection Brian crouched up on the seat, hoping to sweat out the female intrusion. He just could not face the embarrassment of forcing his way through THAT crowd. As the needs of the ladies became urgent some women checked under the door, they rattled the handle incessantly and even tried forcing the door. With each desperate assault Brian's future looked grimmer; the longer he stayed, the worse would be the pain when discovered. He could only wait, and as each impatient gal banged on the door, his nerves shot again to a fever pitch. Well, after a torturous half hour, Brian saw the room was finally clear and quickly dashed to freedom. Brian has a final comment on the whole affair though: "Some of you gals," he says, "ain't no ladies!"

VALERIE and MERLE SOMERVILLE

Valerie and Merle Somerville MPA of Vancouver, British Columbia, illustrate how a rare snow fall on the west coast of Canada can upset the whole community. Recalls Valerie, "We had a wedding in February when usually it is very nice weather in Vancouver. But this particular day brought a heavy snow fall and it turned our life into a disaster. Most roads were closed and people just weren't going to work. Despite that we still had a wedding to do, so I went along to help Merle. The bride asked us to shoot prebridal portraits at her home in the afternoon, and to do the formal pictures there at night. It was an elegant home with settings absolutely ideal for pictures. Merle set up extra strobe lighting to be prepared for the evening pictures, then we headed off to the church. Everyone was soaking wet and the bridesmaids were slipping on the ice at the entrance to the church. Some people never arrived even though the minister delayed the services, hoping to pull everything together. It just seemed to be one problem after another making it a totally miserable day."

"After the ceremonies were complete, we all dashed for the house to squeeze in the formal group shots, in the time that remained before the reception. As we pulled up to the house, the electric doors on the garage wouldn't work. That should have given us a hint as we then found all the electric power was cut off. Nobody had a working flashlight, so they scrounged up three candles with which to find our way around in the house. The candles dwindled as guests ran off with one to the washrooms while the groom's mother used another to entertain her new inlaws in the kitchen. The lack of electric power ended Merle's use of the big strobes, so he resorted to his portable flash unit to make his group photographs. But it was so dark he couldn't focus; so I ended up holding the one remaining candle in front of the bride and groom so that Merle could get the focus. Then I went down the ranks to check that everyone was in position and their clothing was in place. As I moved out of the way Merle yelled into the darkness,

'Is everybody smiling?' He couldn't see if they were blinking or not and just hoped for the best. We went through that charade for half an hour then packed up and headed for the reception. Thank goodness they had electrical power there. When the proofs came back from the lab they were excellent with no blinks and everyone was quite relaxed despite their ordeal in the dark."

MARK and CONNIE ROBINSON

Mark Robinson of Palmerston, Ont., recalls a busy Saturday when his studio had three weddings booked for the same afternoon. "While one photographer worked in the studio," says Mark, "my wife, Connie, teamed up with another photographer and I, with an assistant, covered the third wedding. When the day was over, we all landed back at the studio at the same time to unload film. Asking if everything had gone OK, the studio photographer explained that he had endured a terrible experience. While changing film, someone bumped his arm and the roll of exposed film fell to the floor. Before his eyes in painfully slow motion, it unrolled right down

to the very spool. He had to reshoot all his pictures! The photographer accompanying Connie had not fully charged his flash battery, with the result it took forever to build up a charge for each flash picture. Connie was annoyed and embarrassed. I listened to their tales of woe, chuckling with sympathy, and said proudly that not a thing had gone wrong with me. I turned away to unload my camera smug with confidence. That was when everyone burst into hysterical laughter. The joke was on me, as they pointed out I had ripped the back seam of my pants, from the crotch right up to the belt. I visualized how I must have looked, standing up on the church pews to take pictures with all the guests peering at my backside. So much for MY problem free day!"

GURJIT PROOTHEE

Gurjit Proothee of Mississauga Ont., remembers photographing an East Indian wedding where the ceremony requires the couple to walk around the Holy Book, at which point they are officially married. "Everyone was sitting on the floor of the temple and it was exceptionally crowded. There was a small table in a corner where they burn the incense, so I moved it away to give me the best angle to shoot. I got the critical 'walking shots' and realized that everybody was staring at me. I couldn't figure out what I had done wrong... there were so many eyes on me. Well, finally

someone suggested I wipe my face off. As it turned out, when I lifted the table the bottom was covered with soot. Then I apparently wiped my face and it became smeared with jet black soot! I was so embarrassed I must have looked like one of the singers from KISS!"

Gurjit arrived at a bride's home to shoot the pre-church photographs. "I set up my equipment and was ready to shoot when I realized that I did not know the name of my bride! A little boy walked into the room and I reasoned... Great! I'm saved. I will get the information out of him. I coyly asked, 'Who is getting married today?' Proudly he answered, 'MY AUNTIE'. I tried again, 'What do you call your Auntie?' 'JUST AUNTIE,' replied the child and skipped out the door before I could make any headway. At that point I rushed to the car to find my assignment sheet. It's amazing how smoothly conversation goes when you have a simple thing like the name of the bride!"

JOHN E. MITCHELL

John Mitchell MPA of Cambridge, Ont., laments, "You get one wedding a year that's like a wedding from hell; nothing seems to go right. A week before the wedding, the bride phoned to tell me

her parents had argued with the groom's parents, so there would be a change in the location for getting dressed. When I arrived at the groom's home, he wasn't even there and we wasted 45 minutes before starting the photography. Everything seemed to go wrong; I finally got to the bride's house and while bending over to reload film into my camera, I tore the ass out of my pants. It ripped open from stem to gudgeon. The rest of the day was a complete embarrassment for me, trying to remember never to bend over and to keep my coat tail tucked down at all times. Every time I looked around, the video camera was ZOOMING in on my rear-end. I've worked through some pretty tight situations, but that was the epitome of all problems during a wedding."

John was assigned to take publicity photographs of a tiger which was to appear at a shopping malls. "The client wanted pictures of the cat as if it was out in the wild. So we chose a setting in the back lot of a local farm. It was marshy and the cat was enjoying walking through the tall grass. I was busily shooting with a 150mm on my Hasselbald, slithering in the mud and trying my darndest to keep up to him. The cat eventually climbed up on a mound of earth and it gave me the opportunity to get some great shots from a low angle. The image was so large and clear on the viewing screen that it looked like a television shot, just before the tiger attacks its prey. All of a sudden there was this blur, and I instantly looked from the camera just in time to see the tiger leaping towards me! He caught me around the legs and in an instant had me down on the ground with my knee clamped in his jaws. I thought I was finished.... I was a goner for sure... I froze! The trainer threw himself on the cat and finally freed me. But the worst part came later. I was so shocked when I saw the tiger leaping through the air at me, I tripped the camera shutter.... alas, the picture was out of focus!"

Photographers do have a sense of humour, which comes to the fore with its own photographic twist. John recalls when he worked for the local police force in the Identification Branch. "When one of our all-male technicians was to be replaced by a female, we decided to make sure she was thoroughly initiated (welcomed) into the department. In the finger print room, we used a slimy green soap to remove the ink after taking finger prints. I got a great idea of putting this slime into a film box, and then chilling it in the refrigerator to turn it into a gel. When the change-of-shift came I put the box in the darkroom, and told the new recruit to process the mug shots for the day which were in the box. In the dark she opened it up, reached in for the film and got a handful of very cold slime. We heard this god-aweful scream from the darkroom.... but nothing else seemed to happen. Our young lady was in quite a dilemma. She knew it couldn't be film, but still couldn't take the chance to turn on the lights. She must have stood in the dark for ten minutes before finally venturing to turn on the light. Well, the next day my name was mud as the detectives had sleuthed out the mystery. They complimented our young lady for her excellent screaming ability!"

MICHAEL GUILBAULT

Mike Guilbault of Barrie, Ont., had a request for prebridal portraits with the couple dressed in their wedding outfits while sitting in a ski lift. They both were avid skiers and worked at a local winter resort; however, the couple chose to shoot the picture in the middle of August. Conveniently, they arranged to have a fork lift on hand with a platform to raise them up into the chair. For the added touch they brought along their skis and strapped them on for the photo. "I started shooting pictures but found it difficult to move them about in the ski chair and compose the billowing dress with the lengthy skiis. The picture just wasn't working at all. I wanted a better angle and finally found this one spot that was perfect. The sun was just right and it looked excellent, but from my particular angle I could hardly see any of the skis. I was about 50 feet away so I yelled, 'Heather... lift up your tips!' At this she immediately sat up straight and thrust forward her chest. Her fiance just shook his head and as sweet as possible said, 'TIPS, darling, not your TITS!' The guy driving the fork lift broke up with laughter and was rolling on the ground, but the bride-to-be took it all in good sport."

WILSON and MARGARET ROBBINS

Wilson and Margaret Robbins of Hamilton, Ont., were commissioned to photograph a wedding in Toronto with the reception held at the Royal York Hotel. They decided to make a "dry run" the day before the wedding, in order to check the location of the church and see the layout of the hotel reception area. "At the hotel," says Margaret, "we parked at level H10 in the underground area and visited the Ontario Room where the reception was to be held. Satisfied that we had everything under control, we took the elevator back to parking level H10 –but our car wasn't there! That was not funny as we had left all our camera gear in it. Besides, we needed to get back to Hamilton and of course return to Toronto the next day for the wedding. Finally, a kind gentleman explained that there are three types of parking at the Royal York: one for the boutique owners, one for monthly parking and one for casual day parking. We had to go up to a different level for 'casual parking'. I suggested that we climb up the one flight of stairs, but that was a big mistake! On reaching our floor we found the door was locked. On reaching the next level, also, the door was locked, and for every floor thereafter it was the same until we reached the very top of the building. There we gratefully found an unlocked door marked 'maintenance'. We surprised a number of workers as we paraded through their office to the elevators. Well, we finally got to the proper level and thankfully found our car. Next day everything went without incident. Thank goodness for a 'dry run!'"

SID CALZAVARA

Sid Calzavara of Woodbridge, Ont., arrived at a bride's home to be told there was a delay because the bride's dress was "broken". It seems that the zipper was stuck and just would not close. The dressmaker arrived in a flurry, wrapped the dress in a bed sheet and dashed away to make the repairs. "To pass the time, I was asked to go up and talk with the bride to rework our schedule of pictures. When I entered the bedroom, I was quite surprised to find her twisted round and round in the drapes, which were still hooked to the curtain rod. In this makeshift covering she carried on our conversation!"

DOUGLAS WILKINS

Have you heard about the story from Doug Wilkins CPA of Hamilton, Ontario? The wedding guests were assembled at the church, the groom waited patiently in the vestry but after a full hour the bride still had not arrived. "We all wondered if she had changed her mind. The minister was quite agitated because of the impending arrival of his next wedding. I took off for the bride's home to seek the answer. There the bride still did not have her dress on, in fact the dress was not even ready for her to wear! Apparently her mother had made all the wedding dresses. The bridesmaid's dresses, being created first, had consumed all the time and as I arrived she was frantically cutting and stitching the bridal gown. I warned them to leave immediately or lose out on the wedding completely. Well, the bride did make her trip down the aisle, but ONLY by pinning the pieces onto her to achieve the final result. Everyone came through the episode quite well, except the Best Man... he fainted from the long wait!"

ELISABETH MARTENS

Elisabeth Martens of Saskatoon, Saskatchewan, remembers a wedding assignment where the mother of the bride had taken on the task of making the dresses for the three bridesmaids. "On the day of the wedding she hadn't finished the dresses and was STILL sewing them in the building next to the church at the very hour set for the ceremony to begin. The wedding commenced a good hour late, while the mother assembled and stitched the garments, then fitted them onto the bridesmaids. Incredibly, the bride maintained her composure through the whole crisis while the guests waited ever so patiently. The mother was all cheery when it was over, and remarked that she wasn't stressed out by it at all. But I'm sure the bride wouldn't want to relive that again!"

DOROTHY and DOUGLAS TAYLOR

In the wedding game the photographer must be prepared to meet every type of situation. Dorothy and Doug Taylor of Guelph, Ont., proved their dedication when they arrived at a bride's home for the prebridal portraits and were informed that the bride was still in the bath tub. With only half an hour until wedding time, the maid of honour was still dressing and the bride's father who spoke no English just sat in the living room patiently waiting... never speaking, never moving! Finally, the bride emerged from her bath, hair dripping wet; she also spoke no English. Dorothy realized her shooting time had vanished, so offered to help dress the bride. She got more than she bargained for, as all the clothes were still in their boxes. The two Taylors set to work unpacking and removing labels from the garments, sorting out shoes and even ironing the gown. When finally ready, Doug asked how everyone was getting to the church; but no one had thought to arrange transportation. So, you guessed it, Dorothy and Doug drove the wedding party to the church. The bridegroom, at least, spoke English and everything thereafter went smoothly so that the Taylor's could finally complete their wedding coverage.

STEPHEN and ROSA GAZAREK

Stephen and Rosa Gazarek of Wallaceburg, Ont., have a collection of stories from the many weddings they have photographed over the years. Steve starts with a very personal story. "I was shooting a wedding in mid November and had completed both the house pictures and the church pictures, then headed to a park for some final group photographs. I arranged everyone together in a beautiful setting and had taken only one exposure when the film ran out in my camera. I had to dash back to my car for more film so ran across the damp grass and, in stepping onto the pavement, my feet slipped from under me and my legs flew into the air. I landed squarely on my back while trying to protect the camera in my hand. It completely knocked the wind out of me and I couldn't catch my breath for quite a few minutes. The wedding party gathered around to see if I was alright, but I couldn't even talk. When they finally got me to my feet my back was really sore, I could hardly move my arms or turn my back. I did reload the camera and completed the wedding photographs but with much pain. On Monday I went to the chiropractor and he found that I had dislodged three ribs out of my spine; he put them back in place but I was sore for about four weeks. Needless to say the bride was very happy with her pictures, but with that amount of pain I wouldn't wish an assignment like that on my worst enemy."

"On another occasion I arrived at the bride's home for the prewedding shots and found four young ladies in cut-off blue jeans, standing out on the lawn, crying their eyes out. When they recognized me they cried even louder. One girl stopped long enough to say they were the bridal party and were locked out of the house. When the mother of the bride left to get her hair done, she had forgotten to leave the door unlocked for the girls. With the bride's agreement I broke a small window and crawled into the house to open the door. They had only half an hour left to dress, so there was no time for the formal portraits. The bride arrived at the church with only a minute to spare... quite nervous, very happy and much relieved. She pulled me aside to thank me, then wished

I had taken a picture when I saw them crying on the lawn. I told the bride I had, in fact, captured that memorable photograph on film."

"I was taking a picture of a bride and groom posed with the wedding cake. My hip jolted the table causing the cake to wobble so I grabbed the top of the cake to steady the whole thing. But suddenly one of the supporting pillars of the cake gave way and despite trying to support the second tier with my elbows it went crashing to the floor. I was left with only the top tier in my hands. With all the mess I set it down on the nearest chair for safe keeping. It just so happened to be the chair for the father of the groom and he, having missed all the excitement, arrived at that moment and

promptly sat on the cake. He got a real surprise but calmly asked whether anybody had any ice cream to go with it!"

Steve tells of a wedding reception where everything was proceeding smoothly with the evening's festivities half completed. The bride and groom had been dancing separately with all the guests. The bride was first to finish with her male partners, while the new husband continued to swirl about with several remaining ladies. Steve overheard a woman suggest to her husband that he dance with the bride because she looked so lonely out on the floor by herself. The gentleman must have imbibed a bit too much and galloped forth in his stocking feet to greet the bride. He soon realized he was in trouble as the floor had been liberally sprinkled with slip-powder and there was no way of stopping his forward charge. Losing his balance he flipped onto his back and sailed across the floor, bowling over the bride with a great flurry of white billowing tafetta as she fell on top of him. We last saw them disappearing beneath the skirting of the head-table like a stage curtain closing after a final act. There, he confronted the startled bride with 'Would you care to dance?'.... and they did!"

Steve remembers a church wedding that was set for 3 pm. "Arriving at 2.45, I entered the rear of the church where the groom and best man were waiting. I asked for the ring in order to photograph the groom looking at it. Checking his little finger, the best man blanched with horror as he discovered the ring wasn't there. He ran out to the car to look for it while everyone joined in the search scanning the floors and the walkways... but with no luck. The time was now 2.55, so the priest suggested they borrow a ring from someone; a quick consultation produced a stand-in ring. The bride's father had the task of telling his daughter the ring was lost, at which news she broke down and cried. Being an emotionally charged day, the mishap did not bode well. The wedding had to be delayed for ten minutes and when the bride finally walked down the aisle you could see the disappointment in her eyes. This was a Catholic wedding which had a twenty minute mass before the actual wedding service. I decided to search through the car for the ring myself. I looked under the seats, into every crag of the rugs... but nothing! Then I sat in the seat where the best man had been, trying to visualize his every move. I pulled down the arm rest... and, behold, out popped the ring! Now I had to get the ring up to the altar, but the priest had insisted that no photos be taken during the service. Not wanting to let the congregation know that anything was amiss, I walked to the front as if I was about to take a photo and slipped the ring to the best man. They were just reaching the part where they bless the rings. Everyone was so happy, I just had to take a photo and even the priest had a big smile! After the service the priest commented that it was one of the greatest moments a photographer could ever capture with all the joy that shone from the party. But then, with a little hesitation, he cautioned: "But please don't let it happen again." At the reception everyone was thanked: the mothers, the fathers, the brothers, the sisters, caterers, disc-jockey, bartenders... everyone but the photographer! I had lived my brief moment as a hero. We photographers are the only ones to capture for posterity the joys of the wedding day. Maybe that IS all we need."

THIES and AUDREY BOGNER

Thies and Audrey Bogner MPA of Welland, Ont., were commissioned to photograph the wedding that would join two prominent families, the groom was from Niagara Falls while the bride resided in Toronto. The bride chose to be dressed at her home, so Thies had to leave by 6 AM to drive to Toronto for the prenuptial photographs. When he arrived he found no-one was ready. The mother was delayed, collecting the flowers after completing her trip to the hairdresser; of course, no flowers meant no formal bridal shots. Some quick family groupings finally had to suffice in the remaining time, then Thies dashed off to Niagara for photos of the groom at his home. As fate would have it, a massive traffic jam on the Queen Elizabeth Way tied up all the traffic and he never did get to the groom's home. Similarly, the bride's car was held up in the traffic, leaving Thies to explain to the waiting party and officials, the reason for everyone's delay. An hour and a half after the appointed time, the bride finally arrived for her wedding. They thought they had covered all contingencies, but the delays cut drastically into the photography shooting time. To make matters worse, guess where the reception was held? You got it... back in TORONTO! All those hours wasted, driving back and forth, for the sole purpose of pleasing both sets of parents, the one from Toronto the other from Niagara Falls.

ALEX ROSS

Alex Ross CPA of Downsview, Ont., has seen a lot of years go by since he reentered professional photography after the Second World War. He has a never-ending supply of stories that flows from his mind.

"I was shooting a Catholic wedding with about 350 people gathered in the church. The priest, the altar boys, the groom and the best man were waiting at the altar; the bridesmaids had come down the aisle and had taken their positions. Then the music changed to the Wedding March and the bride made her entrance to begin the slow walk down the aisle. Everything is elegance, she's holding her flowers with her left hand and she's resting on the arm of her father. I'm waiting in the aisle to get the traditional entrance picture. Half way down the aisle, the bride stepped on the front of her gown and fell flat on her face, crushing her flowers beneath her. There she was lying in the middle of the aisle and no one - absolutely nobody, was making any attempt to help her. Her father never missed a beat and just kept walking. With the little Italian I knew, I called to him and he stopped. Still, no one in the congregation made any move to give assistance while the poor bride made no effort to get up. So, I went to the her and urged, 'Come on, please get up, we have a wedding to go to here!' Her tearful response: 'I wanna die!' So I took on the attitude of a Sergeant Major and lifted her briskly to her feet. I felt sorry as the tears were streaming down her face, mixed with running mascara. I got the father back, made the bride take his arm and together they continued down the aisle. Since I was left behind them, instead of in front, I could not get my traditional walking picture. That was when someone whispered to me, 'Why didn't you take a picture of her lying on the floor?' In that trying moment I didn't have the heart, my concern was more for the bride than shooting the actual aisle shot."

"When shooting a wedding group I warn everyone. 'I will count to three, and it is up to you what you want to look like.' So I say, 'Ready, One....' And at that, I flash off my strobe as if I have taken the picture. Everyone is surprised and I say, 'Well, I lie a lot!' It catches them every time and all react with a broad smile... so I immediately grab the real shot which is spontaneous. I don't have to say all those repetitive Cheese phrases."

"I was covering a wedding reception that took place in a three story house," recalls Alex. "It was a really hot summer and back in those days there was no air-conditioning. The house was crowded with people with a lot of heavy drinking going on. It was so boiling hot, my assistant and I headed outside to get some fresh air. As we were standing on the lawn, we could hear loud arguing coming from the wide-open second-story window. The name calling and yelling continued then, suddenly, a body came hurtling out of the window and landed six feet in front of us. We all were in utter shock with no one making any effort to check if the guy was okay.

I finally yelled to someone to call an ambulance then went to see if I could help the victim. He wasn't moving at all and it looked pretty grim. But just as the ambulance drove up he rolled over and opened his eyes. He wasn't hurt one bit! He was dead drunk and had survived the fall without a scratch. The ambulance attendants pronounced him OK and left him to party on!"

"At another wedding the guests had arrived but only one of the wedding couple had shown up. The other principal didn't appear. We waited... still didn't appear... we waited some more... finally, someone made some phone calls as the priest was getting fidgety. A member of the family , quite agitated, came to me and said, 'There is not going to be a wedding. Will YOU please tell the priest?' So I walked down the aisle and told him. The priest then asked, 'Will YOU make the announcement to the guests?' So I was the one to make the stunning announcement: 'Ladies and gentlemen I regret to say that we're all going to have to go home. The wedding has been cancelled!' Boy, did I get out of there in a hurry!"

"Every Saturday we averaged ten to thirty sittings in our studio, all kinds - wedding groups to babies. A couple came in to pick up their finished order of baby pictures and they marvelled how beautiful the baby looked. They paid for their order and they went away –oh so happy. The following Saturday the same couple returned and my receptionist guessed that they wanted to order more pictures. I left her to handle everything, but she called me back to the counter as, apparently, there was a problem. Whatever it was I knew it would surely be a simple matter to correct. The couple exclaimed, 'This is NOT our baby!' They were ecstatic with the results the previous week, but it took a whole week to recognize that it wasn't their baby!"

"A thirteen year old girl was brought in to have her portrait taken and she was distraught about the whole affair. She was self conscious of the braces on her teeth and felt everyone would laugh at the results. She just did not want a photograph with the braces. So I confided to her, 'I will guarantee that you will not have braces on your teeth. Just leave it to me!' We completed the sitting and she chose from the proofs with the braces still on her teeth. Once

more, I had to assure and promise her that there would be no braces in the final photos. I asked her to have faith. I put a lot of extra effort into finishing those pictures. When the family picked up the order, I ceremoniously unveiled the prints and the little girl burst into the biggest smile, like a flower coming into bloom. I had retouched out all traces of the braces and she saw herself with a beautiful set of teeth. Her eyes were an absolute dazzle, she flung her arms around her mother then she hugged me, too. They paid and left all happy but twenty minutes later she was back with a gift of a box of candy for me. I found that gesture so warm and appreciative; needless to say, I loved it! I had made a happy person who is still a customer to this very day."

JOHN LAIDLAW

In Toronto, John Laidlaw tells of the time he was to cover a wedding in Collingwood, Ont. With the intention of staying overnight, he arrived early, booked into a local hotel and leisurely changed from his driving clothes into his wedding outfit. But horrors of horrors, he found that he had left the tux pants at home! "I immediately phoned the front desk," recalls John, "and the lady clerk sent me scurrying to a store in town. She phoned ahead so they quickly had me outfitted with a pair of dark trousers to match my suit. The pants were too long so the saleslady had me run up the street, right through the centre of town to get them altered. I think the party phone-lines must have been busy and everyone seemed aware of my predicament. They were looking out and cheering me on. At my next stop, a seamstress was waiting; she measured me, shortened and ironed the pants to perfection. Then, it was another panic run back to the hotel to get changed and head for the bride's home. Of course, everyone at the wedding had already heard of my troubles and were waiting patiently. After that everything was perfectly normal."

ROBERT STREETER

Bob Streeter and his wife, Marg, ran a studio off the main Lakeshore Road in what was then called New Toronto. It was a converted house with the studio on the second floor and a camera store on the ground floor. A counter was located right at the bottom of the stairway which, because of tight space, was a convenient place to stand and serve the customers. If anybody was ever leaning there, their backside blocked the entrance to the stairs. Recalls Bob, "Every time I came down the stairs, I would give Marg a little pat or a pinch on the derriere as I squeezed by. It was particularly painful when she was serving a customer and had to maintain a straight face during the ordeal. Dozens and dozens of times I used to do this, but she kept her composure while trying to sell somebody a camera. One Friday night we had this customer come in to pick up an order; he was an airline pilot, a typically good looking young fellow. It had to be 9 o'clock as we were just ready to close. So I locked the door and was talking with him for some time, I just couldn't get rid of this guy. Marg disappeared upstairs to get her coat, hoping it might suggest an end to the visit. As Marg came down the stairs, she saw the usual back side in the doorway leaning over the counter. It was her golden opportunity to make up for all the pinches suffered over the years. Marg jabbed her hand between his legs and gave an almighty pinch! But by accident she grabbed his private parts. With a shriek, the body literally shot over the counter. But to Marg's dismay when he turned round... IT WAS THE CUSTOMER! They were both dancing around all red faced, the pilot desperately clutching his crotch while Marg pleaded, 'I thought it was Bob! I thought it was Bob!' Well, it DID make enough impression to end the visit!"

"When I started in photography in 1955, my main business was weddings. I had this wedding to shoot at the bride's home which was a large house with reflecting pool and just reeked of money. The bride's mother had the worst nose you could ever imagine. I did everything, including standing on a ladder, to improve this woman's appearance. The bride picked up the proofs and asked that I later come to the house so she and her mother could both give their orders. On the appointed evening, it worked quite well as I took down the bride's order then prepared to get the numbers for the mother's album. I looked up at the mother and asked, 'Now, what about the bride's mother's NOSE?'... Even forty years later, I still get a terrible sinking feeling at what my mouth said. Oh! how I yearned to sink into the ground at that moment."

"For another wedding I arrived at the bride's home really early, with plenty of time to spare. When the bride let me in she was wearing a house coat. I sat off in a corner of the room, just sitting there, when a door opened and the bride's mother walked across the room, stark naked, and into a room on the opposite side. I just sat there. Fifteen minutes later she came back out and finally saw me. She immediately asked how long I had been waiting there. Of course, to be courteous, I had to say that I had just arrived!"

"We used to pull some great pranks on each other in the old black and white days. We would be visiting somebody in their darkroom and when they weren't around would open their 500 sheet box of paper, go down about five sheets, stick our finger in the hypo and write on the emulsion of the paper: 'The phantom strikes!' Of course when he printed that sheet of paper he couldn't figure out where the wording came from. We would be long gone!"

"I lived near Oscar Peterson, the famous pianist. "We were masters at playing tricks on each other. I had mysteriously 'borrowed' Oscar's Christmas tree that decorated the outside of his house and it took some time for him to realize I had blatantly displayed it in front of my house. Eventually he retaliated -in spades! I came down to my darkroom one day and it stunk to high heaven. I actually couldn't work there and spent days trying to find out the cause of the stench. I tore everything out and finally found some limburger cheese melted all over the radiator. Oscar had hidden the cheese there and the heat had melted it. You can't imagine all the crevasses that runny, smelly cheese can get into and I had to get every last bit of it out."

"One time I was with Oscar Peterson in Tokyo at a time when he was doing really well. We went into a camera shop and he asked to see the Topcon cameras. When shown the camera he said that was just what he wanted. Then he asked if they had a carrying case for it. The guy brought out one of those fancy aluminum cases with all the padded compartments. Oscar said, 'I'll take that too!... and all those little holes, just fill them up with whatever goes in them!' "

PETER W. NORTHCOTT

Peter Northcott MPA of Barrie, Ont., tells us that: "After working without an assistant on weddings for so many years I decided to take along my lady friend and show her exactly what I was doing in the business of photography. To help speed things along, I showed her how I changed film in the magazines and had her take the silver wrappers off the film. About twenty minutes into the wedding I asked for more film and looked down to discover that Jane, in all her sweetness, had taken the paper stickers off the 'EXPOSED' rolls, and was now ready to hand them back to me as fresh unexposed film. Fortunately, and much to my relief, I caught it just in time –so there was no disaster!"

LOU FERRIN

We all have bad experiences some time in our lives and Lou Ferrin CPA of Oakville, Ont., tells of his "best" bad day. "I left for a wedding one Saturday afternoon and drove along the Queen Elizabeth highway to the bride's home. I was in a hurry to get there and, on arrival, was upset to discover that I had no film with me. I rushed back to the office, got the film, then made a hasty return. By this time I was really flooring it to make up the lost time. I completed the bridal portraits at the house and then it was back on the QE highway to the church... rushing as usual. Well, just as I was swinging in to park beside the church the STEERING gave out completely! The wheel just spun in my hands like a turntable! I was flabbergasted to think how close I had come to eliminating myself. It could have been a major accident and I can only say: 'Someone, up there, must be looking after me!' "

TERRY HRYNYK

Terry Hrynyk and Jeanette Metler of Gravenhurst, Ont., were photographing a wedding where the groom was seriously troubled by his appendix; yet he was determined to see the wedding through, so a doctor was in attendance, just in case it burst. "I had difficulty getting good photographs," says Terry, "as it was impossible to perk the groom into a smile -he was in such constant pain. Under the circumstances, he did quite well and we were still able to create some memorable pictures. To wrap up our coverage at the reception, we were photographing the cutting of the cake and I asked the groom to lean over a little bit... to bend towards the cake. THAT was the moment when the crisis came to a head. The offending appendix burst at that moment, and in a flurry of excitement the groom was rushed away in an ambulance. That left the bride to carry on alone, hosting the rest of the reception. The groom spent some time in the hospital, and when he was finally recovered, we returned to the scene to take additional pictures. This time there were plenty of smiles on all faces!"

HARVEY HORTON

On the other side of the coin, Harvey Horton of Brampton, Ont., tells of a wedding he covered where the bride drank most of the champagne while travelling back and forth in the limo. "During the reception she wasn't seen at the head table for more than five minutes during the whole evening. Under the circumstances, the poor groom did the best he could and had to complete the First Dance without his bride. That certainly was not a very exciting reception! But I saw far more excitement at an Italian reception where the best man (a Hungarian) had been drinking too much. As he stood to begin the toasts, there was quite a bit of noise and he unfortunately began his opening remarks with... 'Shut up you wops'. Well, all hell broke loose with fights all over the place and it turned into a real shambles!"

Harvey recalls the very first wedding he ever photographed. "I arrived at the bride's home to find only the father there... alone and drunk! He welcomed us in and we waited for over half an hour until the bride and brides maids finally arrived in their blue jeans from somewhere. They were ready with just enough time for me to rush through our pictures. I learned the girls had gone shopping down town for hats that morning. On their way home, one of the hats blew out of the car window and was crushed to bits on the 401. That necessitated going back to shop for more hats. Well with that little snafu out of the way, everything went smoothly on, until the best man punched out the groom's father during the reception. Then the groom decked the best man and it spread into a general brawl. That was the point where I decided it was time to leave!

WILFRED OBERTHIER

Wilf Oberthier is from Gloucester, Ontario and tells of a wedding involving, what he considered to be, the mother from Hell. "I was to photograph a wedding on an island in Algonquin Park. It turned out to be the hottest, most humid day of the year and to get to the location required being transported by barge, with all my equipment, across this big lake. The ceremony was to be held on the pier which had been decorated with some four thousand dollars worth of flowers. With no contingency plans for an alternate location, the heavens decided to open up with a deluge of rain that poured down, like you never would believe. The mother started screaming at the hotel staff to get her flowers inside. But there was only a single 12 x 30 room that could possibly be used for the ceremony, and that was the hotel's restaurant. They cleared out all the tables and brought in the flowers which were dripping wet. In no time there was an inch thick puddle over the whole floor. After an hour's delay the bride appeared and the wedding went on... weddings always go on! I don't think the mother ever stopped bitching all day long: -lack of help from the hotel, -half of her expensive flowers still out on the pier, -on and on! I was carrying an armload of equipment to a special area for some portraits when she berated me and demanded. 'You put a smile on your face right now.' Yet she never cracked a smile all day long!"

Wilf continues, "While shooting bridal photographs at the Experimental Farm in Ottawa, I lost a 220 camera magazine with 24 valuable exposures in it. I didn't realize it was lost until I got home. I checked through all my equipment and was sweating bullets when I couldn't find it. The only thing to do was to head back to the location and retrace all my steps while shooting the wedding. It was early the next morning when I got back for the search. After a good hour I was getting desperate at not finding the prized equipment. Finally, I remembered a spot by a bridge where I had crouched low to shoot the couple. I swept apart the long grass with my hands and finally grasped the missing magazine which was sitting dangerously at the water's edge."

J. MARCEL HAGEDORN

From Hull, Quebec, Marcel Hagedorn HLM recalls shooting his first Greek Orthodox wedding. "It was quite a few years ago," says Marcel, "in fact it was well over 25 years ago and I quite embarrassed myself because I didn't know the rituals of the service. It might be a story that happens to every photographer at least once in his lifetime. Part way through the ceremony, golden crowns are held over the heads of the couple and they begin to move away. I thought they were going off to sign the register, so I joined right in behind them... the Priest, the bride and groom and then me. But instead they walked completely around the altar... and I walked behind them. Every time they changed direction I thought they were heading off to some other room in the church. They kept walking around the alter for three whole times. Well, I finally woke up to the fact that I didn't belong there and said to myself: 'What the hell! I'm a nut being here.' I was so embarrassed I ran off into a corner and hid myself, and was next to crying in front of all those people. Those who look at you, think its the funniest thing ever; but being in the procession in error was no laughing matter to me. I did, though, continue with the photography and finished the wedding."

"On another occasion, my wife and I were photographing a wedding for a friend who was the father of the bride. He went quite heavily into the cognac, and that tended to make him extremely heavy in the middle. For the wedding he was wearing a beautiful suit which was a little too tight in the pants. He was waiting with his daughter at the back of the church, ready to make their entrance and to walk down the aisle. I noticed that he had some problem with his undershorts causing "something" to be squeezed to one side creating a big bulge on his leg. I whispered to my wife: 'I just can't photograph him like that!' At the moment, guests were mingling around him. I looked again to my wife and then she, too, spotted the problem. I didn't know how to bring it to the gentleman's attention to rectify the bulge, but my wife, on the other hand, walked up to him, took his pants by the waist band and shook them... REALLY... REALLY good! Everything fell properly into place. 'Now!' she said, 'you can proceed to walk down the aisle towards the photographer.' What bravery my wife has! I'm not sure whether his beaming smile was from escorting his daughter to the altar or from his experience with my wife."

"Some years ago, I had a wedding assignment in which both the bride and I received a last minute call from the groom saying not to come to the wedding the next day as he was calling it off. 'What's this!' I cried, 'calling me at the last minute. I'll have to charge some of the money for a late cancellation.' The groom suggested I keep it and if he decided to get married again, he would call me. So that looked good to me. I was quite surprised when only a week later I got a phone call from the same guy saying he's getting married the following month. 'Well that's fine,' I said, 'you just come by and we'll rewrite the contract so you can increase the deposit. In going over the details, he said the bride's address was wrong. 'Oh!' I said, 'someone has moved?' He finally explained that he had been courting two girls. He was going to get married to one, then changed his mind, and was now marrying the other. As it turned out, one bride had money while the other one didn't. In the end it made no difference, as several years later they were divorced."

MARGARET LANSDALE

Margaret Lansdale of Etobicoke, Ont., is the author of this book and draws upon her own experiences as a photographer. These are some of the tales which caused her to seek out other photographers and set their stories to these pages.

"As a dedicated teen, I worked for a wedding press-agency with seven other photographers. In the course of our work we travelled all over Scotland taking along a portable darkroom in order to have finished B&W proofs (bridal and guests) by the time everyone rose from the dinner. Each photographer used approximately forty glass plates (3 1/4" by 4 1/4") for convenience of processing and enlarging the wet negatives to 5" by 7" proofs. That was the advantage of glass plates. B&W negatives were used until the advent of colour."

"On what must have been the 'wedding of the year', five of our photographers were assigned to give full coverage to this major social event. With so much film to process, and the urgency to get proofs back to the reception, we all gathered in the main darkroom rather than in our individual processing rooms. All were silent in the darkened room as we unloaded our plates, each concentrating on the job at hand. Suddenly WHITE light flooded the room and a tiny voice rang out: 'Tea anyone?'.... We were stunned in our tracks as hours of precious work was obliterated in that instant of light. No one had remembered to lock the door, and there stood the tea-lady in all her innocence! That numbing memory haunts me to this day."

"In my early days I was prepared for all emergencies, as I carried practically everything in my kit. On one wedding the bride arrived without her flowers; there would have been a lengthy delay to retrieve them and another wedding was scheduled to follow immediately. The minister was pleading with the bride to proceed with her wedding but she would not start without her flowers. With all at a stalemate, I skipped out to the garden next door and gathered up flowers which I decorated with ribbons from my bag. On

presenting the bouquet to the bride, she was quite delighted and consented to proceed with the ceremony. But the minister gave me a thunderous look as he recognized his cherished PRIZE-WINNING ROSES. I am sure he could have killed me on the spot or, at least, blasphemed throughout the rest of the day."

"Being a lady photographer, at times brought its own advantages for the bride. I always seemed to be loaning my shoes to them, when they realized that they had left home in their slippers. I would end up padding about in the bride's slippers, while the bridal car was dispatched for the real shoes."

"I was quite elated when assigned to cover a distant wedding on an island across from Oban, in Argyleshire. After the train journey, I boarded a small boat for the final leg to the island. My enthusiasm quickly vanished as the choppy waters made me terribly sea sick for the whole trip. As I arrived at the wedding hall, the bride's father greeted me with the words: 'I have never seen such a white faced girl in all my life' and he thrust a large whisky into my hands to settle my stomach. For a non-drinker, on a much emptied stomach, that proved to be my undoing. As far as that wedding goes, the next thing I remember with clarity, was standing on the deck of the boat... HEADING BACK HOME! I can not remember shooting anything of the wedding. I agonized to think that I had muffed the job and failed my company. To add to my pain, I was deathly sick again. I languished in my misery the whole trip back to Glasgow and headed immediately for the darkroom to process the film.

Praying for a miracle, I pulled the first test negative out of the hypo and to my utter amazement, the image was sharp, centered and properly exposed. I rushed the rest of the films through and they all came out OK. To this day, I thank my sub-conscious for having guided me in taking the pictures!"

"I was sent to photograph a Scottish Highland wedding in a lovely little stone church. Everything was fine as the organ commenced the march to signal the end of the wedding. I was using a large press camera with a focal plane shutter and as I prepared to take the first aisle shot... the shutter jammed! Absolute panic swept over me and I wondered why I ever chose to become a photographer. As usual, I asked God to get me out of this situation, but help seemed not forthcoming. In desperation and anger I banged the camera against the stone wall, and to my amazement the shutter released and came down. Breathing a sigh of relief, I captured the smiling couple as they reached the doorway. I had survived yet another day. So maybe He did hear my prayer! For all the many crises, there seemed to be a new adventure every day with many a happy memory."

LYLE W. MCINTYRE

Lyle McIntyre MPA of Bracebridge, Ont., relates that he had a photographer working for him who really did nice work. He was photographing his own daughter's wedding by the local locks with the group spread out across the top of the gate in a dramatic setting. The photographer was, in this case, in full dress for this special wedding and was backing up to get everyone into the picture and create the best composition. But then, he took one step too far and tumbled head over heels right into the water. A brand new suit, all his cameras and strobe gear... everything went down with a splash. When he crawled out the cameras were still at the bottom of the muddy channel. To make it worse they printed the story in the local newspaper thus upstaging the social side of his own daughter's wedding. He hadn't expected to be the headline maker of the family."

JOHN J. RAUDSEPP

John J. Raudsepp of Montreal, Que., was assigned to photograph a Bar Mitzvah for a very prominent Montreal family. "I was asked," recalls John, "to take some family groupings at the home before heading for the services. I went out and scouted the area for a good outdoor setting and then, when the women used up all the time to prepare their hair, I was under pressure to complete the photography. While trying to compose everyone in my viewfinder I took a step sideways and fell head long over the edge of a wall into a swimming pool some eight feet below. I splashed down with two Nikon F-3's, extra lenses and two flash units. I tried to save the equipment by getting it to dry land but it was thoroughly soaked. It looked like the end of that assignment! Everyone was more concerned about me, offering warm blankets while I, on the other hand, was more concerned about my equipment. I borrowed all their hair blowers to dry out everything as much as possible. Then the family loaned me one of their cameras and I picked up another old Nikon when they chauffeured me home to change my wet clothes. While they headed off to the synagogue, I did this mad dash home and rejoined them in time to begin coverage of the reception. So I was able to recoup my missing group pictures. When I took my equipment into the Nikon people for repairs they nearly went berserk. Water and pool chemicals in a camera is a definite no-no to them. It proved to be an exceedingly costly visit. The strobe repair technicians were, at least, a little more sympathetic, saying that if the units had been 'ON' when I contacted the water, I could have had a bad shock to my nervous system. I was cursing for three days all of the grief and repairs the accident was costing me. But later, I came to realize just how lucky I had actually been! I learned that my client had filled the swimming pool only one day before the shoot. Without the water, it would have been a fifteen foot drop to the bare concrete floor. I count my blessings to have survived unscathed and still be alive!"

EARLE KEATLEY

Earle Keatley MPA of Oshawa, Ont., recalls, "I had a country wedding and travelled out to a farm to shoot the prebridal portraits. When the photography was completed, every one dashed out to the cars and joyously headed off to the church. So I was expectantly waiting to shoot the bride's arrival and entrance into the church, but for some reason there was no bride. I see the father, I see the bridesmaids, everybody else is there... but no bride! So I asked the father: 'What happened to Jackie?' You could see a light suddenly turn on as the father exclaimed: 'Oh my God, she went to the bathroom and we left her there!' So he hopped in the car and roared away to retrieve his daughter. At the start of that particular ceremony, the wedding party was overcrowded at the front of the church; it was a small country church with a very narrow aisle. The minister asked: 'Who gives this woman to be married?' The father replied with the traditional: 'Her mother and I do.'... then moved away from the bridal party. But as he stepped backwards he got tangled in the bride's train, a long extension from the veil of the headdress. I banged off a shot showing the father, off balance on one foot, while the groom grasped desperately to the bride's hand as she was pulled backwards. When the couple came to view the proofs, they saw this picture and both looked at each other in amazement. 'When did this happen?' was the mutual query. Neither could remember anything about that near disaster. Being a bad experience, I guess they blanked it out while enjoying the good memories of their wedding. It wasn't until they talked with family members that they believed it actually happened. They seriously thought I had cooked it up with trick photography."

BARRY SCHEFFER

Barry Scheffer of Downsview, booked a wedding to be shot in Midland, Ontario. "But I got a phone call from the couple saying they were cancelling all the services here, and were taking a small wedding party to a different location. That was fine with me, but where was the new location? The couple excitedly exclaimed, 'It's in GERMANY... will you come?' As it turned out only the bride's German parents lived in Toronto while the rest of the relatives lived in Europe. It was easier to transport the bridal party there than bring all the relations to Canada. I readily agreed on the assignment and expanded the trip into a ten day holiday, touring the Spas, castles and historic sites. I joined up with my bridal couple the day before the ceremonies in Freiburg, a lovely small town next to the Black Forest. On the wedding day, the hotel asked me to also photograph their dining room and the food displays. I made sure to combine much of the scenery with the ancient church, a garden area with a bridge and the cobble stoned streets. The church service was magnificent. Then it was on to the hotel for the reception where we captured more of the German essence, the festive foods, the drinking and the dancing. The trip was memorable because I took on the assignment with a special purpose."

On another wedding, Barry was photographing the evening reception, accompanied by his assistant. "When the sweet table was ready I had the couple stand behind the elaborate food display for a special photo. My assistant was to do the shooting while I set up a fun shot. I chose a chrome plate that held a luscious cream cake and handed it to the bride. She was to simulate throwing it to the groom. Well, the paper doily under the cake was very slippery and as the bride went through the motion the cake slid off and went flying through the air. I tried to stop it but it just shattered through my fingers and hit the groom. Gobs of cream went streaking down the front of his suit and onto the floor. Thankfully, the couple had a good laugh at it all. But the caterer was totally 'cheesed off' to put it mildly. My assistant captured the whole thing with a sequence of shots showing the horror on all our faces."

DAVID CHOO

David Choo MPA of West Vancouver, British Columbia recalls where good intentions at a wedding reception turned definitely sour. "Some 600 guests at an Italian wedding watched as the bride's father rose to speak and, with a grand gesture, opened the lid of a mysterious black box. Loud cheers and applause filled the air when two symbolic white doves flew up and made an impressive fly-pass around the hall. Uneasy at the clamor of the guests and their strange surroundings, the love birds swooped and dove when they could not find an easy place to land. One bird chose to perch on the chandelier, causing it to swing like a pendulum, sending the people below scurrying for cover lest they be hit by falling glass or other droppings. The second bird chose, as its landing site, the top of the five tier wedding cake. The flapping wings sent a shower of cream and icing in all directions. When the wedding cake was finally served as dessert, everyone wiped away all traces of the icing... lest it be some other form of bird decoration!"

DOUGLAS A. GROSE

"On a wedding I was shooting in Ottawa it seemed I was jinxed not to get the Bride and Groom together for their official portrait. They were delayed at the church by well wishers; so time was short when we went to a park for the group photographs. Everything else was completed and we were just about to pose the couple when the heavens opened up pouring with rain. Everyone ran away and headed off to the reception at the Chateau Laurier. I followed and set up my camera there and finally had them posed. But when I checked the viewing screen I could not see the image; it was totally dark. I thought the lens cap was on... but no lens cap! I took the camera apart... but nothing was out of place. I looked at the prism finder but it was OK. Everyone was getting impatient with me as the dinner was getting cold and they couldn't figure out why I was delaying the final photos. Since I couldn't see the image I just guessed the focus and framing for the whole series of pictures. Luckily all the photos turned out beautifully. The problem turned out to be a drop of rain that had seeped into the focussing screen and blackened out the view completely. I now carry a spare screen with me all the time!"

ANDREW W. R. SIMPSON

Andrew Simpson MPA SPA HLM of Abbotsford, British Columbia, has a cute story about the time he was arranging a bride's train. "I knelt down to flip and arrange the folds of the dress but it didn't quite work out the first time. So I went back, knelt down and this time began to billow out the skirt, flipping the material to get air under the folds. A little three year old train bearer was watching my actions intently and walked up to me until she was about two inches from my nose. She wagged a stern finger and admonished, 'NO-O-O-O PEEKING!'"

BERT FISHER

Bert Fisher of Owen Sound, Ont., tells a revealing story of one of his weddings. He was preparing his bride to exit the limousine at the church. It was exceptionally windy, so Bert cautioned the bride to wait a moment until the wind had died down; but she tired of waiting and chose to make her entrance. Just as she stepped from the car a great gust of wind caught the dress and billowed up the skirt. It completely blew up over her head, revealing to all that she was not wearing any undergarments! "Being a gentleman," says Bert, "I turned my head and looked off to the side. But once turned, I was looking directly at the mother of the bride who had the most knowing look on her face, and stood slowly shaking her head."

NELSON SIMARD

Nelson Simard CPA SPA of Woodstock, Ont., joined the wedding guests as they stood to receive the blessing at the beginning of the reception. The minister of the Dutch Reform Church had been asked to say grace and he spoke on... and on... with everyone getting painfully tired on their feet. "I timed him at 22 minutes before the sermon ended," says Nelson. "With sighs of relief the guests were just about to sit down when the minister started up again, but this time in DUTCH! It lasted a total of 45 minutes. It was the longest blessing I have ever had."

Nelson was photographing another wedding and had started to take the family groups when a little sweetheart of a gal in a maternity dress joined the party. "Nelson," she pleaded, "would you put me behind my husband so this doesn't show."... "Well!" said Nelson, "I think pregnant women are the most beautiful things in the world! You shouldn't be hiding!" She caught Nelson off guard with her retort, "I had the baby last Monday!"

BRIAN LITTLE

Brian Little of London, Ont., was photographing a wedding where the bridesmaids wore gowns held up by elastic above the bustline. This party was particularly jovial, so when it came time for the bride to throw her flowers all the young women gathered excitedly for the big moment. The maid-of-honour was particularly determined to catch the bouquet so positioned herself in the forefront of all the others. As she leapt into the air to catch the flowers someone, unfortunately, was standing on the hem of her dress with the result that the wedding suddenly changed into a "coming-out" party. "Being the fine-moment photographer that I am!" says Brian, "I captured the whole exposure. There, poised in mid-air, was the maid-of-honour half-out of her dress, but with her hands triumphantly clutching the bouquet. I did the most honourable thing, of course, and presented the deleted negative to the young lady."

KEVIN DOBLE

Kevin Doble of Sault Ste. Marie, Ont., shoots videos of his weddings during which he attaches a wireless microphone to the groom in order to pick up the voices. Says Kevin, "I wear a head set at the camera to make sure the microphone is working and sometimes I hear the darndest things. At one wedding the bride and groom were bickering with each other during the actual ceremony. The groom kept nudging his bride and telling her to shut up. She was obviously irritated by this and icily scolded him, 'What do you mean shut up?' The groom explained that he was wired. 'What do you mean you're wired?' chirped the bride. 'I've got a microphone on,' said the groom, 'and its going over to the video camera.' At that the bride peeked slowly towards me and to the camera. I wagged my finger, admonishing them, and they both broke into embarrassed laughter."

CONRAD and GLORIA MIRON

Here is the favourite story that Conrad Miron MPA of Sudbury, Ont., tells about himself. "While photographing the reception of a

large Ukrainian wedding, I was invited by a couple with young children to sit at their table for the meal. Not wanting to miss the cabbage rolls, perogies and shishkabob of their national cuisine, I readily accepted. As usual, I was up and down, three or four times during the dinner to grab various shots of the activities. Due to the frailness of one of the grandmothers, I was called upon to shoot the family group photo so that the grandmother could head for home. Wedding photographers will appreciate the scene, as I organized some 40 relatives in the middle of the banquet hall, while, at the same time, providing light entertainment for the 300 guests who had nothing else to do but watch my antics. The session completed, I rejoined the family at our table. It was at this point I realized something was wrong, everyone was decidedly quiet and downcast. The father would not look at me while the mother's face was as red as a beet. Fumbling, she kept repeating how sorry she was. But I had no idea what she was apologizing for. Finally she blurted out, 'I'm so sorry Mr. Miron.

When you were up earlier, taking pictures, one of the children dropped a cabbage roll on your chair.... and YOU sat on it! But worst of all... I'm afraid it stuck to the seat of your pants the whole time you were taking the family picture.... and to tell you the truth, it didn't exactly look like a cabbage roll!'... Wow! all I could say at the time was: God bless those little children!"

Conrad replayed a prank that was handed down from a previous generation. "I found some old flash bulbs that looked as big as house bulbs, so I decided to pull a joke on visiting relatives. In the evening I screwed one of these flash bulbs into the bathroom light socket. During the evening one of our guests made his way up the darkened stairs to the second floor and threw the switch for the bathroom. The bulb went off with a brilliant flash of light and caused our startled guest to have a bit of an "accident" before achieving the purpose of his visit to the bathroom."

Gloria Miron had an encounter with a young man while attending a convention in Toronto in the early 80's. "My son was attending school in Toronto, so I made double use of our visit by arranging to meet him in the hotel lobby. As I stepped out of the elevator, there was this young man waiting to get in. He looked me square in the face and smiled, and I smiled back at him. I couldn't help thinking that I knew him, and during the next fifteen minutes I encountered this same chap, four or more times, while I paced the lobby waiting for my son. Everytime we passed it was, 'Hello, how are you? Nice day, how are you keeping?' I kept wondering how did I know him. Was he a customer from back home?... another photographer?... or some friend of our family? When my son finally arrived, I explained my puzzle and dragged him by the arm over to identify the stranger. As we approached the front counter, my young stranger turned around and again gave me a broad smile. My son then explained, "Mom, THIS is Wayne Gretzky!" Wayne smiled from ear to ear, as he knew he had 'caught' me. It was part of his beautiful personality to be friendly to everyone."

CAROL HEBERT

Carol Hebert MPA of Windsor, Ont., related this story where her husband, Ray, had a wedding assignment and, since she wasn't busy, accompanied him to assist with the setup of the group photos in the park. "I did all the posing, setting the bride and groom under a tree. I was arranging them into some lovely, gentle, emotional love poses. The bride was a tall girl, and with myself being tall, we were at perfect eye contact. Suddenly, I felt something thump on my head which I thought was just a branch or leaf touching my hair. So I continued to set little refinements with the tilt of the bride's head. Our eyes met and I saw a look of horror as they widened in shock. I couldn't understand why she was looking at me like that as I continued, getting the groom to tilt his head ever so slightly towards the bride. Then her mouth fell wide open as something oozed down onto my nose and I suddenly realized what had happened. That thump on my head was now dripping down onto my face; it was a gift from a bird in the tree as it pooped all over my head. I've relived that squeamish nightmare everytime I'm reminded of the bride's changing expression."

WILLIAM E. HART

Bill Hart CPA of Rothesay, New Brunswick, reveals this story about himself. "I was involved with a wedding where I felt like a movie director in a Hollywood set. After the ceremonies I was shooting group shots from a vantage point in the balcony of the church. I was a fair distance from the bridal party and had directed most of the pictures with great success. But I ran into trouble when, for one particular shot, I yelled some specific instructions to the bridegroom. To my surprise, he turned to the bride and with great gusto started hissing at her like a snake! Puzzled, I ran down and queried what he was doing? 'I told you to kiss her!' 'Oh!' said the surprised groom, 'KISS her.... I thought you said HISS AT HER!' I must say that some days are filled with surprises."

RUSSELL POWELL

Russ Powell MPA of Scarborough, Ont., recalls the worst thing that happened to him. "I was ready to leave on two wedding assignments and had everything packed in the car. To be at the first bride's home for 10.30 I hopped in the car precisely at 10.05. But then, I remembered one last item and dashed back up to the apartment. Just before closing the door, I checked my pocket for my car keys... yes, they were there. So I pulled the door shut and headed back down to the car. That was when I discovered I only had my office keys in my pocket. My car keys were still up in the apartment on the dining room table, and that meant trouble as my apartment door key was with them. Oh panic! But I calmly walked to a nearby pay phone and phoned to warn the bride

of my predicament and that I would arrive as soon as possible. I was apprehensive being away from my car as I had to leave it unlocked with all my equipment inside. The next thing was to call my cousin who I remembered had an extra set of keys. He lives some distance away and it took forty minutes to come and rescue me. I finally got to the bride's house an hour late with my stomach tied in knots by that time. But when I arrived SHE STILL WAS NOT READY to be photographed. You have to live through it personally, to appreciate the pain and the irony."

ANTHONY ATTANYI

Tony Attanyi MPA HLM of Calgary, Alberta, was photographing a wedding in a small town out West where he came up against a very strict United Church minister. "He was against any disruption during his ceremony, especially by photographers! He demanded absolute silence and waited until all was quiet before he would proceed with any of the services. At this wedding there was a two year old ring bearer, the nephew of the bride who was given the task of carrying a satin cushion festooned with ribbons to which the ring was securely tied. But temptation was too strong for the little tyke and he couldn't resist the knotted ribbons. The intonations of the minister and the calm peacefulness of the church seemed to pause at the very moment when the tiny fingers released the bow and the ring fell to the floor with a CLACK! You could distinctly hear it roll across the hard flooring. Immediately the little boy dropped to all fours in search of the run-a-way treasure. Where did it go? He scrambled amongst the wedding party, receiving encouragement and directions from some of the congregation. A titter of laughter spread contagiously, much to the consternation of the minister whose face became longer and darker. For a moment the little guy disappeared and then made a very triumphal appearance. He made a sudden appearance exiting from beneath the gown of a very startled bridesmaid... and she wasn't his mother. With that the congregation roared with laughter and the minister had lost ALL control."

JOHN TSOUROUNIS

John Tsourounis of North York, Ont., recalls the day he got the fright of his life by going to the wrong church! "We completed the normal coverage at the bride's home then headed for the church to be ready for the arrival of the wedding party. But when we arrived the bridesmaids, somehow, were wearing gold dresses instead of pink. I ran to the rear of the church and found even the groom was different. How and where was I to find my Greek wedding in all of Toronto? It could be at any of four locations that I knew. I phoned the Greek church closest to the bride's home and found, YES, my bride was to be wed there. Racing to the new location, I estimated I would miss the arrival and the aisle shots. I reproached myself for making such a stupid mistake. But then I reasoned it wasn't my error... it was their fault and their problem. As I pulled up to the church, I saw the bridesmaids still standing outside. How considerate, I figured they must have held up the ceremony just for me. But apparently the wedding rings had been forgotten and the bride's brother was rushing back to pick them up; the couple refused to get married without them. My nerves slowly eased back into place, so I strolled into the church to where the groom was waiting. I coyly asked: 'And what church did you tell me you were getting married at?' You could see the surprised look come over his face. 'Oh my God!' he exclaimed, 'I was supposed to call you Friday.' Well, I guess God must have been looking after all of us, as the rest of the day went beautifully."

ROBERT J. NEPHEW

Bob Nephew of Goderich, Ont., cautions all wedding photographers with this story so they may warn their brides of potential dangers. "I was photographing a wedding reception and had just finished the formal groups and the cake shot. The bridal party was gathered at the head table which was beautifully decorated with several candelabra. The bride was talking, moving her head from side to side to reach everyone. Her veil, which was a mass of tulle, swept across the candles and immediately went up in flames. She had the presence of mind to rip the head-dress off but it was ruined. The fire scorched her dress and burned her back where some of the melting nylon stuck to her skin. Luckily, the bride was a nurse, as were half of the guests, so she got plenty of first aid and attention."

VERNE A. HARVEY

Verne A. Harvey is from Ingersoll, Ontario. "I was asked to photograph some displays at the Elmhurst Inn, which would be used to promote their wedding facilities. I might say that Elmhurst is reputed to be haunted, so you might wonder, as you read this story, whether the ghost was making itself known. Since my own photographs were to be included in this promotion, I was eager to do the assignment thoroughly and arrived at ten o'clock on a Sunday morning, when I knew I could spend more time lighting it elaborately. The displays, lit with spotlights, covered quite a large area. So I made a series of tests on Polaroid to work out my exposures and was just about to take my first real picture when, suddenly, I had no power in my strobe lights."

"I went down to see the manager, believing a fuse had blown. To get to the fuse box meant going from the gift shop, through a maze in the basement to a panel in the back furnace room. Since the manager was the only one tending the gift shop, I had to wait for a lull in customers before he could skip down for me. It seemed to take forever, but when he came back the power was back on. I got all set again and just when I started to take another photo, the lights went out again... I had no power! Frustrated, I tried some of the other outlets, sometimes I had power and sometimes I didn't. I couldn't figure out what the problem was. I reasoned that with my lighting added to the existing overhead lights I must be overpowering the circuit fuse. So, I told the manager I would wait until there were no customers in the gift shop, turn off all the general lighting and then surely I would have power enough to light everything with no trouble."

"So, as the last customer left we turned out the lights and were eager to finally get on with the job. I switched on the strobes but, would you believe it, there was no power! Frustrated but still determined, I went home to get a longer extension cord to bring power from a more distant outlet. No real success even with that, as again, sometimes I had power and sometimes I didn't. That was

at 2 pm and reluctantly I told the manager that I was going to wait until he closed the shop completely at 6 o'clock; then we would have full control of all power."

"On my return, I systematically tested all the outlets to see which ones had power. Using a small radio I found that outlets would have power one moment but not the next time I tested them. I was driving the manager crazy asking him to make so many trips down to the panel box where he found the fuses still perfectly OK. The fuses had been blown the first trip but never after that. That was when he jokingly mentioned the legendary ghost that is supposed to haunt the carriage house. Well, that didn't help my spirits at all. We were still tinkering with those lights at 7 pm when we realized that turning off the overhead lights, in order to shoot our photographs, was the very moment when the radio went dead.

For the first time we clued into the answer to our problem! Turning off the light switch also cut the power in the wall outlets for my strobe lights. Finally at 10 o'clock we had the job completed. And that my friends is my short story of The Haunted House In Ingersoll!"

JOHN A. JENKINS

One Saturday in Toronto, John Jenkins HLM finished his first wedding and had an hour to spare before commencing the next one. He thought he would pass the time by getting a coffee and snoozing in his car at a local plaza. Says John, "I enjoyed my coffee, then eased back in the recliner seat of my car for a nice forty winks. Fifteen or twenty minutes of this solitude had gone by, when I was startled by a knocking on my car window. There, peering through the glass, was a policeman calling: 'Are you all right?...Are you all right?' Believe me he looked as surprised as I felt, particularly when I climbed out of the car to see what all the commotion was about. That was when I got a real shock and would have loved to crawl down the nearest mouse hole. There, waiting at the back of my car, was: one ambulance, one fire truck, two police cruisers... and a whole crowd staring in my direction! Someone must have dialed 911 to report a man sick or dead at the wheel of his car. From now on I'll choose a quieter location to take my afternoon snooze."

HAROLD RYDER

Harold Ryder operated his photographic business for thirty years in Norwich, Ontario. Daughter-in-law, Beverley Ryder of Brantford, also became a photographer and absorbed these charming stories while working along side of the elder Ryder.

Harold was the photographer for a large wedding and was bestowed the honour of being seated at the head table with the wedding party. As the banquet proceeded the two grandmothers were found to be missing and only showed up long after the first course had been served. The family was aghast at the sickly appearance of one of the ladies and it seemed she wasn't wearing her false teeth; everyone expressed concern. "Whatever happened to you, Grandma?" was the question asked. "Oh!" spoke up her companion-in-arms, "while we were waiting during the reception we had a bit too much to drink. Grandma, here, started to be sick to her stomach so we rushed to the washroom. I'm sorry to say I flushed the toilet before I knew that she had also tossed her teeth into the bowl. She lost everything. So now, you all enjoy your dinner!"

Harold relates another anecdote where he went to a bride's home for pre-bridal photographs. He spent considerable time arranging the furnishings and decor to a setting for the bride, then meticulously groomed every detail of the gown down to the final adjustments of the veil and flowers. He felt he had achieved perfection for a stunning bride's portrait then stepped back to his camera to record the scene for posterity. At that beautiful moment the bride blurted, "I've got to go wee-wee!" and ran off to the bathroom leaving a dismayed photographer stunned in his tracks.

E.M. TED DAWSON

Here is a cute anecdote from Ted Dawson MPA of High River, Alberta, which tells of a wedding where all ages of the family were involved. One of the ring bearers was a little fellow about three years old; he was quite rambunctious and everyone was trying to keep him quiet by presenting him with little bribes. They gave him a roll of Lifesavers, then chewing gum and other candies to chew on during the service in order to keep him occupied. Just before the services the Elder came by and organized every one to begin the trip down the aisle. At that point the best man slipped the ring safely into the little fellow's pocket and the party proceeded into the sanctuary. In mid-service they arrived at the part where the couple was to exchange their vows. The minister asked for the ring and they all turned to the little ring bearer. He dug into his pocket and the first thing he brought out was this package of Life Savers, next thing out was the chewing gum, third thing were some mints. This went on for five handfuls until he got to the bottom of his pocket and finally produced the ring. The whole congregation was rolling in the aisles and loved every moment of it."

D. LYLE WEBB

Lyle Webb MPA,SPA of Trenton, Ont., shares these wedding stories with the remark that: "Fires seem to have cropped up at a number of my weddings. I photographed a bride who was dressed in her grandmother's 50 year-old wedding gown and veil. The head table was elaborately decorated with Christmas bunting and many candles. As the bride turned to greet a friend, the veil brushed over a candle and immediately burst into flames; I couldn't believe how fast it spread. I pounced at her and smothered the fire, then was rewarded with the nicest kiss. A photographer rarely gets kissed by the bride... but that was the situation."

"After a wedding at Stirling, Ontario, the recessional march started and down the aisle went the bride and groom followed by the parents, grandparents and wedding party. Unknown to them, a drama was unfolding at the altar. A display of artificial flowers, a fixture for many years in the church, caught fire as a draft of wind touched the flame of the candles to the silk flowers. The Minister started beating the blaze with his hands and the whole mess fell to the floor, badly burning the rug. The bride didn't see this excitement, but when she returned from her honeymoon, the first thing she did was phone and ask, 'Did you get the fire on the video tape?' As a matter of fact, I had recorded it all from my vantage point in the balcony."

"An example of things going wrong – this took place during a wedding where everything was supposedly 'totally organized'. The wedding party lived close to the church and when they arrived for the services, it was discovered all the bouquets had been left back at the home. It was just as well in this instance, for in retrieving the flowers from the house, a small tot was found under the kitchen table crying its eyes out, forgotten in the excitement by its mother."

"Most photographers will agree that it is a small forgotten item that throws a monkey wrench into any wedding. I was covering a beautiful wedding with the cream of society in attendance; the mayors from two cities were included guests. The reception was held in the finest hotel. During the ceremony, the bride remembered that a special knife to cut the cake had been forgotten and she was almost reduced to tears. Her father, resplendent in his tuxedo, drove 25 miles back home to collect the family heirloom. Meanwhile, the guests waited for the receiving line to begin, and suffered the increasing humidity of the hot summer's day. The father was gone almost an hour and everyone wondered what caused such a lengthy delay. He found that the housekeeper had closed up the house and departed. Dressed in his tuxedo, he didn't have any house keys; so he resorted to forcing open one of the basement windows. But just as he was climbing into the house the window fell down, smashing into his face. He did get in, cleaned himself up, got the knife and drove back to the reception.... one hour late. By this time, the party was in total disarray. I wonder if the knife was really worth it?"

Elaine Webb tells of an amusing twist to one of their promotional ads. It was prepared to go in the local newspaper reading: "We capture the heartbeat of your wedding". But through some slip up it became: "We capture the HEARTBREAK of your wedding". Maybe there is more truth there than was meant to be. At least the Webb ad was different!

ALFRED NICHOLS

Alf Nichols of Thamesville, Ont., remembers when he had a young fellow working with him who had never photographed a wedding on his own. A lady had inquired about shooting her son's wedding, months before the actual date, but never confirmed the assignment. So I figured she had contracted another photographer. She reappeared to confirm the details, just days before the wedding which happened to be on the Labour Day holiday week-end. Since I already had made elaborate plans to be away for that time, I could only offer my young partner as her photographer. Being his first solo wedding, my son offered to accompany him as an assistant. This is the story of their 'first' wedding. They arrived at the bride's home and entered by the back entrance to find a blanket in an archway to separate the kitchen from the living room where a water bed and chaise lounge were located. The maid of honour was sitting on a chair while the bride was sprawled on the bed smoking one of those "wacky" cigarettes. Our young photographer suggested that the pictures be taken outside. They had quite a challenge as the bride was much overweight and every time she moved she ripped another seam out of her dress. Before departing for the church, the photographer asked if there was any special picture she wanted taken. 'Yes!' she said, 'I want to be photographed with my snake.' The boys expected a stuffed toy or some gift from her boy friend, but the bride came out with a real live boa constrictor draped, around her neck. They successfully negotiated the challenge and recorded the beauty and the beast. To this day, both my partner and my son think I set them up for that wedding. It was so unusual the colour lab asked if they could add a sample print to their "UNUSUAL BRIDE BOOK".

They said the snake lady deserved a page all her own! The best shot would have been my son's face; he is petrified by anything that crawls and I am sure his eyes must have been the size of saucers when he saw that snake. I never did get to meet or see the young lady but when I talked to her on the phone she had the sweetest, sexiest voice I have ever heard."

JOHN M. BODNARUK

Here's another story which proves that brides can't be too careful when they decorate their reception with lighted candles. John M. Bodnaruk of Hamilton, Ont., recalls, "I had this wedding to photograph where the bride was in her 50's. The bridal party was exquisitely dressed for the occasion and I was setting up the cake shot, concentrating on arranging the bride's long veil. I noticed the bride's 80 year old mother was positioning a pair of elaborate candelabra into the background as an extra touch to the photograph. The bride suddenly stepped backwards catching the flame of the candles and setting her veil on fire. Well, gallantry must still be alive as immediately six male guests leapt forward knocking the bride to the floor and smothering the flames. Tragedy was averted and the bride laughed it off, telling the guests it would be a wedding well worth remembering. Besides, it was the first time in her life she had six men scrabbling over her!"

John recalls setting up another wedding group where he had the bride and bridesmaids nicely arranged. The father was requested to join the group and John tried to get him to kneel down on the floor. He refused to do so but he wouldn't say why; he just wouldn't comply with the request. So John got him to sit on a chair with the girls gathered around him. John asked the father if he would mind closing his legs as it looked like an impolite crotch shot! The man didn't reply or do anything, so John very patiently went over and put the man's legs together and right away the two legs flew opened again! He impatiently asked, "Can you please close your legs?" Still no results. "Finally I went over and grabbed one leg and put it over the other. At that, the bride's mother came to me and whispered, 'He has a wooden leg so please do be patient!' "

H. BRUCE BERRY

Bruce Berry MPA of Truro, Nova Scotia, looks back to his formative years recalling the first job he ever had in professional photography with the Harvey Studios in Fredericton, New Brunswick. "The studio was owned by Ted Atkinson SPA HLM and family at that point but on my first day I was taken under the wing of venerable Frank T. Pridham to help him in the darkroom. Mr. Pridham, at 83 years of age, was a storehouse of experience and a national treasure from his 70 years in Maritime professional photography. Filled with the confidence of youth, my first task was to process the prints which Frank was exposing. As the first piece of paper hit the developer, I started agitating as I had learned in the local Air Cadet photography course. 'Well!' piped Frank. 'You'll never be a photographer.... You're left handed and that's a physical handicap.' My career might have ended right then and there had I not immediately changed hands and set myself correct with Mr. Pridham. After that, Frank went on to show me everything that his years of experience had accumulated; it was an education which I have valued highly. It proves that sometimes we all have to adapt and change our habits."

"I was later employed by the Crandall Studio in Moncton, N.B., which had been run by Wallace B. McAdam until he turned the reins over to Mike Bailey. Wallace was around in an advisory role during my employment there. He was a true gentleman in every sense of the word and was one of the original founders of the Maritime Professional Photographers Association. During that particular Christmas, life seemed to be turning more than glum as my new bride was stricken with a painful infection and my car had decided to lie down and die. Our first festive season was spent in pain and poverty. It included a long hike for miles through the pouring rain to get a prescription filled for my wife. We were just about to sit down to our Christmas dinner which consisted solely of a can of beans when the doorbell rang. There stood Wally McAdam with a basket which he pressed into my hands, bid us a Merry Christmas and drove off into the evening. That basket contained a ham, potato scallop and peach upside-down cake, all the elements that went to make our first Christmas dinner a most memorable and warming occasion. That was 1973, and every Christmas since then, I have honoured Wally's memory by an anonymous act of kindness. I hope I am living up to his legacy."

"In my life as a wedding photographer," says Bruce, "I was preparing to photograph the ceremony from the back of the church and happened to be standing under a spotlight that illuminated the entrance. When the minister came to the part where he asks: 'Speak now or forever hold your peace', a man sitting in a dark corner jumped up and started yelling. It was the groom's estranged father and he bellowed out that NOBODY should ever get married as it all was a big mistake. Then he quickly slipped out of the church. Of course everybody turned around and stared back. In the glare of the spotlight I was the ONLY one they could see and assumed that I was the nasty culprit. Their withering stares burned through me and I was helpless in the situation. I could only mutely plead: 'It wasn't me... it wasn't me!' "

TERESA PAPP

Because so many people thought she didn't dress to fit the rough image of a photographer, Teresa Papp of Swan River, Manitoba describes herself as a 'visual designer in Northern Manitoba'. Swan River is a fairly small community where she

started photographing weddings eight years ago. One assignment required her to travel an hour further north to a community that boasted a total population of ninety-eight and that included all the cats and dogs. "The reception was well underway when I realized I needed another lens from the car. When I got back to my locked car I discovered I had not only left the keys in the ignition but my spare keys were in my purse that was sitting there on the seat. In a regular city or town this might not be a major ordeal but in the isolated north, with civilization a round-trip of two hours away, this was a crisis situation. Guests offered assistance with the coat-hanger treatment but newer vehicles are not as accommodating to that technique. I decided to play the odds and asked everyone with a GMC or CHEV vehicle to try to unlock my car with their keys. It was as if we were in a lottery playing the odds to the limit.... but it worked! A key from a GMC 4X4 truck opened my door. It's too bad the '649' isn't that easy!"

"I've often been asked how I got into photography; I don't mind sharing the secret because of its philosophical meaning. It appears to be a perfect example of my belief in destiny and fate. When my first son was born, ten years ago, so was the photographer born in me. I took hundreds of rolls of film and started reading every photo book I could lay my hands on and applied all the experiments and lighting techniques I could find. A neighbour was getting married with their reception to be held outdoors on their acreage. While dropping off an engagement gift I asked if I might be allowed to take some practice bridal shots on their wedding day as long as I didn't interfere with their hired photographer. They readily agreed.

"The day of the ceremonies was gorgeous, just perfect for an outdoor wedding. We were all waiting patiently but nothing seemed to be happening. I kept checking my watch and realized they were already delayed twenty minutes. Everyone was restless and hot and were certain that something had gone wrong. That was when the bride's brother came out of the house looking for me.... and my life changed forever! He explained that the photographer's camera had jammed and he was unable to complete the coverage of the wedding. I, of all people, was asked to complete the coverage."

"Was this fate?... or wasn't it? I had no time to think, back away or get nervous. I had brought every lens I owned with me and eight rolls of film. The hired photographer felt so bad, he assisted me throughout with the posing and lighting. Could this be fate?"

"I took my films to the local Photo Mart processing center and I was so nervous waiting to see the results. I was like an anxious father pacing up-and-down, waiting for the arrival of his first born. I have to say I was so-o-o pleased with the results. Had this incident never happened I am sure I would not have had the confidence to become a wedding photographer. I would have thought I had rocks in my head to take such a bold step. So I'm sure it must have been fate!"

JOHN PRETTIE

Did you ever get in a situation where you knew an assignment wasn't going right? Well, John Prettie of Owen Sound, Ont., had that feeling while waiting at a church to shoot a wedding. As John explains, "The bride was over an hour late while the two ushers, both with broken legs, were hobbling down the aisle in walking casts to escort the guests to their seats. Then the minister entered and they had to practically carry him in because he had thrown his back out. But he made it and the ceremony proceeded without incident. When it came time to take the group photos I found that all the parents had been divorced and had married new partners. When I called for 'the parents', eight people stepped forward. But we got through that OK. Next it was on to the reception which was held in a room with a very low ceiling; the food and decorations were laid out in buffet style. Everyone seemed to be smoking up a storm and pretty soon the smog built up to such a level that the sprinkler system went off. The guests all scattered for

safety but the food was ruined and it did put a damper on the proceedings. But someone came up with the brilliant idea to call Kentucky Fried Chicken and the party was soon back in business with a new buffet. Now with all that, I should have realized that it was developing into a catastrophe. As it turned out, the bride and groom separated three weeks after their wedding and worst of all, I never got paid!"

John had a wedding to shoot in Niagara Falls so felt he was out of familiar territory with nothing conveniently at his finger tips. The groom and his family brought him down from home-town Owen Sound to shoot the wedding. It was a lovely big Catholic church and just as the bride got to the front to commence the ceremonies, the father of the groom took a heart attack. He was being very discreet about it but was beet red in the face and was starting to get panicky. So I dashed off and called 9ll for help. The ceremonies continued while they eased the ailing father out the side aisle. As the wedding finished and the couple came down the aisle, I wanted to get one good picture of them smiling before they realized what had happened; my last chance was when they came out the church doors. Well, you know that when you call 911 the fire department comes with their trucks, the ambulance comes, everybody comes! All hell was breaking out, just as the couple made their exit. And all I got was this picture of them standing with their mouths wide open. My wife witnessed what happened inside the church. A gaggle of firemen with their

hell-fire gear and hoses came charging through the church. They smelled the smoke from the altar candles, that had just been snuffed out, and they were determined to seek out a fire. They weren't really needed as the ambulance was looking after the father. It seemed like a real disaster, but it did have a happier ending. The father had suffered a bad anxiety attack, not a full blown heart seizure. So, he was able to make it back about midnight to say goodbye to everyone. The sad part was that I was never able to get the father into any of the photographs!"

CLAIR PERRY

Clair Perry CPA of Prince Edward Island, was shooting a wedding in the Basilica in Charlottetown. Located on either side of the main entrance are metal doors as thick and as heavy as those of a

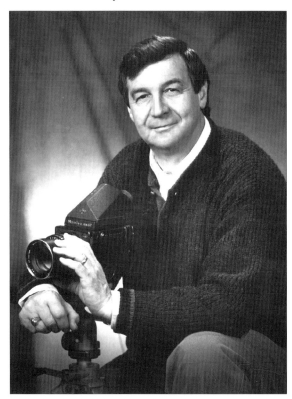

jail, these open to a stairway that leads to the balcony. "I wanted to get overhead shots during the ceremony," recalls Clair, "so I went up to record the full view of the church interior. Well, while I was shooting someone closed the door and locked me inside. I found myself trapped, and there was no way to get out. The ceremony would come to an end and I wouldn't be there for the photographs. Luckily, there was this tiny window through which I could see several people decorating the car outside. I finally attracted their attention and they scurried off in search of the caretaker. With time ticking away, they finally found him, but he felt it necessary to tell the priest, passing the message up via the altar boys. At this point, the priest made the grand announcement to the congregation that: 'We are going to have to slow down our services, here, as the photographer is locked in the balcony!' When finally freed I ran to the front of the church to capture what remained of the ceremony. I was so embarrassed I am sure I was a blazing shade of red."

JAMES MIKLOS Sr.

James Miklos Sr. of Brantford, Ont., recalls a country wedding just outside their city limits. A lovely wedding and truly a lovely bride. The house had a wonderful setting with the garden

being chosen for the actual wedding ceremony. Jim waited until the bride came down stairs for her formal photographs. She descended with a flow of elegance, swishing softly as the folds of her gown cascaded the stairs. S o m e t h i n g caught Jim's eye and he said, "When you get your shoes on we will proceed with the pictures." The bride replied, "But this is it!" She then raised the front of her dress to reveal two bare feet but with a large white ribbon around one big toe. A fantastic vision... but no shoes!"

JAMES MIKLOS Jr.

Jim Miklos Jr. of Brantford, Ont., recalls that at the end of last summer's drought he was to do a wedding out in the country and it looked like a real storm was brewing. "You could hear distant thunder as I arrived at the farm house to take the prebridal portraits. By the time we had worked our way through to the photograph of the bride on the stairs with all the bridesmaids, the thunder and lightning had arrived overhead. It was so bad, everyone was cringing in fear with each clap of thunder. I was in the middle of the living room, framing a shot, when lightning hit the house. It blew up the chandelier, immediately over my head, and I can't tell you how scared that made everyone. We moved to another room and, would you believe it, lightning hit the house for a second time. It blew out the telephone answering machine in the corner of the room; it literally smoked! The lightning finally cleared away just as we were ready to leave for the church. The wind was blowing so strong we couldn't open the back door. At the front door, the limousine had to drive right onto the lawn up to the steps as water flooded everything to a depth of three inches. The bride was soaking wet just trying to get into the car. It was quite a treacherous ten mile drive over country roads that were so inundated with water we couldn't see where the ditches were located at either side. Everywhere was a sheet of water, so we were forced to creep through at five miles an hour. We must have followed the storm into town as it was just as bad inside the church and the guests were worried the windows might cave in at any moment. We did most of the photography inside the church then returned to the house for the rest of the wedding. It wasn't until I read the news reports that I learned a tornado had swept through the area, yet we had successfully completed our assignment through all that mayhem!"

–With the passing of photography from one generation to another, this seems to be the perfect place to end my presentation of photographers' true stories and anecdotes. –Margaret Lansdale.

Epilogue......by Michael McLuhan MPA

For over a decade Margaret Lansdale teased the members of the Professional Photographers of Ontario with her levity. I have no doubt that her column in "Exposure Ontario" was more widely read than my own. It had to be.... It was hilarious.

The book you have read is a work of the love and devotion which Margaret has for our great profession. She knows by personal experience the trials and tribulations of making a living in photography. The economic vagaries of our profession ensure that we all suffer for our art. There is always time enough for that. Margaret has taken great pains to ensure that we take the time to laugh – and laugh I am sure you have.

Many of the photographers in this book I am proud to call my friends, while there are many, I have never met. They are all our colleagues, however, and this cannot be denied. Their careers span more decades than I have lived. Yet we all share the same heritage. Our lineage can be traced back perhaps to 1839. We all share something with the great pioneers of our craft as well as with the aspiring novice: It is the subtle seduction of the mystery of shadow and light. We cannot help it if we are obsessed! Photography is like a cult – a Brotherhood or Sisterhood of Light. We must be slavishly devoted to our craft to be good at it. I am convinced that this brings out the most altruistic tendencies in photographers. In creating fine portraits we must be prepared to surrender our own wants or desires to accommodate an empathetic ability to feel and see those of our subjects. To show their beauty, we must be able to see the truth and beauty in their lives. To show their love, we must love them. This complicates our lives a little and sometimes this obsession can lead to a kind of tunnel vision. We see that which is in front of us acutely in supreme detail. We become oblivious to the other events which occur peripherally.

This is probably how so much of the weird stuff which is detailed in this loving look at our lives can happen to us in the first place. Face it, you couldn't have had a book like this for accountants.

Since I have known them, the Lansdales have spent their lives in the service of our profession. This book enshrines forever many of the humorous moments of our professional lives. It makes me laugh. It makes me proud to be a photographer. It makes me grateful to be able to call Margaret Lansdale a colleague and a friend.

Sometimes in our rush to stay in business we forget why we became professional photographers. Periodically, we must each rediscover our obsession, a marvellous obsession with light and shadow, line and form, the sheer joy of creation, but we must still remember to laugh.

Michael McLuhan MPA is known internationally as a writer, educator and photographer. He has operated a portrait studio in Owen Sound, Ont., since 1987. The son of the late Marshall McLuhan –"Guru of the Electronic Age" and media theorist, Michael's personal obsession is shooting ballet dancers of all ages – thus the setting for this portrait.

Index of Photographers and Personalities.....

PHOTO CREDITS:

We thank the following photographers and studios who have supplied the portrait photographs in this book.
All photographs are copyright and may not be reproduced without the permission of the studio or photographer.

Page **8**: Ewald Richter. **9**: Gilbert Studios Ltd. – Eugenio Medeiros. **10**: Margaret Lansdale Collection. **13**: G-W Photography Ltd. **16**: (left) Bochsler Photographics + Imaging.
16: (right) Erik Singer Photography. **17**: British Institute of Professional Photography. **19**: Attanyi Colour Photography Ltd. **23**: Fred Lum. **26**: Anne Marie Sorvin.
37: Boris Spremo Collection. **45**: (left) Pro Photos. **45**: (right) Photographic Associates - Cliff Wright. **46**: SRT Photo Inc. **47**: Eric Trussler Collection.
48: Wilmot Blackhall Collection. **49**: Sandy Barrie Collection. **54**: Ron Smith Photography. **55**: David James Photography. **57**: Mark Laurie Collection.
60: Ronald Miller Photography Ltd. - Donna Miller. **61**: Simone Portraitistes. **62**: Averill Lehan. **64**: Panda Associates Ltd. **65**: Polar Studio. **66**: William Meekins Photography.
67: The Station House Studio of Fine Photography. **69**: Arranel Studios Ltd. - Lianne Morgan-Sands. **75**: Hines Proguide - Sherman Hines. **78**: Yousuf Karsh of Ottawa.
81: Bochsler Photographics + Imaging. **82**: Boily Photo. **83**: Richard Bell & Associates Ltd. **89**: Hines Proguide. **91**: Stirling Ward Photographic Design.
97: Bochsler Photographics + Imaging – Mike Lalich. **99**: Bert Hoferichter Photography Ltd. **102**: Charles van den Ouden Photography. **104**: Douglas Boult Photography.
106: Foley's Studio of Photography. **108**: Photographic Imagery. **109**: Coral Studios Ltd. – Bill Davey. **110**: Narvali Photography Ltd. **111**: Silver Studios. **112**: East End Studios Inc.
113: Brigden's Ltd. –Ev Roseborough Collection. **123**: Hamilton Civic Hospital – Roy V. Cooke Collection. **127**: Ray Baker Collection. **128**: The Art of Photography – Robert Bray.
131: Stone's Studio. **132**: Photographic Associates – Cliff Wright. **133**: Winnipeg Photo Ltd. **135**: David Brown Photography. **136**: (right) Helen Trotter Collection.
138: D'Angelo Studio – Joan Herron. **140**: Hilda (Onions) Gee Collection. **142**: Livingston Photo. **145**: Adam & Eve Photographers Inc. **146**: John Paisley.
149: (left) Ron Smith Photography. **150**: John Mitchell Photography. **152**: Dorothy Taylor Studio. **153**: Gazarek Photography. **160**: Studio Marcel Enr.
164: Clearbrook Photographic Arts Inc. **165**: David James Entwistle. **169**: Mary-Ann Harvey. **171**: Webb Studios. **172**: Nichols' Photography.
173: BerryHill Fine Photography. **174**: Papp Innovations. **175**: (left) Prettie Portraits. **175**: (right) David MacNeill.
176: Jim Miklos Photography. **177**: Michael McLuhan Master of Photographic Arts.

Pages: **11, 31, 34, 35, 161**, FEDNEWS Photos – James David Lynch Collection.

Pages: **21, 25, 41, 43, 51, 63, 70, 71, 73, 77, 85, 87, 93, 95, 114, 117, 121, 124, 129, 134, 136** (left)**, 137, 139, 141 149** (right)**, 155, 157, 166, 167,** Robert Lansdale Photography Ltd.

THE PHOTOGRAPHIC HISTORICAL SOCIETY OF CANADA

The printing of this book was supported, in part, by one of the first Publication Grants awarded by
The Photographic Historical Society of Canada. This is but one of the services offered in their goal to support
the research and preservation of Canadian photographic history.

The PHSC was formed in 1974 for people interested in photographic history and camera/image collecting. They have members across Canada, the United States, Australia and Europe. The membership includes individuals, libraries, archives, museums, and photographic companies. Members are provided with five issues per year of Photographic Canadiana, a quality journal covering all aspects of photographic history – with a Canadian emphasis.

The PHSC holds two Photographica Fairs each year (spring and fall) which attract over 1200 of the public to inspect and buy photo-antique wares on 200 tables. Similarly an annual public auction is held in the spring which is of interest to both collector and photographer.

Monthly meetings are held at the North York Central Library featuring educational speakers covering a wide variety of photographic topics.

Activity continues to expand as the Publication & Research Awards program was initiated to encourage Canadian photographic research. The society now has a world wide web site to augment its efforts to provide information to all who seek it. The Canadian Stereoscopic Collection of books and stereo images at Sheridan College, Oakville was similarly co-founded to provide a source for research and education.

For information write:
PHSC, Box 54620, RPO Avenue/Fairlawn, Toronto, Ont., M5M 4N5

PROFESSIONAL PHOTOGRAPHERS OF CANADA INC.

The initials following the name of a photographer in the body copy indicate honours awarded by the Professional Photographers of Canada Inc. The awards are:
F/PPOC – Fellow, MPA – Master of Photographic Arts, HON MPA – Honourary Master of Photographic Arts, CPA – Craftsman of Photographic Arts,
SPA – Service of Photographic Arts, HON SPA – Honourary Service of Photographic Arts, HLM – Honourary Life Member. Association members accumulate merits by their participation in the National Print Show, by working for the association or its provincial member association, and by promoting professional photography within the community. Returning something to the profession, which provides their livelihood, is part of the responsibility of the title holder.

The Professional Photographers of Canada Inc was formed to establish a strong national identity for all those involved in the photographic industry. It affiliates the provincial associations in British Columbia, Alberta, Saskatchewan, Manitoba, Ontario, Quebec, the Maritimes, plus the Professional Military Photographers of Canada into a single voice when dealing with legal matters, government agencies or legislation. PPOC provides its members with educational publications, national conventions and print show competitions to upgrade the quality of photography and the talent of the individual.
Members gain in the presentation of merits, awards and professional recognition.

For information contact: PPOC Inc., PO Box 337, Gatineau, QC., J8P 6J3

1997

Notes & Autographs

Notes & Autographs

———⊄⊕⊅———

Notes & Autographs

1997

Notes & Autographs

— ❧ ❦ ❧ —